CONTENTS

A GUIDE TO
LOW-BUDGET FILM AND VIDEO PRODUCTION

by Helen Garvy

Illustrated by Dan Bessie

Third Edition

SAVE-A-BUCK PICTURES
DIRECTOR
I.M.A. GENIUS

SCENE	TAKE
1	127

Library of Congress Catalogue Card Number: 94-69890
ISBN: 0-918828-17-1

SHIRE PRESS
26873 Hester Creek Road
Los Gatos, CA 95030
(408) 353-4253

INTRODUCTION

Before You Shoot will save you time, money, and aggravation when you make your next film.

Making clear, sensible decisions and planning a well-organized shoot are essential to the success of any film, but these are often overlooked as filmmakers concentrate primarily on artistic and technical challenges. In *Before You Shoot*, I'll clarify what decisions need to be made and on what to base those decisions. I'll also discuss what needs to be organized and how to do it. Although the jobs I discuss usually belong to the producer, the production manager, their assistants, and assistant directors, this book will also be very useful for directors — and, of course, any independent filmmaker who, of necessity or by choice, will fill many roles.

In preparing this book I've drawn on my experiences as producer and partner (along with Dan Bessie) in Shire Films, a two-person independent production company that has produced over 22 films. Our projects include a dramatic feature film, children's programs shown on both network and cable television, a documentary, and many short educational films. I've presented the information in this book at workshops and seminars throughout our area. I've learned some lessons the hard way and I hope that by writing them down I can spare you from having to learn the same way.

Much of this book is just simple common sense, written down and organized a little. I used to take common sense for granted. I assumed things would just "work themselves out.". But I've learned that by not figuring things out carefully in advance, you generally lose time and waste money — and can even ruin a film. As I've gone to film festivals and markets, I've seen filmmakers who've put years of their time and too much of their own money into producing films (some quite worthwhile) that never made it to the local movie house, that never got distributed. The tragedy

1

is that most of those mistakes were preventable. *Before You Shoot* will help you avoid those mistakes.

While I can't tell you how to make your film, I can help by creating checklists, suggesting alternatives, and alerting you to potential problems.

This book does not cover the technical side of filmmaking — cinematography, lighting, sound, or editing, except in general ways that relate to the decisions a producer must make. Nor does it cover directing or script-writing, again except as they relate to the role of the producer. What's left? That's precisely why filmmakers get into trouble and have chaotic shoots and go over budget. What's left is the very important decision-making and organizational side of filmmaking.

The order of things in this book is somewhat arbitrary — but that's simply because so much in filmmaking (as in life) is inter-related. I'd suggest reading through the whole book and then going back and using specific sections as you need them. Not everything in this book applies to every film project or to every person. Take what applies to you and ignore the rest — perhaps it will be of use in your next project.

I can't tell you what decisions to make, and I don't want to because what's right for me may not be right for you. But I do hope to let you know what decisions need to be made and what some of the problems are, as well as to give you some ideas about how you might approach solutions for your film.

A few specific notes:

1) I've tried to write this book for both the novice and those who are already involved in filmmaking. Those with experience may want to skim certain areas while novices might find other sections too detailed and overwhelming at first. Take your time.

2) This book is geared more to independent filmmakers than to those working within the system, although I hope it will be useful to both.

3) This book is primarily for the "low-budget" filmmaker, although that phrase can mean many things, and money is usually an important issue on even the biggest Hollywood shoots.

But those working on low budgets need to be especially frugal — and above all they need to be flexible and creative. This book stresses both.

4) This book focuses on scripted films but most of it also applies to documentaries, where creativity and good planning can cut costs significantly.

5) Terminology. Every field has a language of its own and film is no exception. I've tried to define words that might be unfamiliar. Use the index for cross-references.

6) A word on gender. The terminology in this book is the terminology I use. I'm aware that film has traditionally been a man's world (except for "'script girls," "wardrobe ladies," and such) and words have reflected that. But times are changing and my world of film has not been totally male. Many of the crews I have worked with have included women in key roles and so my terminology reflects that. It's difficult to say cameraman or soundman when the people you have worked with in those jobs have sometimes been women. I've tried to use neutral terms and although I realize that "he or she" is unwieldy, I use it sometimes for lack of anything better. If my terms seem awkward, perhaps they'll be less awkward as women become more accepted in the field and our language adapts. If my terms help question stereotypes, so much the better.

7) I sometimes ask a lot of questions without providing specific answers. I don't do this to frustrate you, but simply because the

answers depend so much on particular situations that it would take forever to cover all possibilities. But I do want to make you aware of questions to ask yourself and things to think about. Once you do that, the answers should come fairly easily.

8) A note on the films mentioned in this book. I use specific examples from my own experience in order to illustrate certain points, drawing from the following films, all produced by Shire Films.

"PETER AND THE WOLF" — a 30-minute live action version of Prokofiev's famous tale that also introduces the instruments of the orchestra. Features Ray Bolger as the on-camera narrator — and a real wolf. Budget: $50,000. This film has received numerous awards and has been seen nationally on CBS and HBO. Distributed to both the educational and home video markets by Pyramid Films.

THE TIMES WERE HARD... DECENT MEN WERE DRIVEN TO DESPERATE ACTS.

HARD TRAVELING

A TRUE STORY.

NEW WORLD PICTURES PRESENTS A SHIRE FILMS PRODUCTION HARD TRAVELING STARRING J.E. FREEMAN ELLEN GEER • BARRY CORBIN DIRECTOR OF PHOTOGRAPHY DAVID MYERS EDITOR SUSAN HEICK MUSIC BY ERNIE SHELDON BASED ON THE NOVEL "BREAD AND A STONE" BY ALVAH BESSIE PRODUCED BY HELEN GARVY WRITTEN AND DIRECTED BY DAN BESSIE NEW WORLD PICTURES PG PARENTAL GUIDANCE SUGGESTED SOME MATERIAL MAY NOT BE SUITABLE FOR CHILDREN ® © 1986 NEW WORLD PICTURES. ALL RIGHTS RESERVED.

"HARD TRAVELING" — a feature length dramatic film based on a novel by Alvah Bessie, *Bread and a Stone*. A tender and moving love story set against the tensions of the 1930's depression, "Hard Traveling" stars J.E. Freeman, Ellen Geer, and Barry Corbin. Directed by Dan Bessie and produced by Helen Garvy, the film was shot in 35mm in six weeks in Santa Cruz, California on a total budget of $425,000. It was distributed theatrically and in all

5

other markets by New World Pictures and is now available on video from Starmaker Entertainment.

"BEWARE THE JABBERWOCK" — a 30-minute original story introducing poetry to children and using our version of Lewis Carroll's imaginary "Jabberwock" as the principal character. Features Ray Bolger. Budget $35,000. Sold to CBS, cable, home video, and the educational market.

"TURNABOUT" — an hour documentary about two 92-year old gay men and their 70 years together in the theater. Budget $16,000. Sold to PBS stations. Distributed to the educational market by Filmakers Library.

Other examples in the book have been drawn from some of our other films, including "The Ugly Duckling," "The Immune System: Your Magic Doctor," "The Birth Control Movie," "Child Abuse: The People Next Door," "Teenage Pregnancy: No Easy Answers," and "Physical Fitness."

I hope that sharing some of my experiences with you will make your film shoots more pleasant and successful.

WHAT IS A PRODUCER?

Hollywood has rigid job categories. For example, there are very specific tasks that a second camera assistant does and doesn't perform, and the same is true for most of the technical jobs. The title "producer," however, is much looser. Although the functions that must be performed to produce a film remain pretty much the same, they can be divided up differently and given different titles on different films.

Let's begin with job titles. There are different kinds of producers. There are plain "producers" (which can mean a whole variety of things, as we'll see later), "executive producers" (generally those who arrange the financing or even put up the money themselves), "line producers" (usually does the nuts and bolts of organizing the production, but usually without making the major decisions), and "associate producers" (a catch-all title that may be used to reward a relative, a person who put up some of the money, or an especially hard-working production manager or producer's assistant). Other people on the production staff include the "production manager" (deals with the nuts and bolts of the shoot, similar to a "line producer"), "location manager" (finds, secures, and deals with the filming locations), "assistant director" (assists the director but also runs the set and bosses the crew during the shoot), "production assistant" (assists the production manager or others in the production department), and "post-production supervisor" (supervises the post-production stages).

Other, more specialized, roles in the production department include publicist, researcher, technical advisor, accountant, book-keeper, and script supervisor.

The lower your budget, the more likely it is that some of these jobs will be combined, sometimes with jobs outside the production department. No problem — we're concerned with functions, not titles.

A producer's job can often include both creative and organizational functions. To a large extent, the size of the producer's role, especially his or her creative role, will be determined by who initiated the idea for the film. If the person who had the original vision (perhaps the writer or director) hired the producer, the original person will probably make the basic creative decisions and may take on some tasks that would normally fall to the producer. The producer's role, then, may be largely organizational, perhaps including fund-raising. If the producer originated the idea, he or she may make most of the creative decisions in the film and the writer and director may be relegated to more limited technical roles. A line producer may also be hired to deal with the organizational aspects.

So what does a producer actually do? The following functions are often included under the role of producer. Again, who does them is not so important, as long as they get done.

1) **Make basic decisions.** Someone has to make basic decisions such as what the film is about, who the intended audience is, what level of quality is desired, etc..

2) Maintain an overview. Someone has to hold on to that vision, once it's defined, and mesh the different aspects of filmmaking together so that the finished film will resemble the original vision. Someone has to maintain perspective and view the project as a whole.

3) Obtain financing. Someone has to get the money to make the film. This may involve making deals, pre-selling the film or selling it afterwards, obtaining grants, or fund-raising from private sources (often through limited partnerships or donations).

4) Be financially responsible for the film. Someone has to determine costs and keep the production on budget.

5) Plan the production and make all related decisions. Select the cast and crew (alone or with the director or others) and plan the logistics of the shoot.

6) Run the shoot. Make sure that what is supposed to happen does — and as smoothly as possible. Make sure all tasks are covered and nothing falls through the cracks.

7) Set and uphold standards. Make sure you are getting the quality you want during every step of the process.

8) Set priorities and balance everyone's needs. The producer is a juggler, sometimes of an impossible number of conflicting things. The director, director of photography (DP), and actors (not to

9

mention the editor, camera operator, assistant camera, gaffer, grip, sound person, etc.) all seem to have different and often conflicting needs and ideas. Everyone fights for time and money. Often each will want to show off his or her specialty (fancy camera work, unique lighting, innovative editing style) so that it will be noticed in the finished film. Your goal may be to make sure that each person's work is appropriate for your film — and in the best interests of the film as a whole rather than any one particular individual.

9) **Keep the shoot on schedule and on budget.** That's the bottom line.

10) **Supervise post-production** in the same way as the shoot itself, balancing everyone's needs and keeping an eye on quality and the budget.

11) **Follow the film through to the end**, which usually means until it is distributed.

In sum, the producer is responsible for holding the whole show together from start to finish.

HOW TO MAKE A GOOD MOVIE

Your job as producer is to make a film. But I assume you don't want to just make a film — you want to make a *good* film. Some of that, obviously, is subjective. Excellence will depend on your ability to successfully combine the various elements, including a good script, good acting, good directing, good camera work, and good editing. But there are other things, under the control of the producer, that will help you achieve excellence.

1) **Aim high.** Try to obtain the best possible script, crew, cast, equipment, and locations. Don't assume that because you have limited money you can't get the best. It never hurts to try: the worst that can happen is people will say "no." Let them say it, but don't refrain from asking. Don't give up without trying.

2) **Plan well.** Planning is the key to good filmmaking (assuming, of course, that you have a good idea, good script, good acting, good directing, etc.). The tighter your budget, the more essential planning becomes. Planning means arranging to make the most efficient use of time and resources (which includes money and energy). It means knowing all the things that need to be done and arranging them in the best possible way. It means using people efficiently and in a way so as to conserve as much energy as possible. Getting stuck and having to produce on short notice is often possible, but it also usually causes headaches and costs more money. Planning can prevent this. Good planning can let you foresee most problems and probably prevent them.

3) **Go slowly and carefully.** Give yourself time. Take as much time before and during the shoot as you can afford. Take time to rehearse — allow the director and actors time. Rehearsal before the shoot, without a crew standing by, is cheaper than if you're paying a full crew. Rehearsal with the camera off is usually cheaper than wasting film with the camera on. Give yourself plenty of pre-production time and adequate post-production time

as well. You don't need to use all the allotted time (especially if you're paying people by the hour or week), but have time available if you need it. Working to meet deadlines is nerve-wracking and costly.

4) Choose your cast and crew carefully. Since a good film depends on good acting, directing, cinematography, editing, etc., the people who will carry out these tasks should be selected with great care. Choose people with the experience and ability needed for *your* film. If possible, hire people who care about the project and will work hard for you. Once you've selected good people, help them to do their best work. See to it that they have the time and resources they need (within the overall limits of your film).

5) Evaluate regularly. Assess your strengths and weaknesses at various stages along the way. Maximize the strengths and compensate for the weaknesses.

6) Learn as much as you can about all aspects of filmmaking, from directing to acting, camera work, sound, lighting, and editing. The more you know, the better you'll be as a producer. I believe this is good advice for anyone working in film in any capacity. The more you know, the better decisions you'll make, and the better you can supervise and teach others. If you set a tone that values and fosters learning, others may also be inspired. This is especially important if you're working with less experienced people. There are specific things you can do before the shoot to help others increase their knowledge. For example, I often give workshops for interns who work on our films. I also let people know they can take time to learn new skills on the set — as long as their responsibilities are met.

7) Set high standards for people working with you and check to see that these are upheld. This means you have to know how each job can and should be done in order to set the standards. It also means you have to pay attention to every detail of what everyone is doing (as much as is humanly possible). To some extent, hiring good people can take care of this. Working with people you trust and whose work quality you know will make your job much easier.

8) Make sure you have good communications. Filmmaking is people working together — and that necessitates good communication. Communication to the crew needs to be explicit and clear. The clearer your instructions, the better they can be carried out and the less energy (and time and money) will be wasted. For example, if you want someone to find a prop, give them a clear enough idea of what you want so they don't waste time looking for the wrong thing — or protecting themselves (also known as "covering your ass") by finding extra things. If you know how or where to find what you need, tell them.

But communication needs to go in more than one direction, not just down from the top. Artistic, technical, or organizational ideas can also move up — from the crew to you or to the director. Let people know how much feedback you want, and how and when to offer it. You might want to set up a structure to facilitate or channel this, such as regular production or crew meetings.

9) Get advice at all stages, but use it wisely. By that I mean that you should seek advice and listen to it, but remember that advice is usually subjective (not purely objective) and should be taken in that spirit. Even advice from "experts." Technical experts may know a lot about their field and may be invaluable — but experts are often followed too blindly in our society. Like you and I, experts are only human and they come to conclusions based in part on the information they have — but also based on their own values, experiences, priorities, and needs, which may not be the same as yours. You need to sort out the experts' information and mix it together with your (and your film's) values, priorities, and needs to arrive at *your* decision. Unfortunately, experts don't always recognize this and are often all too eager to make your decisions for you. What they should do is share their knowledge in a way that helps *you* make the decisions.

10) Maintain your sanity. Last, but certainly not least, try to stay sane and healthy during the process. You have a difficult job and need to be clear-headed. Take care of yourself and your crew. This will pay off in the quality of your finished film — and it will certainly make the process far more pleasant.

THE IDEA

The starting point for a film is usually an idea — based on a book you read, a true event, or an original story.

BOOK

When your idea comes from a book, the main issue is whether the book is under copyright or in the "public domain."

If your idea comes from a book that is in the public domain you are free to use it. This usually means the book is more than 75 years old, although you should check the details of the copyright law carefully (write Registrar of Copyrights, Library of Congress, Washington, D.C., 20559). A specific book may be copyrighted but may be based on material that is in the public domain (a news story, for example). You are then free to go back to the original sources and base your script on that. If you're unclear about anything, check with an attorney.

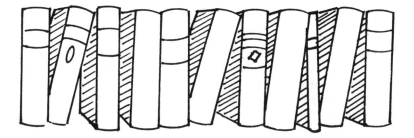

If the book is protected under the copyright laws, you need to secure the rights in order to use it. Rights for some books are easily available. It's good old capitalism — supply and demand. If the book is popular, you'll likely be bidding against other people, some probably richer than you. If it's a little-known book that you fell in love with, or a book that's been around for a while and nobody's noticed, then you might have a better chance. Write to the publisher and ask if the film rights are available. The publisher may refer you to the author or the author's agent. If the rights are available, you can make an offer, either to purchase them outright or for an "option."

An option is the right to develop a project, based on a book or true story, for a limited amount of time, usually for a percentage of the cost of the rights (10% for one year is common). At the end of that time, if you decide to go ahead with the project, you usually pay the remaining 90% and proceed. Otherwise the rights revert back to the original owner and you lose your 10%. An option basically lets you tie up a property while you try to put a package together. You can use the time to write a treatment or a script, locate funding, line up distribution, and gauge whether other people share your assessment of the viability of the project.

Whether you want to option a property or decide to buy it outright, determine what you can afford or what you want to pay and make an offer, specifying the type of film you want to make and what markets you want the rights for. It's like any other kind of bargaining. A low offer may insult someone in addition to getting you a "no." But if you ask very nicely and make clear that you are honestly offering what you can afford, you're less likely to antagonize someone even if they find your offer too low. And you can negotiate. Perhaps there is another way to make up the difference, such as offering a percentage of profit, deferred payment, some sort of barter. If they have no other offers, you are at least offering to make their project into a film. If you can convince them that you'll do it well, so much the better. Take care to present yourself well — serious, talented, professional, and committed to the project. If they reject your offer, you can always raise it and try again.

A TRUE STORY

This might be a friend's personal story or the story of a famous person. Depending on your relationship to the person or the popularity of their story (whether, for example, it's your grandmother or someone who's currently on the front page of the newspapers) you might want to contract with them formally for the film rights to their story.

ORIGINAL STORY

This might be a fantastic dream you had the other night or a carefully concocted plot you spent months working out. In this case you obviously don't have to worry about obtaining rights at all.

Some people come up with ideas easily while for others they are very rare. In any case, before you go on to formulate a master plan, it's worth stopping for a moment to evaluate your idea. See p. 35 for more on this but for now all you need is an evaluation of whether your idea is sound enough for you to proceed to the next step. Will the idea translate well to film (not all do)? Is there a market for the film (unless you don't care about selling it)? Is it a film you really want to make? Can this film be made with the general level of resources that you have available?

THE MASTER PLAN

The decisions you make about your film should reflect a balance between your **goals** — both personal goals (such as making money, obtaining fame, creating art, influencing others, or gaining experience) and goals for the film (such as the type of film and the audience or market you want to reach) — and the **resources** you have available (money; time; cast, crew, and equipment available; and personal experience).

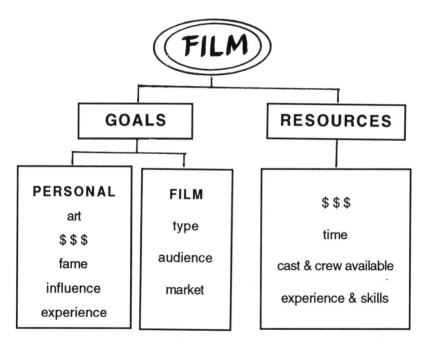

As you begin your project, you should stop and ask yourself some basic questions about how you view the project and what you want out of it. Some people know this clearly and immediately, but for others the following questions will help clarify a master plan — the basic concept (and goals and resources) — for your film.

PERSONAL GOALS

What are your goals for this film? Do you want to: 1) get rich (or at least make some money), 2) obtain recognition as a filmmaker (for its own sake or in order to receive offers of other work), 3) create an artistic masterpiece (by whose standards?), 4) influence people (in what way?), 5) fulfill a course requirement, 6) learn more about filmmaking by doing it, 7) work on a project with some people you like, 8) produce something useful with the degree you just earned from film school, 9) do it because someone hired you to do it, or 10) simply have fun? This is quite a varied list, and it is neither all-inclusive nor are the categories mutually exclusive — but it does show the variety of reasons people make films. Why do *you* want to make your film?

GOALS FOR THE FILM

TYPE OF FILM. What kind of a film will it be? Will it be entertaining or educational, or both? Will it be a love story, mystery, horror film, science fiction, or children's story?

What type of material will you be filming? Will it be dramatic material from a script that you will shoot on sets or on location, documentary footage that you will shoot, documentary footage from archives, stock footage of other kinds, or animation or special effects that you will create?

PURPOSE OF THE FILM. Why are you making the film? Are you trying to entertain or educate — or both? A wonderfully written educational film that is clever, funny, and tells a good story is useless if its purpose is to educate and it doesn't do that well. Do you want to raise questions or recite facts — or both? What is the age and level of sophistication of your intended audience?

AUDIENCE. To whom is the film geared? To what kind of people do you think the film will appeal — young or old, a mass market or a more limited one, just friends and family, a specialized audience (who?), American only or international?

MARKET FOR THE FILM. To what markets do you expect to sell the film — theatrical (wide release or limited), television (network, cable, or public television), schools (what age level), industry, or home video? Or do you not expect to sell the film at all, but hope to be able to show it at festivals, or to special interest groups, or potential employers, or future financial backers?

What are the requirements and preferences of your desired distribution markets with regard to 1) length, 2) rating (based on language, sex, and violence level), 3) size of screen and screen ratio, and 4) quality. One difficulty with this is that many films today try to fit several markets — and the different markets may have different requirements. Most producers of theatrical feature films also hope for television and home video sales, while some educational films can also sell to television.

1) Length. How long will the film be? Is it a 10-minute short or a 90-minute feature? Your answer should fit with your intended audience and market because length requirements vary for different markets. Theatrical films are usually 1 1/2 - 2 hours. Television is programmed in half-hour units. Networks have very exact length requirements (sometimes down to the second) because they leave room for commercials. They may want a half-hour show to be 23 minutes, 30 seconds. Because public television has no commercials, they may want 26 minutes, 40 seconds. Individual half-hour shows may be difficult to sell. Check current requirements and preferences.

The educational market for schools is geared to the length of classroom periods. If the class is only 50 minutes, they can't show a 55 minute film without wreaking havoc with their bureaucratic system. Twenty to 25 minutes works fine, leaving room for discussion (which teachers like). Younger kids have shorter attention spans (at least for educational films!) and need shorter films, usually 10-15 minutes. There are always exceptions to every rule, but don't assume your film will be that exception!

2) Ratings. Each market has different standards, formal or not, for sex, violence, and language. Pay attention to these — it can make a difference when you get ready to sell your film. Distributors can be a good source of information.

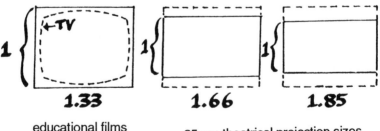

educational films
& television cut-off

35mm theatrical projection sizes

3) Screen size and screen ratio. The size of the screen your film will be shown on will (or should) affect the action you plan. Large theater screens allow you to see a lot of details that get lost on a small television screen. Long shots and scenic panoramas can work well in theaters. You can see subtlety of acting on a big screen that might not be noticed on television. Films made for TV tend to have more close-ups so you can see emotions clearly.

24

Screen ratios (the relationship of height to width of the frame) vary for different markets, which should affect the framing of your shots when you get to the actual filming. Television sets also normally cut off a little all around the frame ("TV cut-off"). Be especially careful if you're shooting film that will be shown both in theaters (especially 1:1.85 ratio) and television — unless you want heads cut off or important things at the bottom or sides of the frame left out.

wide screen   wide screen film as
                               seen on television

4) Quality. What general level of quality are you aiming for? This will obviously depend a lot on the amount of financing you have available — or, on the other hand, it can tell you how much financing you need to obtain. Quality will also depend on your skill as a filmmaker and the skill of those around you — or it can tell you what type of people you need to get to work on the film. Do you see this as a roughly made film that simply gets its idea across or do you see it as polished "Hollywood" quality (acting and technical quality), suitable for theaters or television. Some roughly made films do make it into theaters, but the vast majority don't (and don't assume your film will be that rare exception).

If you're making a film only for yourself, that's fine, assuming you can afford to do that. But if you're making it with the hope of selling it when you're done (or even having it shown), you need to pay attention to these questions. Otherwise you may have a very nice but very expensive film sitting on your shelf.

Each market has quality standards, both artistic and technical. There are always exceptions, but the general standards exist and not meeting them is the easiest way to kill your distribution chances.

RESOURCES

MONEY. How will your film be financed? Your options here will depend to some extent on the answers to the above questions. Will you look for funding from a major studio ("Hollywood"), a smaller company, an independent "executive producer," grants, private investors, loans (from banks, credit unions, friends, relatives), or savings? Will you seek deferments from cast and crew as partial financing?

Before obtaining financing you'll probably need to assess the money-making potential of your idea (see p. 37). That in turn will depend on what markets your film will fit as well as the quality of the film.

How much money will you have available, from whatever source? Are you beginning with a set amount of money (and have to tailor the film to the money available) or can you decide how much money the film requires and then assume you will be able to raise that amount? Reality is often a combination of the two — but it's senseless to spend a lot of time planning a $5,000,000 film if you have no hope of ever raising that amount. If you know you could probably raise $50,000 - $75,000, it may make sense to plan a film that can be made on that kind of budget.

Somewhere in here you need to think about your own finances. When you think about the film, think about how you (and perhaps other key people) will be supported during the time it takes to complete the project (perhaps years for a feature film, when you include fund-raising and distribution). If you will include money for yourself in the budget, fine. How much do you need, for how long a time? If there's no money for you, how will you support yourself? Think that out clearly and realistically now and avoid pain later.

TIME AVAILABLE. What is your time line? Do you have outside deadlines or only your own? Are you free to work full-time on the project or will you have to fit it in with other commitments?

PERSONAL EXPERIENCE. What skills and experience do you bring to the project? Will any of these influence the type of project you choose or the way in which you do it?

CAST, CREW, EQUIPMENT AVAILABLE. Do you have any particular cast, crew, or equipment available that will influence the planning of your film? Is your best friend a fantastic composer of a famous actor? Does your favorite camera person have her own equipment that she'll rent to you cheaply? What kind?

"GIVENS." What are the "givens," if any? What ingredients are fixed from the outset? Do you begin your project with specific people connected to it (writer, director, cast, crew), or with specific money you either have or have targeted? Does any of your money have strings attached? Is any of it "in kind" services, rather than cash (such as equipment, post-production facilities, or services of cast or crew)? Is some money contingent on your using a particular actor (or writer, director, etc.)?

DECISION-MAKING STRUCTURE

What will be the basic decision-making structure for the film? Whose film is it? Who's the boss? Who determines the shape of the project? Who hires the other people? Will there be only one boss or will power be shared? If it will be shared, how?

Once you've answered all these questions, even tentatively, you'll have a better idea of where you're headed. At this stage, do a quick evaluation. Does it hold together so far? Do the answers you gave to one question fit with the answers to another? Does it all balance? If your available budget is $5,000 and you expect a top quality feature length film, stop right now and re-think the project because that's not realistic. But let's assume your project makes sense at this early stage and you've made any adjustments you want to make. You're now ready to go on and develop the script.

THE SCRIPT

This section won't tell you how to write a script or about screenplay format or character or plot development. There are plenty of books about that and it's not my purpose here. But there are things to keep in mind when writing a script that are directly related to producing it. These are worth considering if you're not just writing a script in a void but writing it with a view towards actually making a film.

The script is the basis of a film. That's not to say that acting, directing, cinematography, etc. aren't important — but your script is the foundation. And just as with a house, a weak foundation will affect everything built upon it. Begin with the best script you can get. Don't go on to the next step until the script is as good as it can be. Changes at the script stage are fairly simple — a little time and some extra paper — but they become harder and more expensive in later stages. Trying to re-write quickly on the set when you find that some things just don't work is at best disruptive and can create enormous problems. Changes you might like to make when you get to scene 54 might not fit with earlier (or later) scenes already shot. Although post-production editing can often work wonders, there are limits to the problems it can fix. Don't simply assume you'll fix it later.

HIRING A WRITER

Who will write the script? Will you or someone already connected with the project write it, or will you look for a writer to hire (for cash payment, deferred payment, or a combination)? If you'll be hiring a writer, there are other things to consider besides writing skill. Do they understand writing for film, and the type of script you want written? Dramatic films, television sitcoms, documentaries, and educational films are all very different. Do they really understand the characters in your film and what makes them tick? Can they write realistic dialogue for those characters? If it's an educational film, do they thoroughly understand the subject matter of your film — and educational concepts in general? How well do they understand the ideas of the producer (or whoever the "boss" is)? A good writer whose ideas differ from yours may write a great script — but not the one you want. How fast do they write? Some people can whip out a good script quickly, while others labor forever. If you have a deadline, this may be important. Don't assume anything.

How will the writing process work? Will the writer just go off and write a script or will you work closely together to develop characters and story line? Will you read scenes as they are written or wait until the script is finished?

If you don't like the finished script, what then? Talk that out with the writer and reach an agreement beforehand. Will the writer do a re-write as part of the original price or will there be an additional fee? How many re-writes? What if you prefer to give it to someone else to re-write? Who will get what credit? If you're using a writer who is a member of the Writers Guild of America, there are rules and regulations which cover all this, as well as rates. If not, think out carefully what arrangement meets your needs.

THINGS TO CONSIDER

The primary things a producer has to consider about a script are: 1) its purpose, 2) various decisions made at the master plan stage, and 3) cost.

PURPOSE OF THE SCRIPT. Before you (or someone) begin writing, you need to know the purpose of your *script*, not just the purpose and market for the film. If the script will be used to impress people (either to help finance the film or to attract actors or others to your project), then you'll want to write something that reads well and stands on its own — something that not only contains dialogue but that also conveys a sense of the film. If you're writing a shooting script to guide a director, you'll want to include shots and specific action, but prose style may not matter at all. Or you may just need the basics of action and dialogue and let the director take it from there. For documentaries you proceed differently and the "script" (usually only a narration) is often written last. However, the clearer an idea you have of what you want to end up with (even if not the exact words), the less film (and money) you'll waste.

MASTER PLAN DECISIONS. Your script will be affected by decisions you made as you formulated your master plan, including: 1) purpose of the film (entertainment, education), 2) audience (age and sophistication), and 3) market considerations (such as length, ratings, screen size). (For more details on these decisions, see p. 21.)

COST. When writing a script that you intend to produce, pay attention to potential costs — based on ease of shooting and availability of resources. This doesn't mean you always have to write as "cheaply" as possible, just that you should be aware of costs as you write and make those decisions consciously. The key to that is an understanding of the filmmaking process and an awareness that there are alternative ways to do most things. The more easily you learn to think of alternatives, the more choices you will have (whether you're concerned about costs or not).

1) Understanding film costs. In order to be able to write with costs in mind, a writer has to understand enough of the process of filmmaking to know how much things cost. If the writer doesn't know that, a first draft (or treatment or outline) might be a time for you to catch expensive things and make alterations. It's hard to talk abstractly about costs, because costs will depend on your resources. Things that might normally be expensive might not be in your case — so you'll need to know what you can get free or cheap. A film with a lot of antique cars, for example, might be very expensive to do in Los Angeles but much easier in a small town with several old car clubs.

2) Know your alternatives. One of the joys of filmmaking is that there are so many different ways of doing things. Let's say, for example, that you want to begin a film by introducing the viewer to a certain city. You could open with a helicopter shot, circling around the city; or go to the top of a hill or tall building and shoot down on the city; or use a montage of shots showing various aspects of the town (which shots you select will determine the image you convey); or buy some picture postcards and shoot them on an animation stand with camera moves; or have a few visuals and have someone tell about the city; or simply have a shot of the sign at the entrance to the city which gives the name,

9412

elevation, and population. Which alternative you choose can depend on preference, what impression you want to give, or your artistic taste — but it can also be influenced by the resources you have available. The more you train yourself to think about alternatives, the more choices you 'll have.

3) **Use illusion** if appropriate. Film is often illusion, and that can be very helpful in expanding your choices when you are looking for alternatives. In "Peter and the Wolf" there is a part of the story where the wolf eats the duck. A writer who doesn't think about the producing end might just write, "wolf eats duck." Now we probably could have done that, but for obvious reasons we didn't want to (just think of how many ducks we would have had to kill if we needed several takes — not to mention that the duck we used was someone's pet!) So we wrote the script to give an impression. We first see the wolf running, and then the duck running as if being chased (in those shots he was being chased by a production assistant and finally, when that didn't produce enough sense of the duck running in fear, by a chimpanzee, a pet of the animal trainers who was delighted to get into the act). We cut back and forth between those shots, with the pacing and the size of the shots (and the music) adding to the sense of pursuit. Then, right before the fateful moment, we cut to a shot of Peter watching, first in fear and then in horror, with appropriate

music. The next shot shows the wolf sitting and licking his chops (in actual fact he's licking off peanut butter) and the camera pans down to a pile of duck feathers (from a pillow) on the ground. It worked fine. Much of that film was based on illusions of things we couldn't get the animals to do. But we had thought it all out beforehand and discussed with the animal trainers what the animals could do (with the gentle methods both we and they were willing to use, which was an important consideration working with the animals).

4) Know your resources. Knowing what your resources are — in terms of actors, crew and equipment, locations, and props — is very helpful in adding production value to a script without adding huge costs.

a) Actors. Know the limits and talents of your potential actors. Will you be using top-notch actors who can do anything, actors who have limited abilities, or total amateurs?

You can also enhance your script by incorporating special talents your actors may have into the script. Our film "The Birth Control Movie" featured a group of high school kids. As I was writing the script, I had one particular boy in mind for a leading role — a saxophone player with a local high school jazz group who was a natural ham. After he auditioned and got the part I wrote his saxophone into three scenes. The script would have worked fine without it, but the sax added a nice touch (and we tied it into the music for the film, for which we used his band). The better you know your actors and their strengths and weaknesses, the more you can adjust for them.

Do you have a lot of inexpensive extras available? If so, that will allow you to do things you might otherwise never be able to do. For example, a scene with 1000 extras could be very expensive (depending on the length of the scene, what they have to do, and what kind of costumes). But you might also be able to do it for next to nothing. Perhaps you can use a crowd that is gathered for some other occasion. Or you might invite a crowd and give them some non-monetary payment such as a free concert. Or maybe you have 1000 friends who would love to help you out. But if you have only 50 friends, there's always the possibility of faking it — using close-ups and large crowd sound effects so you get the impression of a crowd but with many fewer people.

b) Locations, props, equipment. What do you have available? Do you have easy access to a plane, or helicopter, or a dolly? Do you have a trained monkey, special props or costumes, unusual locations?

In Santa Cruz it's fairly easy to find small town period locations (late 1880s on) and so we don't hesitate to write period scripts which might be prohibitively expensive for other people to produce. "Hard Traveling" is based on a true story that originally took place in the 1930s in Pennsylvania, over a period of about a year. But to film it on the east coast would have been very costly for us, especially to film a variety of seasons. One way we save money is by filming locally and we felt the story was a generic one that could just as easily have happened here as anywhere. So we changed the setting of the film — to Santa Cruz County. We had to make some adjustments, of course, but we didn't really lose anything by the change — and we were able to make the film for the amount of money we thought we could raise.

READ AND TIME THE SCRIPT

Once your script is written, you should do two things. One is to read it out loud, preferably with actors, to see if it works as you imagine it does. The other, which can be done at the same time, is to time the script. The general guide of one page of script equals one minute of screen time is only very approximate — so don't rely on it. The time to adjust the length of the script is now. Yes, you can cut the film down in the editing room, but not as easily as you can now — and probably not as smoothly. In addition, if you wait to shorten it in the editing room, you'll waste precious time and money shooting extra shots or entire scenes that you won't use. You might as well put that money into what you *will* use. If your film is too short, you would have to add material later (and find a way to do that smoothly). Fix it now!

EVALUATING YOUR PROJECT

A very important part of your planning should include an evaluation of the strengths and weaknesses of your project — and all the components that you are sure of at this time — as well as an evaluation of potential markets. The evaluation of the project should be made at different stages — to help you in planning and also to guide you in the fund-raising, production, and distribution stages. Your assessment will change as the project develops and as you add ingredients (for example, a script or cast) and as the theoretical becomes real (for example, when the composer actually writes the music and it is better, or worse, than you imagined). I'm not advocating that you go overboard and re-assess everything formally every two weeks — but I hope that talking about the evaluation process will let you keep thinking about it on some level throughout all the different stages. I do suggest at least one thorough, probably even written, evaluation at an early stage. The best time to do this is probably when you have all the basic elements put together, but at least after you have a script. For our purposes, let's assume that you have a script and the basic plan for your film as you do this evaluation.

The purpose of this evaluation is not to discourage you from making your film — it's to help you make it better.

Can you evaluate your project honestly? Some people maintain a fair amount of objectivity about their projects but others can't at all. If necessary, ask for help from colleagues and friends. I believe it's good for friends to give praise and be supportive and we all need that at times — but friends can also be invaluable for constructive criticism. Ask them to help you — and let them know that you really do want honesty and constructive criticism, and that you need their help to improve the film. Show people what you have — a script or treatment, and any other elements already in place. You can also get feedback on your casting ideas and other things as you go along. It's much better to know early on that no one but you likes the leading lady than to discover it after the film is finished. Ask for feedback again during the editing process with both the rough cut and also with the fine cut.

Don't let your ego get in the way of good judgment. The more honest and objective you can be in your assessment, the better off you'll be later on. The ostrich principle (burying your head in the sand) isn't useful, even though the evaluation process might lead to conclusions that you don't want to face. Perhaps the project shouldn't continue, at least as it is. But, if that's the case, it's better to know before you invest a lot of time, energy, and money. Or you might decide to continue in spite of the evaluation but with different (and more realistic) expectations. Or you might decide to make changes to strengthen the project.

Be systematic and specific about your assessment. Take five pieces of paper and label them: 1) strengths, 2) weaknesses, 3) resources, 4) needs, and 5) market potential. Write down as much under each heading as you can. Keep the lists around for a while and add new things as they come to mind. You may discover things you never thought about before.

STRENGTHS AND WEAKNESSES

Strengths and weaknesses are relative terms and depend on your goals, desired markets, etc.. A lot of violence might go into the "strengths" column for one kind of film while it would be a "weakness" for another. Characters that are good role models might be much more important for an educational film than for a horror movie. Look at all parts of the idea and the script (story line, characters, locale) and the rest of the package that you have together at this time (director, cast) and extract all the possible strengths and weaknesses. You can list tangible things here — but also intangibles. For example, if you have a lot of patience and stamina, that's a strength that might allow you to do things (such as take risks or a longer and harder route) that you might not be able to do otherwise.

RESOURCES

Some of this might fit under strengths, but I prefer to make a separate list. Resources might include people who will work directly on the film or who might help in other ways — cast, crew, or publicity, marketing, or distribution contacts. These might be people whose names alone are of value, or little-known but talented people whose skill is the resource. Make notes about access to equipment, locations, props, money — anything you might be able to use. The resources could be actual, that is people who've already committed to the project, or potential, people to whom you might go at some later stage. Keep this list. Add to it as you or your friends think of additional resources. Write it all down, otherwise you really will forget some of these things.

NEEDS

Your list of needs can include everything from financial needs (how much money do you personally need or want to make while doing this project) to professional and emotional needs. It's useful to write these down clearly and keep them in front of you as you do your evaluation.

MARKET POTENTIAL

You may also want to evaluate the market or commercial potential of your film. This involves determining to which markets the film could be sold, the likelihood of such sales, and the potential income from those sales. Be realistic. It's better to make a realistic assessment and then tailor the film to your budget than to be surprised after it's completed.

If someone else is funding your film, *they* will probably evaluate its money-making potential. If you've already done that, you can make sure they don't overlook any of your positive findings.

Talk with distributors and buyers if you can. Show them your script and tell them your plans. Ask for their evaluation and suggestions. Make clear that you aren't asking for money (if you're not) but would like their feedback.

EVALUATION AND ADJUSTMENT

Once you have these lists, evaluate them. Now that you know the strengths and weaknesses of your project, what you want to do is make the most of what you have. You want to maximize your strengths and compensate for your weaknesses (keeping in mind your resources and needs). I'm not advocating turning your film into something you don't like in order to make it saleable — but you should strive to make it as good as it can be within your limits and goals.

Are there things you can add to your film to strengthen it? For example, adding music by a popular rock group might help an ordinary teenage film. Adding excellent acting to a serious adult film might draw audiences to see the acting if nothing else (although excellent acting in a teenage movie might not help as much as a good musical score!). An ordinary story might be set in a unique and interesting location. A film that involves skiing might include a lot of outstanding ski footage as an added incentive for ski buffs to see the film. Go over your list of weaknesses and think of what you can do to compensate for them. Suppose that some of your financing is contingent upon using a particular actor, but he's far from perfect. That's a weakness, but you don't have to just stop there. Do what you can to compensate for it. For example, if the director is good at working with actors, wonderful. Leave plenty of time for rehearsal (perhaps well in advance of the shoot). Or you might want to consider bringing in an "acting coach" to help. Casting seasoned actors to work with a weak actor might also help. Plan staging, camera angles, and editing that will aid the actor.

Suppose you have selected a director who is wonderful with actors but not very experienced with film editing and camera moves. You can compensate by choosing a DP (director of photography) who has a good understanding of shots and of what will work in the editing process (for example, what kinds of shots will inter-cut well, where to begin and end a shot to give the editor good cutting places, and what coverage the editor will need). You might also consider having the editor on the set. Suppose you have a DP who is great at selecting shots but weak on lighting. Compensate by selecting a strong gaffer who can work independently. If you have a DP who is good at the above tasks but is not very steady with a camera, make sure to have a camera operator on the crew (even if the DP could do both jobs).

Another example of compensation, this time from "Hard Traveling." We were doing a period piece and many colleagues had questioned whether we could obtain authentic-looking sets and costumes on our limited budget. Although our budget was small, we knew we had resources that would make our task simpler — a small town with friendly people and many depression era items stashed away in people's homes and garages. Our method would take time, but we had time — or, more precisely, we *made* the time because we knew that time would be the key to doing a good job.

We had a costume person who regularly scoured local thrift shops for vintage clothing. Long before we had raised all our money we told her she could begin buying clothes whenever she found them, up to a certain amount, and we'd reimburse her even if we failed to make the film. That meant taking a chance but we knew we wouldn't have a very long pre-production period once we had raised the money, and allowing her to begin early meant that we obtained better costumes at a much lower cost than we could have otherwise. At first she collected general clothes of the period. As soon as we selected our two principal actors, she concentrated on their wardrobes. In the end, we even cast some extras to fit specific clothing she had found.

We also began looking for our key locations well in advance. We didn't make a crusade of it, but anytime we went anywhere we tried to take different roads — and I always kept a little notebook in the car with notes on potential locations.

By giving ourselves time in this way, we achieved a more authentic look than we would have been able to do otherwise — and certainly at less cost. We succeeded in turning a liability into an asset. We didn't ignore our friends' doubts, we just tried harder.

Your evaluation may lead you to change the goals of your film, as well as change the film itself. If the consensus is that the story will never be a big financial success, you may decide that you really care most about the film as a showcase of your and other people's talents, and you may still think the film will be a good vehicle for that. You might still decide to go ahead with the project — but perhaps on a much smaller budget than previously anticipated.

You can make changes and adjustments at any time during the filmmaking process — but the reason to do an evaluation near the beginning is that it's much easier (and cheaper) to change things early than later on.

EXAMPLE: "PETER AND THE WOLF"

Here's what our evaluation of our film "Peter and the Wolf," a half-hour version of Prokofiev's famous tale, looked like.

Strengths. The list of strengths included a well-known and loved story and music, an original concept that would work both as an educational film and also as entertainment for television, cute animals, and a script that the animal trainers we selected felt was very workable (in terms of what their animals could do). Later we added Ray Bolger, a talented actor/dancer who will always be remembered for his role as the scarecrow in the "The Wizard of Oz," as our on-camera narrator.

Weaknesses. The primary weakness was the relatively high cost. Kids and animals are not easy to work with, and we required some very specific and tricky things from the animals. We knew they were possible, but they would take time and a relatively high shooting ratio. And since wolves, cats, ducks, and birds are not predictable, we didn't know how long it would take us to get the necessary footage of the animals. Because the budget for the film was high for an educational film, we knew we'd be unlikely to obtain complete funding from an educational film distributor (as we often had in the past). That meant we'd have to search for additional funding sources.

Another weakness was that although we considered trying for television distribution, at that time we had little experience and no track record in that area which made it unlikely that we'd get advance funding from those sources. We were also neither accustomed to nor good at hustling money in that world. In addition, our film already had serious competition — Disney had made a classic animated version of the same story years before that was still widely used in schools and libraries.

Resources. Our most valuable resource was a couple of animal trainers we had met while using their chimpanzee in another film. They owned several wolves, felt the project was feasible, and were eager to work with us. We also knew that we had period locations, costumes, and props easily available in our area.

Needs. Our needs were 1) to make back the costs of the film reasonably fast and ultimately make a profit for the investors (we hoped to build a base of satisfied investors for future projects), 2) to begin building a reputation for our films in areas other than the educational market (again looking towards future projects), and 3) to make a film that both we and the investors would be proud of. Although we hoped to make a profit in the long-run, our personal financial needs were low and we could cover those by doing other projects while we worked on this one.

Market potential. Because the film would be appropriate for both television (at this time we thought only of cable although the film was ultimately sold to CBS as well) and the educational market, it stood a good chance, if made well, of earning back its costs and then some. (We did not consider the home video market at that time because it was not widely used for that length film. Nor did we consider foreign sales because at that time we knew very little about the foreign market.)

Evaluation and adjustment. We did various things to compensate for the difficulty of working with animals. We began with animal trainers whom we liked and trusted and we checked each scene with them, adjusting the script where necessary. Because

41

wolves are generally skittish, we planned to accustom the wolf to the boy who would play Peter, to us, and to a camera before the shoot. (The trainers feared that a cameraman crouching behind a camera might be very threatening to the wolf so they set up a camera next to the wolf's cage for two weeks before the shoot.) We insisted on a calm and quiet set whenever the wolf worked (with crew out of sight as much as possible) and we used women to move lights or props near the wolf because he was more at ease with women. We scheduled shots carefully around the animals' needs and schedules. For example, the cat was more active in the morning and lazy in the afternoon so we scheduled those shots accordingly. We planned the shoot so that shots of animals without people came last, to be filmed with a reduced crew.

Although we had faith in the idea, in our script, and in our ability to make a good film, the high budget scared us as much as the project excited us even. We decided to fund the film through a limited partnership, keeping costs low and doing as good a job as we could. We thought we'd be able to sell the finished film in both the television and educational markets and thus recoup our costs. We knew we'd have to walk a fine line to make the film entertaining enough for television yet educational enough for schools. The desire for TV sales meant that we added an introduction before the beginning of Prokofiev's music to make the film closer to a half-hour in length. We also decided to find a name personality to be the on-camera narrator to improve our chances of television sales. We knew this would increase our costs somewhat, but we thought it would ultimately be worth it. We didn't attempt to set the film in Prokofiev's Russia, but instead chose turn-of-the century California — a setting that was easy for us to create successfully, hopefully adding "production value" to the film. We added a line to Ray Bolger's introduction saying, "The original story took place in Russia, but it could have happened anywhere...."

The difficulties we knew we would face with "Peter and the Wolf" led us to proceed cautiously and in the end we probably produced a better and more commercially viable film than if we hadn't stopped to carefully evaluate the project.

FINDING THE MONEY

Each film project is different — and how you raise money will also be different. Where to look for funding will depend on the type of film, the strengths of the film, the track record of the filmmakers, the markets for which it's appropriate, the level of funding you want, and your own personal preferences and abilities.

SOURCES OF FUNDING

The primary sources of funding for films are 1) your own money, 2) money from family and/or friends, 3) grants, 4) loans, 5) investors (generally through a "public" or "private" limited partnership), 6) funding from distributors or film studios, 7) funding from a private company or corporation, 8) pre-sales of the film to certain markets, and 9) crew and/or cast donations or deferments (of labor and equipment). You can also combine two or more of these.

1) YOUR OWN MONEY. Some filmmakers have enough money (or inexpensive enough films) to be able to fund them by themselves, either all at once or slowly over time. Some people work at one job to earn money while shooting their own film on the side, using any spare funds to buy film or for other expenses. The limits to this are obvious — you have to have money to begin with and you have to be willing to risk it on a film project. In addition, if your money dribbles in slowly, your film will proceed at the same pace. But if no one else is willing to give you money, it's a way to get your film made. And it has advantages — you may then receive all the profits (unless you have given deferments or profit-shares to others who worked on the film) and you will also generally have total control over your film.

2) MONEY FROM FAMILY OR FRIENDS. This can be either gifts or investments. It's nice if you can get it — but be careful not to burn your friends, intentionally or not. Remember that film is usually a high-risk investment and that for all the glorious success stories you hear (which may be exaggerated) there are many untold stories of financial disasters (which almost never get publicized, except for outrageous Hollywood boondoggles).

3) GRANTS. The big advantage of grants is that they are just that — gifts that usually don't have to be paid back (although some strings, such as showing the film on public television, may cause you to lose other potential income, and some grants do have payback conditions). Grants are also often very competitive but they do exist from many sources. Some grants are very generous, others are small; some are simple to apply for, others are very complicated and involve much paperwork and long waiting periods; some grants have strings attached, others don't; some grants require completed scripts, some will accept ideas; some provide start-up money, others may give only completion funds; some require experience, others want to encourage new filmmakers.

Grant organizations will often tell you their guidelines and requirements in advance so that you can determine if your project is appropriate for their grants. There are organizations that give grants specifically to filmmakers (such as the National Endowment for the Arts or the American Film Institute) and others that are general foundations and may fund films as well as other things. If you are making a film on a specific topic, check organizations and foundations that give grants for that subject as well as film grants in general. Grants are usually easier to obtain for projects that are not inherently commercial (although there are exceptions) and that have some social or artistic worth, as determined by the grant donor. Grant writing is an art in itself and requires skill and time.

4) LOANS. These can be from banks, credit unions, friends, or family. Terms and conditions can vary greatly. Some will have many stipulations and stiff payback terms, while others may be generous and flexible. Some loans can be paid back all at once at some future time, while on others you have to make regular payments from the time you take out the loan (which can be a heavy burden, although you can allow for loan payments in your film budget).

Numerous films have been made on credit cards — but beware that the interest rates are very high.

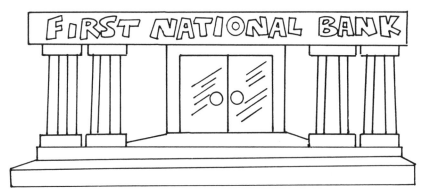

Loans can be a great source of financing, giving you a high degree of control over your film and a high percentage of the profits (above the fixed interest you agreed to pay) — but they can also be a disaster. Make sure you can pay the loan back, and that you'll have sufficient income to make the periodic payments if you'll have those. Otherwise you can lose friends, or any personal property that you put up as collateral. Remember that film is a high-risk business. Give yourself plenty of time to sell your film (and receive payment) before you have to repay the loan. Don't count on selling your film the day after it's completed.

5) PRIVATE INVESTORS. This method of financing will usually be structured as a "limited partnership" — a common legal structure that has many variations but where the "general partners" (usually the filmmakers) contribute their knowledge and experience and usually have creative control while the "limited partners" (the investors) put up the money and only share in the profits (or losses). These partnerships are governed by state or federal laws (or both) depending on the size and type of partnership. Whether the partnership is "private" or "public" relates primarily to whom and to how many people the partnership is offered. Regulations governing partnerships differ, with public ones being more complicated and costly. Consult a lawyer for details on your particular state and situation. You can also obtain information on your own by going to a law library (try a law school or the local courthouse — and ask the librarian for assistance). Also check out your state taxes on partnerships.

Expenses for setting up a partnership vary with their size and complexity. Partnerships usually involve writing up a lengthy "prospectus" which clearly outlines your project and the background of the general partners, and also contains a lot of standard legal language pertaining to the rights and duties of both the general and limited partners. Limited partnerships are common in the business world and you should be able to find a qualified lawyer to put one together even if you don't live in a major film center. You may be able to cut your legal costs by providing your lawyer with a sample prospectus from another film project and also by preparing some of the non-legal sections about your film and the general partners on your own.

Partnerships are merely pieces of paper, agreements between people, and they can be written in a variety of ways (in conformity, of course, with state and federal regulations). A standard type of arrangement is one in which the first money made from the film will go to pay back the investors and then the profits will be split according to some pre-arranged formula (for example 50% for the general partners and 50% for the limited partners, divided among them according to each partner's share of the total investment). You can also offer a percentage (of profits or of total sales) to actors or crew members or others involved with the production. This is often referred to as "points." Before you write out your agreements, think out the financial structure carefully and seek the advice of other filmmakers who have gone through the process as well as the advice of your lawyer. Remember that although your lawyer knows the law, *you* should decide what terms you want for your partnership. Be aware that all this may involve complicated book-keeping later on so it's in your interest to keep the terms simple. Remember also that these are legal documents and you are bound by principles of "full disclosure" to include all relevant information, negative as well as positive, in your prospectus. One thing this means is that you must mention the "high risk" nature of film investment. Last, but not least, remember that if the partnership makes a lot of money, everyone will probably be happy, but if it doesn't, even good friends may take you to court, so follow legal requirements carefully.

Finding investors. If you know a lot of rich people looking for investment opportunities, that's great. If not, you'll have to be more inventive to locate potential investors. (A potential investor is anyone who has enough money to meet your minimum investment and legal qualifications.) Do you know any people who might be able to invest in your film? Do your friends know any potential investors? Do any people associated with the film project (in any capacity) have friends who might be useful for funding? Some people are likely to know potential investors simply because of the nature of their work. Lawyers, accountants, stockbrokers, investment counsellors, or realtors are some of the kinds of professionals who might know potential investors.

Think about your particular film. To whom will it appeal? Be as specific here as you can — this will give you clues as to where to look for money. Does the film have special appeal to women, men, swimmers, doctors, or any particular special interest group? A film that involves important subject matter (whether a documentary or a dramatic film) can sometimes appeal to people based on its content. In addition, are there any people to whom the film will appeal because of special connections — to the script, the story, cast, crew, or locale? The next step is to figure out how to reach these people. Are you a member of any groups where you might meet them? Do you know someone who might host a party for potential investors? Do you know people who know people...?

Convincing investors. Once you have contacted appropriate people about investing in your film, you have to convince them that it's a worthwhile investment (based on whatever their criteria is — social or artistic worth, financial soundness, or whatever). Film is both intriguing and scary as an investment. When you mention the idea of investing in a film to some people, they may run scared because of bad experiences of their own or those of friends, or because they know that investing in film is risky. Others may light up and become intrigued because film has an air of excitement and glamour about it. If you're dealing with someone who has had bad experiences, it's important to find out the details because their experiences may not be relevant for your project. For example, their experience may be with a worthwhile but not financially successful documentary while you may be planning a very commercially viable dramatic film. Or their example may be a film by an eager but inexperienced novice that ended up disastrously, while you have a long and successful track record. They may only know about high budget Hollywood film partnerships that use "creative book-keeping" and were never really intended to benefit the investors.

On the positive side, some people are excited at the chance to be involved in the making of a film, which is an opportunity most people don't have (especially outside Los Angeles). We've found people who like the idea of investing in a film simply to diversify their investment portfolio — they have a few pieces of real estate, a business or two, maybe an oil well, but they never "had" a film. It's something different and intriguing, great cocktail party conversation. Maybe they hope their daughter can be an extra. A word of caution: some of these people can be quite naive and you should be careful not to take advantage of that. You don't want unhappy investors later.

A film that will be made locally might be an added attraction. Investors might enjoy watching the action from the sidelines, meeting the actors, or even participating as extras if appropriate. And you can appeal to local chauvinism. If the cast and crew are at least partly local, you can appeal to people to support local artists and craftsmen (local businesses will also benefit). Film is, after all, an art form worthy of support by people who support other arts. Investing in film allows them to support the arts and hopefully also make some money at the same time.

Prepare a formal presentation about your film that you can give to individuals or groups. Include some "show and tell" — film clips of previous work, a script, production board, photos of potential cast or locations — anything that might excite the person or help convince them that the film, and you, are a worthwhile investment.

6) DISTRIBUTORS OR FILM STUDIOS. This option is as varied as the distributors or studios that might fund your film. Some want large amounts of control, others demand relatively little; some want the rights for all markets, others desire only one market; some have large amounts of money available, some don't. When you negotiate, be clear about what both you and they want. Get it in writing and, if necessary, have a lawyer check it over. This can be an easy way to finance a film — the studios or distributors do, after all, give you the money to make your film. But they are not likely to fund your film unless you have a solid track record and it's a project they deem to be very saleable. They may also want more control than you're willing to give them.

7) PRIVATE COMPANIES often sponsor industrial films, either for training or publicity purposes. As with distributors, the amount of control they desire varies, although you are usually making their film, not yours. Sometimes private companies also fund films on other subjects as a public service or for public relations reasons.

8) PRE-SALES. This method involves selling off some or all of the rights to your film (for example, foreign or television or home video rights) before the film is made. The advantage is that you make a sale to those markets and obtain some money to make your film. The disadvantage is that you will be left with fewer markets to sell after the film is finished. Be careful if you raise only a portion of your funds this way and must sell the film to other markets when it is finished, since some distributors won't be interested in your film at all if you've already sold off some of the rights. You may also receive a lower price than if you had waited until you had a finished film.

A "negative pick-up" is a variation on pre-sales where you receive a guarantee that a distributor will buy your film upon receiving the completed answer print. The negative pick-up deal won't give you cash before you make the film but it can serve as collateral which will allow you to obtain a bank loan. In general, this can be a good way to fund a film, but read the fine print. A negative pick-up deal may be a definite, air-tight guarantee or it may include conditions (such as requiring an "acceptable" answer print) that may allow the distributor to take the film if they like it but drop it if they don't (or if they are short of money at the time or for any other reason), leaving you with a film and no buyer. Hollywood studios sometimes use negative pick-ups as a way to avoid some union regulations and obtain a film for a lower price than if they had funded it outright.

9) **CAST AND CREW DONATIONS** (of labor or equipment). Films can be made largely or in part cooperatively with crew and/or cast sharing in potential profits or simply deferring their pay until the film is sold. This won't eliminate all costs, but it can cut your cash budget way down.

CREATIVE FINANCING

Creative financing can work as well for filmmaking as for real estate. One basic formula I've used a lot may seem obvious, but it is useful nevertheless — money not spent is equal to money raised. Money can be "raised" by cutting your budget, obtaining deferments, paying cast and crew with "points" (a percentage of ownership in the film or a percentage of profits) rather than cash, or bartering ("I'll work on your film if you'll work on mine"). All this reduces the amount of cash that you'll need.

Raising the money for "Hard Traveling" was extremely difficult, and every time we came to what seemed like an impasse, we sat down and brainstormed and tried to think of ways to find money other than looking for still another investor. At that point we mainly reduced the budget and obtained personal loans. When it became clear that we wouldn't be able to raise our ideal budget ($800,000), we cut costs, little by little, and amended our limited partnership agreement to reflect the lower budget. Some of the cuts were possible because as we got closer to our fund-raising goal we were able to make firm deals for certain services (which is harder to do when you don't know when or even if you'll be filming). Other cuts were simply sacrifices and compromises — but the film got made.

Timing. Filmmaking is usually such a long process that fund-raising can be done in stages — although this can be very risky. If you fail to complete the film, the money you raised at the beginning is totally lost. An unfinished film is worthless. Money can conceivably be raised for four main stages: development (of the idea), production (getting the film shot and "in the can"), post-production, and distribution. Raising lower amounts is certainly easier although it's a drain to have to be raising money when you're in the middle of making a film (unless you have a producer or executive producer whose primary job is raising money and who isn't involved in the actual production). When you raise money in stages, you have something to show potential backers for the next stage, which may be an advantage. But if they don't like what they see, you may be stuck half-way. While you may not need to have all the cash in hand before you begin filming, I'd strongly suggest that you know (for sure) where all the money will come from before you start shooting.

Publicity. Publicity can be very useful in the fund-raising stages. For "Hard Traveling" we began to think about public relations at the very beginning and it was useful in helping us raise funds. Our fund-raising base was primarily local and we concentrated on the local press. Although we couldn't openly advertise that we were seeking investors (a legal requirement for a private limited partnership, at least in California), we received publicity in various local papers about our upcoming project and also about past successes. Our hope was that when we approached people for money, they would know about both us and "Hard Traveling."

FUND-RAISING TIPS

Be organized. Write everything down. Keep all your lists of fund-raising contacts written down, along with information about who gave you their name, when, what material you sent them, how you contacted them, what their response was, if any follow-up is needed (or possible), and any other useful information about the person such as special interests or past investment history. Writing all this down may seem crass, but you'll be glad later. Use file cards or a notebook. You may also make contacts at this stage that will be useful later on — for publicity, production, distribution. Write all this information down in the proper place. Begin your public relations and resource lists.

Make a good impression. The impression you make at this stage will give people an indication of what they can expect later on.

If you propose to make a high quality film, take extra care with your written and spoken presentations. Show people how well you understand the filmmaking process.

Have a well-prepared "pitch." Find a way to describe your project in a clear, concise, but exciting way. You should be able to convey the essence of your film in 3-4 sentences. Be prepared to then give more details, and to present basic financial information about investing in the film succinctly. Stress the strengths of your project, don't just assume they'll be obvious.

Get something from everyone you talk with. A piece of advice given to us was to always leave a fund-raising meeting with one of three things — money, names of other contacts (if the person you talked with liked the project and was willing to refer you to other people even if unable to give you money), or specific criticisms or suggestions (if they didn't feel they could support or recommend the project). That way you always come away with something that can help you.

Don't count money as certain until the check clears the bank. People may promise money with the best of intentions and simply not be able to come through. This may even happen with good friends. If you count the money before you have it, you may be disappointed and perhaps suddenly find yourself in a financial bind if it doesn't come through.

Each film is different. There is no one "right" formula, no "right" way to raise money. Each film is different and each person is different. What works for my film may not work for yours. What I feel comfortable saying and doing may be totally impossible for you. The trick is to find out what works for you and for your project. Try different approaches and learn and re-assess as you go. See what works best and what feels most comfortable.

Chose a project you can live with for a long time. It may be a long, hard road to make your film — make sure you care enough about the project to stick it out through the tough parts.

TAXES

If you're new to filmmaking, check out the tax laws, especially as they relate to small businesses. (One helpful source is *Small Time Operator* by Bernard Kamoroff). Find out what you can and can't deduct. Check out tax implications of different business structures and funding sources. Do this before you begin.

RESPONSIBILITY

This section wouldn't be complete without a word about responsibility — to the people who put up the money, but also to other filmmakers and to yourself. There is, somewhere in the artistic world, a fine line between artistic expression and self-indulgence. It's a hard line to find, and very subjective, but it's there. There is nothing wrong with artistic expression, even in an expensive medium, but if you are just asking people to support that, do so clearly. Don't mislead anyone.

Responsibility to investors or to whoever puts up the money for the film is really a question of morality, and I don't want to preach more than I already have. But I do want to raise a practical consideration — and that is that you can usually only burn people once. If your financial plan (or the film project itself) isn't sound, you won't be able to continue to make films in the same way, burning the same people.

Another moral issue I want to raise is the question of your responsibility to other filmmakers. Each time one filmmaker burns investors with a film that is poorly planned or goes way over budget, other filmmakers will likely feel the effects. As you raise money you'll probably hear tales of past filmmaking disasters. Think about the filmmakers who will follow you. Be realistic with people about what they can expect (both in terms of risks and profits). Responsibility as a producer means more that just being careful before raising money. It also means doing your job well afterwards — budgeting accurately, producing the film efficiently, and making the best film you can in order to maximize its chances of success.

The last area of responsibility is to yourself. That means don't kid yourself about your project — and take care of yourself (financially and emotionally) during the process.

HOW TO SURVIVE A FILM SHOOT

Pacing is very important in a film — but it's also important in the *making* of a film. Filmmaking can be a very high-pressured, stressful, occupation, and one of the things you should think about before the shoot is how to deal with these pressures and how to pace yourself (and the rest of the crew) so that you don't end up physically and emotionally exhausted at the end of the shoot (or worse, in the middle). Many things contribute to the pressures of filmmaking.

Money is a primary pressure, especially for the independent filmmaker for whom it's usually in short supply. You have to deal not only with the difficulty of raising money, but also with the conflict between being an artist and a money person. Because filmmaking is such an expensive proposition, you are constantly aware that everything you do, even stopping for five minutes to go to the bathroom, costs a lot of money. Low budget productions face this even more acutely. And the independent filmmaker often feels personal financial pressures as well — whether it means living at a fairly low economic level in order to do work he or she wants to do or even going into debt in order to make a particular film.

Time is also a pressure, especially on low budget films — mostly because time equals money. There are deadlines to meet and the clock is always running.

Working with people and dealing with personal conflicts can be another source of stress. Time and money pressures are felt by most people on the set, which doesn't make for ideal working conditions. In addition, personality conflicts, ego problems, or power struggles can arise and can sometimes become serious enough to interfere with the film.

Although all these pressures are real, there are actions you can take to improve the situation. Try to remove or lessen any pressures that you can. Five day work weeks are ideal, although usually a luxury that low budget films can't afford (or think they can't afford). Low budget films also tend to work long hours (not to mention that the standard film day is already 10 hours). I understand that paying for equipment by the day or week is an incentive to work long hours and get the most out of the equipment, but what's good for equipment isn't necessarily good for people. Exhausted people don't work at their best — and they don't work cheerfully. More important, tired people are more likely to have accidents (and a film shoot with lots of electrical equipment around is not a good place to have accidents), get sick or simply be cranky. So before you plan to have much overtime, think about whether you can afford overtime in terms of decreased productivity and the toll on your crew.

Now that we know more about the effects of nutrition and stimulants like caffeine and sugar, pay attention to the food you serve. Have healthy foods available for cast and crew, such as fruit and juices for breakfast rather than just the traditional coffee and doughnuts. Provide non-caffeine teas and nutritious low-sugar snacks. You can't legislate peoples' eating habits, but you can offer healthy alternatives.

Do what you can to encourage cast and crew to get adequate sleep. Avoid long hours. Make sure crew can eat and get to sleep quickly if they want to, and that food and transportation are easily available.

Take as many outside pressure off yourself as possible. This is especially important for a long shoot where you have to continue living as well as working. Someone has to feed the cat, wash the laundry, pay household bills. "Wives" were a very handy institution for all this, but times are changing — and that system never helped those of us who were women. Supportive mates and friends can help, but dumping on them is a poor solution and ignores the fact that they may have their own important work. Good advance planning can be the best solution.

Know your limits. Pushing past your limits doesn't help you or other people. Know how much pressure you can take and how much work you can do. Find others to help do what you can't handle — or allow yourself more time.

Part of your master plan for producing a film should include a plan for your personal finances (and those of other key people). Will you take money from the film project? Enough to live on? Do you have other sources of income? Will you have to juggle other work at the same time as this project? Do you have any reserves in case the film takes longer than planned? Having to deal with personal financial crises in the middle of a shoot is no fun.

A special warning to couples working on a film together: the pressures of a several-year low budget, high-stress feature film can lead to divorce or at least severe relationship problems (and has in several instances I know of). So if you're working with a mate, be a little extra understanding, and be aware that some of the relationship problems that arise may be caused by the film.

Producing a film is a much longer project than just the actual shooting. Plan adequate time for rest and recuperation during the process — you'll probably need it.

ORGANIZATION

There are so many aspects to film production, so many details, that it's important to be well organized. The elaborateness of your organization will, of course, depend on the size and type of film you are making. I can keep essential information for a small educational film in one thin file folder or on a clipboard, while my "information book" for "Hard Traveling" was a very full 2" loose-leaf binder (and even then I kept less relevant information in other places). The following is the method I use to keep track of all that I need to keep track of for a film. I use four main tools: 1) the production board or chart; 2) a loose-leaf notebook (or manila folder for small films) that I call my "information book" that contains all the lists, phone numbers, and miscellaneous information I need for the production; 3) a notebook I call my "daily book" (optional for small films) that has a page for each day of pre-production and production, where I can keep track of all the details that have to be done each day; and 4) the "money book" to keep track of payroll and money in general.

COMPUTER PROGRAMS

There are now various computer programs that can help you organize your information. Some can, for example, help you transfer the basic information from the script to a production board — and all the other production forms you'll need. Others can help you budget. These programs are expensive and not at all essential, but they are handy and can save you time. On both the production forms and budget programs, if you make any changes, the computer will automatically adjust everything else affected by that change. Nice. If you have access to these computer programs, you'll easily be able to adapt what follows to your program. The key is still to get the right information to begin with. If you want to get a computer program, ask around to find out which best suits your needs — they are not all equal.

PRODUCTION BOARD

The production board or chart will be discussed in detail on page 78 so I won't repeat that information here. A production board enables you to see all the basic film elements and the schedule at a glance. Unfortunately, the production board for a feature film is large and cumbersome.

INFORMATION BOOK

This will vary greatly in size depending on your film. For a small film all you really need is a file folder with a cast and crew list, a call sheet (see p. 95) with call times and location addresses and phones, and a few other miscellaneous contact phone numbers (for lab, props, etc.). For a feature film I'd suggest a 2" school-type loose-leaf binder with dividers for different sections. A 3-hole punch will be invaluable. For "Hard Traveling" I added or removed different sections as I needed them or finished with them. The following are sections you might want to include.

1)   Schedule. Because the production board for a big film is so unwieldy, I keep a typed summary of the schedule, updating it as needed. If you're using one of the newer small production boards, a xerox should work fine here. You might also want to include a very brief scene summary (one line per scene) for easy reference. If you use a simplified production chart, just include that.

2)   Breakdown sheets. You may want to keep these in this notebook if they contain a lot of information not yet transferred elsewhere.

3)   Cast. This should include name and phone numbers (home, on location, agent,), social security number, and salary information. You can also include information for the casting process, such as potential cast for each role. For "Hard Traveling" I began this section with cast descriptions and then added lists of potential cast (and their phone numbers and agents, as well as other films they'd been in that we might want to look at). After we made casting decisions, I removed all this keeping only the list of selected people. (But keep the rejects filed away somewhere, you never know when you might need them.)

62

4) Extras. This should include names and phone numbers of extras, arranged by scene. I use this to call them if they don't show up and to keep track of who has signed releases and who has been paid. After the film, you can use this list to invite them to a screening of the finished film.

5) Crew. During pre-production this can be a long list of potential crew people, while after selection it can simply be a page of crew names, with phone numbers, social security number, salary, whether a deal memo or contract was signed, and starting dates. Don't throw away names of crew you don't use — in case you need them later.

6) Technical and service contacts. This can include labs; sound studios; equipment rental houses; sources for film stock, office supplies, food; and miscellaneous items such as dry cleaners and doctors — in other words, everything you might possibly need before, during, or after the shoot. This can include price quotes and details in addition to addresses and phone numbers.

7) Locations. During pre-production I use this to keep track of possible locations, while during the shoot it becomes a list of the actual locations we are using and all relevant information such as names, addresses, phone numbers of all appropriate people (including the janitor's home phone if he'll open the place up for you), location fee, dates, and any special arrangements.

8) Props and costumes. Beginning with pre-production, keep track of any and all sources. Anytime someone mentions a prop they have, write it down here. There is so much information floating around during the production of a film that if it isn't written down in a specific place, it'll get lost.

9) Pre-production tasks and decisions. This is a section I use for specific things that need to be done or decisions that need to be made. This is where I kept the pros and cons and relative costs of 16mm and 35mm as well as Kodak and Fuji film when we were trying to make those decisions for "Hard Traveling." I also kept a list of tasks for both volunteers and staff.

10) Budget. I keep the final working budget with me at all times. Referring to this often helps keep costs down. As the production progresses, I add "actual" costs in the proper column and keep close track of how those figures compare with my original estimates. That way I always know if I'm over or under budget for any item, and by how much.

11) Fund-raising. This section can contain fund-raising contacts, copies of printed matter used for fund-raising, and basic financial information you need to give to people. During "Hard Traveling" most of our contacts were on 3"x 5" cards, but I kept lists in the notebook of people I was pursuing or following up on at any given time (along with any information I needed to know in relation to that). I also kept lists of contacts that other people were supposed to talk to and lists of people invited to particular events, such as a film screening or party.

12) Other films. For "Hard Traveling" I kept a section on other films (primarily recent independent or low budget ones) where I wrote down any relevant information I came across, such as costs, profits made (or losses), technical information, distribution information, and contact phone numbers. This was useful simply for me to know what others had done and also as examples when talking to potential investors.

13) Public relations. This can include press and other public relations contacts, as well as copies of press material you send out. For example, if someone mentions a friend who is a film reviewer or a magazine that might be good for publicity, write it here.

14) Editing. This can include a list of scenes, which can be annotated as the shoot progresses. While I was not physically editing "Hard Traveling." I spent many hours in the editing room and when not there I was often thinking about editing and I made many notes to myself about ideas of places to cut or things to change. As the film was cut, I added timings for each scene. When we began to work on music, I added the timings we needed for the music. When we began to plan the titles and end credits, I kept that information here as well. This is overkill for a small film but can really help for a big one. I always had the information I needed with me, which was especially useful because I made numerous trips to Los Angeles for various post-production tasks.

15) Research. You might want a list of things you need to research. For "Hard Traveling" much of our research was historical background for the script and the shoot, but it also included facts on some social and political issues raised by the film (such as illiteracy, unemployment, child abuse, and gun control) that I wanted to be able to talk about both with potential investors and after the film was finished.

16) Forms. This can be a place to keep call sheets, production reports, or any other forms you might need.

17) Distribution. Keep lists of potential distributors, their phone numbers, addresses, and other relevant information such as what markets they cover, what kinds of films they prefer, what films they have distributed previously, and names of their key people. When the film is finished, keep track of who you invite to screenings and their reactions (if known). If you send out mailings, keep track of who they went to and what the response was. At the time it seems easy to remember all this, but there will be a lot you'll forget. Keep track of any ideas you have about distribution and marketing strategy.

18) Festivals. You can begin keeping data on festivals you might be interested in attending (or being invited to), including festival dates, requirements, entry deadlines, screening dates and procedures, addresses, phones, contact people, and any other relevant information.

For "Hard Traveling" this "information book" was essentially the office on a shoot that had no formal office. I kept it near me at all times and it made my life much simpler — I always had the information I needed easily available.

DAILY BOOK

This could be part of the "information book" — but for a big film that book will simply be too much to carry. The daily book should be with you at all times, with the list of things to do each day and any relevant phone numbers right there. For "Hard Traveling" I kept a 9"x 12" spiral notebook in which I had labeled one page (2 sides) for each date, beginning with the intensive pre-production period (about a month before filming) and going through the shoot. I used this so I wouldn't have to keep anything in my head and in order to have daily information closer than the "information book." Anything I had to do, I'd write down. I kept this book on a clipboard with a pencil attached. The notebook and clipboard fit into a small shoulder bag so it could always be with me, even if I needed to have my hands free. This book duplicated some information I had elsewhere, but it was wonderful to always have it so close. And the process of reviewing what should be listed for the next day was an important ritual each night that helped me keep track of things.

MONEY BOOK

This is for your book-keeping. You may have an accountant or book-keeper set it up but you can also do it yourself. The main things you need are a record of all expenses (separated into categories), a record of income, and payroll records. I use a simple loose-leaf notebook with pre-printed pages (you can buy various kinds, depending on how many columns you need, at a stationary store).

One problem with accounting is that the information the IRS (Internal Revenue Service) needs is different from the information you need. For example, the IRS wants to know your total crew costs, total equipment rental costs, total postage and freight costs. You'll want to know the costs by budget category (camera, lighting, sound etc.) so you can keep track of the budget. The trick is to find a system that gives you the information needed for both. I begin with forms from a standard "Accountants Work Sheet Pad," available from stationary stores.

For small films I set up the books more for IRS purposes, with all of the expenses simply listed sequentially (see sample form on p. 67). Since there are so few entries in each budget category, you can easily locate the budget figures you need and keep track of your expenses by filling in the actual costs as they occur directly in the "actual" column of your budget. When your camera department expenses consist simply of one payment each for a camera person, an assistant, and camera rental, you don't need a separate book-keeping page to keep track of that.

For a feature film, however, there are simply too many expenses in each category to be able to add them up in your head and you'll need a separate page for each budget category. The totals for each department are then consolidated on a "summary page" to obtain the totals the IRS wants.

MONEY BOOK — SHORT FILM

date	check #	department #	paid to:	TOTAL	rent	phone	printing	postage	office supplies	talent	crew payments	equipment rentals	production services	film supplies	location expenses	props/wardrobe	travel	entertainment	publicity	legal	insurance	taxes	miscellaneous	owner draw
7/12	822	8	Mrs P. (house)	35											35									
7/14	823	7	Goodwill	17												17								
7/14	824	9	Kodak	630										630										
7/26	825	5	Emily (camera)	750							750													
7/26	826	5	Steve (sound)	675							675													
7/26	827	5	Tom (gaffer)	600							600													
7/26	828	5	Shiela (grip)	600							600						50							
7/26	829	8	Best deli	105											105									
7/28	830	3	Greg (actor)	250						250														
7/28	831	3	Ellen "	500						500														
7/28	832	6	Film Supply Co.	350								350												
8/1	833	11	Merry Music Library	75									75											
8/15	834	4	Sandy (prod mgr)	600							600													
8/15	835	11	Super Sound Studio	350									350											
8/30	836	13	Phone Co.	62		62																		
8/30	837	10	Susan (editor)	800							800													
8/30	838	12	Expert Film Lab	480									480											
9/7			petty cash	168			8	3	18						82	7	50							
			TOTAL	7047		62	8	3	18	750	4025	350	905	630	222	24	100							

67

MONEY BOOK — SOUND DEPARTMENT

paid to:	Jane Doe - sound	Sam Smith - boom	Jane Doe - equip	Sunshine Hotel	On-time Airlines		petty cash		TOTAL
date	3/10	3/10	3/10	3/12	3/12				
check #	183	184	185	192	194				
TOTAL	750	375	150	105	180		7		1567
rent									
phone									
printing									
postage									
office supplies									
talent									
crew payments	750	375							1125
equipment rentals			150						150
production services									
film supplies									
location expenses				105			7		112
props/wardrobe									
travel					180				180
entertainment									
publicity									
legal									
insurance									
taxes									
miscellaneous									
owner draw									

MONEY BOOK — SUMMARY PAGE

paid to:	date	check #	TOTAL	rent	phone	printing	postage	office supplies	talent	crew payments	equipment rentals	production services	film supplies	location expenses	props/wardrobe	travel	entertainment	publicity	legal	insurance	taxes	miscellaneous	owner draw
Script & rights			826			22	4																800
Producer/Director			2250													50							2200
Talent			875						875														
Talent expenses			195											115		80							
Production staff			1150							1150													
Camera dept.			1825							1300	450					75							
Sound dept.			1560							1300	80					180							
Lighting/grip			2175							1800	350					25							
Sets/props/Wardrobe			85												85								
Location expenses			285								55			230									
Film a lab			1645									900	745										
Editing			1160							1000		125	35										
Post-prod sound			680								120	480	80										
Post-prod lab			520									520											
Insurance, acct.			300																	300			
Office expenses			138		83			30															
Petty cash			152			6.50	2.50	7					12	60	8		56						
TOTAL			15,821		83	28.50	6.50	37	875	6425	1015	2025	872	510	93	410	56			300			3000

69

This system is the one I use for feature films and should let you obtain the figures you need to keep track of your budget as well as the totals the IRS will require.

CATEGORIES. I first make up a list of the categories for the IRS, such as office supplies, film supplies, postage, rent, copying, crew payments, equipment rental, travel, and phone. These are my column headings. I use about 20 such headings. The categories I need for *my* use are the ones in my budget (see p. 267). I need to know how much I spent in each area. I make a separate page for each budget category (see p. 287 and sample on p. 68). Sound related items that are listed elsewhere in the budget (such as sound crew hotels and meals, and post-production sound) are also listed elsewhere for this book-keeping.

SUMMARY PAGE. I use a summary page that lists all the categories across the top (column headings) and has a line for each page (corresponding to each budget category) (see p. 69). This summary page then gives me all the information I need for both the IRS and my purposes. The first column down ("total") is the information I need, while the last line across at the bottom ("total") is what the IRS needs.

PAYROLL SECTION. A separate section of this book is the payroll section, in which I put standard pre-printed payroll pages (again, see your stationary store). These include the basic information I need to gather from each person on "payroll" (those people for whom tax deductions are taken and taxes paid). This doesn't apply to independent contractors (see p. 140). If you have no payroll deductions, skip this section.

PETTY CASH. You'll need to keep records and receipts for all petty cash spent. During the shoot, I usually have the production manager keep petty cash vouchers, with a master "voucher summary" list taped to the outside of a big envelope containing all the filled out vouchers — and collect receipts for all expenses. After the shoot, I enter all the expenses on a separate page in the money book (see p. 72). If I have a lot of petty cash expenses for certain departments, I try to separate out what expenses pertain to each department and enter those totals (listed as "petty cash") under the appropriate department (see p. 68), thus using the petty cash page only as a work-sheet. This method makes my department totals more accurate for my budget purposes.

PETTY CASH VOUCHER SUMMARY

#	date	dept	paid to:	for:	amount

	*to summary page	*TOTAL	Russ' Restaurant	Post Office	Super Market	Xerox	Sam's Stationary	Henry's Hardware	Super Market	Goodwill
date			3/10	3/9	3/9	3/9	3/8	3/8	3/7	3/2
voucher #			8	7	6	5	4	3	2	1
TOTAL		152	56	2.50	28	6.50	7	12	32	8
rent										
phone										
printing		6.50				6.50				
postage		2.50		2.50						
office supplies		7					7			
talent										
crew payments										
equipment rentals										
production services										
film supplies		12						12		
location expenses		60			28				32	
props/wardrobe		8								8
travel										
entertainment		56	56							
publicity										
legal										
insurance										
taxes										
miscellaneous										
owner draw										

```
┌─────────────────────────────────────────────────────┐
│              RECEIVED  FOR  PETTY  CASH               │
│                                                       │
│   # _____.                                     │
│                                                       │
│   $ _____        date _____         │
│                                                       │
│   for _____   │
│                                                       │
│   account _____   │
│                                                       │
│   approved by _____   │
│                                                       │
│   received by _____.  │
│                                                       │
└─────────────────────────────────────────────────────┘
```

FORMS

Decide what forms you'll need and prepare them, designing them if necessary. (Note: to obtain 8 1/2" x 11" copies of the budget or other forms in this book, increase them by 150% — or see p. 297.) Minimize paperwork. This is not only in the interest of saving trees — but every form you use has to be made up, xeroxed, and filled out by someone (which is a drain on your resources, especially if it has to be done during the shoot). Forms you need will fall into three categories: 1) forms you are required to fill out for other people, 2) forms for the cast and crew, and 3) forms for the production department.

1) Forms for other people. This category will include forms you are required to have for SAG (Screen Actors Guild) or other unions such as time cards and production reports (p. 290). There may also be forms for the IRS and state tax agencies (primarily if you have people on payroll), other government agencies, or insurance companies. Check with these groups to find out what forms they require. Try to get by with the minimum because paperwork can kill you on an understaffed shoot. Also try to get as much time to complete paperwork after the shoot and/or do as much as possible ahead of time. Always keep a copy of all these forms for your records in case you need to refer to them later.

2) Forms for cast and crew. This area is under your control so it's obviously much more flexible. Again, try to minimize paperwork.

You need to have a clear system of communication, but this doesn't have to depend on wads of paper. I don't think daily call sheets are usually necessary, even on a feature, if you're organized enough to stick pretty much to your schedule. (Call sheets contain basic schedule information, including call time for everyone and location information, see pp. 95 and 288-9.) For a feature film you might want to have an overall schedule and then a more detailed weekly schedule. You can announce any changes at lunch or the end of each day (and post them at some convenient spot such as a portable bulletin board or on the grip truck). Some shoots, unfortunately, are chaotic. If you're having a lot of schedule changes (due to unpredictable weather, disorganization, or an inability to stay on schedule), daily call sheets may be useful.

PERSONAL RELEASE

I, _____ , have agreed to be photographed and/or recorded
by _____ and that they and their successors shall
own all rights of every kind in said photography and/or recording.

Signature: _____ Date: _____

Print name: _____

Parent's signature (if minor): _____

Address: _____

_____

Phone: _____

By: _____

Production: _____

Scene: _____

Date: _____

Fee: _____

Everyone should have a list of crew and principal cast members and their phone numbers. You may also need maps. Make sure to include detailed directions to the locations, if necessary, as well as instructions about where to park and emergency phone numbers. Is there any other information you want to give to the cast or crew that needs to be copied? For short films, I put all this together (schedule, cast/crew list, and any necessary maps) and hand it out as one package at the start of filming.

What other forms will you need? Will you print shot lists for department heads? What will the editor and script supervisor need for script notes (see p. 291)? Consult with them before the shoot. Make sure you have camera and sound reports if you need them. For a 16mm shoot, where you print all takes, you may not need them at all.

DEAL MEMO

Name:_____ Phone: _____

Address:_____ SS #:_____

_____ Production:_____

Position:_____ Starting date:_____

Rate _____

Payment: Invoice _____   or Payroll_____   (check one)

If invoice: Company name:_____

Address: _____

Fed. ID #: _____

Copyright provisions: Work performed under this agreement shall be considered a work made-for-hire under the provisions of the Copyright Act of 1976.

If invoicing as an independent contractor, I understand that I am responsible for my own worker's compensation, disability, social security, federal and state unemployment insurance, and all withholding taxes.

_____   _____

(contractor/employee)   on behalf of:_____

Date:_____   Date:_____

---

3) Forms for the production department. You'll probably need forms for scheduling, budgeting, petty cash (p. 73), W-4 forms (from the IRS) for payroll deductions, deal memos, release forms and/or contracts for actors and extras (p. 74), and release forms for locations (p. 76). The forms in this book are for your guidance only — for legal protection, consult a lawyer.

Will you need some type of production report (daily or weekly) (p. 290)? This is standard for Hollywood but may be totally unnecessary for a low-budget production with less bureaucracy.

LOCATION RELEASE

I, _____, as owner/agent, hereby grant to _____, as lessee, the use of the premises described as follows:_____

for the purposes of photographing said premises and/or recording sound for such motion picture scenes as lessee may desire, or for other purposes directly related to said motion picture production.

The undersigned warrants that he/she is the owner/agent of said premises, and he/she is fully authorized to enter into this agreement and has the right to grant lessee the use of said premises and other rights granted herein.

Lessee may have possession of said premises from _____ at _____ to _____ at _____.

Lessee shall leave said premises in substantially as good condition as when received, reasonable wear and tear and use of said premises for the purposes permitted herein excepted.

Lessee shall own all rights to every kind and to all photographs and recordings made by it on or about said premises and shall have the right to use such photographs or recordings in any manner he/she may desire.

Owner/agent: _____ Date: _____

Address:_____

_____

Phone: _____

Contact person on premises:_____Phone:_____

In consideration of the above, lessor shall receive payment of $ ___

By:_____

On behalf of:_____ , Lessee

Now that your basic organization is set, you can go on to figure out your schedule and budget.

SCRIPT BREAKDOWN AND SCHEDULE

Your goal is to extract all of the relevant information from the script and lay it out in front of you in a clear and simple form so you can then organize it into the most logical schedule. The most common end product of this process is the "production board" although for short films I use a simplified process that results in what I call a "production chart".

RELEVANT INFORMATION

What information is relevant? Although it may vary somewhat with each film, this is the information you'll want on your production board or chart.

1) Scene number
2) Location
3) A brief scene description if there are several scenes in the same location
4) Whether the scene is interior or exterior
5) Whether the scene is day or night
6) Estimated shooting time
7) Number of pages
8) Cast
9) Extras
10) Props
11) Any special information that will affect scheduling.

You might also want to include other information that you don't need at your fingertips all the time but that does need to be pulled out of the script and kept track of somehow. That might include details of costumes, make-up, more prop details, or special equipment needed.

STEPS IN THE PROCESS

The following are the steps in breaking down a script and scheduling a film — read on for details.

1) Read the script and underline all relevant information.
2) Cut and paste the script, scene by scene.
3) Make or buy your forms.
4) Enter information on forms — either breakdown sheets or breakdown chart for a small film.
5) Transfer that information to production board strips.
6) Organize the strips on the production board or chart.
7) Evaluate.

The short-cut. For short films (a 15-30 minute educational film, for example), I skip step 2 and combine 4 & 5, going straight from underlining the script to making a simple breakdown chart on one piece of paper (see pp. 87 and 92). This breakdown chart has the same information as the breakdown sheet (although with less room for detail) and is almost identical to the production board strips (although it is horizontal rather than vertical). When you have all the information on the breakdown chart, simply cut it into strips with scissors. You now have the equivalent of production board strips. Organize these in whatever order you want and glue or tape them down. I xerox the final product for a neat finished "production chart."

Long or short form? As with taxes, the shorter system (breakdown chart and production chart) is simpler to use. But, as with taxes, it isn't always appropriate. Look at the breakdown chart on page 81. Can all the information you have fit on that? How many scenes (or groups of scenes that you'll count as one) do you have? Will these all fit on the form? You might be able to fit one or two more lines, or you could also use two pages — but at some point it's easier to just use the standard system. A simple film can be organized simply — but to try and do that with a long or complicated film will most likely result in losing important details, which will only hurt you in the long run.

Standard procedure. What follows are the steps in the standard procedure. Details on the short-cut are included wherever appropriate. By the time you've gone through all the stages with a complicated film, you should know the details of the production pretty well. It may seem repetitive and boring, but it's precisely knowing your script backwards and forwards that will be most useful later on. If you know the script that well, you'll be able to do the necessary juggling later on much more easily, and probably with better results. So try not to get bored as you go through all these steps.

1) READ AND UNDERLINE SCRIPT. This is the foundation on which everything that follows is based, so do it carefully. Don't try to read the script while watching TV, just getting the gist of it. You want to catch all the elements and all potential problems at this early stage. Underline anything that seems important, including at least all the items mentioned in #8-11 of the "relevant information" list on p. 77. You'll probably develop your own style. You might want to circle some things, underline others, use different colors for different categories, use arrows or stars to mark special things you don't want to forget. I wouldn't go overboard at this stage because you'll soon be going over it all again soon to transfer the information to other charts (either breakdown sheets for a complicated film or the production chart for simple films).

An accurate and complete script is essential for this step. Rewrites will throw you off (and your budget and schedule may then be off as well). If the script itself isn't complete, then sit down with the director or writer now and fill in the holes. You can't do your job well without a final script.

2) CUT AND PASTE. This step will help you for a big film but you might want to skip it for a small one. Cut apart the script, scene by scene. When you have a scene that's only part of a page, paste it on a regular size sheet, preferably in the same position on the page that it was in the original script. If you have a scene that takes place in two locations, split it at this stage and label the parts A and B (or more if there are several locations). From here on, treat each part like a different scene. You might want to treat two or more very similar scenes (scenes at the same location, same time of day, that you will undoubtedly shoot at the same time) as one. If there is any reason why these scenes might not be shot together, keep them separate.

79

BREAKDOWN SHEET

Film: _____

scene(s) _____

scene	hours	pages	int/ext	D/N	location	description of scene

PRIMARY CAST

SECONDARY CAST

SPECIAL EXTRAS

EXTRAS

VEHICLES

ANIMALS

WARDROBE

PROPS

SPECIAL EQUIPMENT

SPECIAL EFFECTS

NOTES

BREAKDOWN CHART

film:

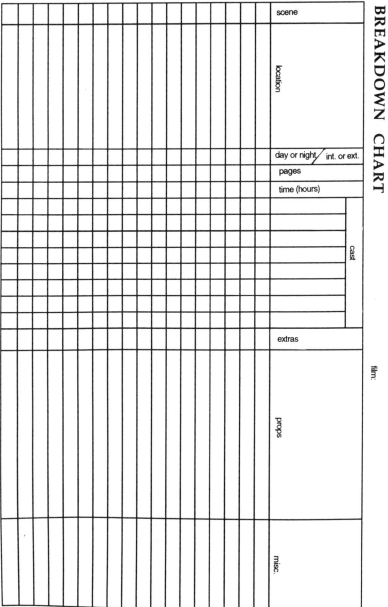

scene																		
location																		
day or night / int. or ext.																		
pages																		
time (hours)																		
cast																		
extras																		
props																		
misc.																		

3) CREATE YOUR FORMS. Now that you're pretty familiar with the script, you should be able to make up your forms to fit the categories needed for your film. If you prefer, various forms can also be bought at some film supply stores. If you don't have local sources for forms and production boards, try: Enterprise Stationers (7401 Sunset Blvd, Los Angeles, CA, 90046), or Alan Gordon Enterprises (1430 N. Cahuenga Blvd, Hollywood, CA, 90028). Also see p. 297 for a packet of forms including the forms shown in this book. You can personalize your forms by adding your company name, address, and logo.

Production boards and strips. You can buy these ready-made, of heavy cardboard or wood. They aren't cheap, although if you do big films it's a worthwhile investment. But if you're struggling to make a film on no money, they can also be home-made (I'd suggest heavy art board and cloth tape). The strips aren't very expensive and it's probably easier to buy them. Strips come in white and also in colors. Use any color code you want, based on the needs of your film. I use white for day scenes (interior or exterior), blue for night scenes that must be shot at night (usually exterior), and yellow for night scenes that can be shot during the day ("day for night" — such as interior scenes with either no windows or where the windows can be blacked out).

4) FILL OUT FORMS. Once you have your forms made up, take your script and fill in the breakdown sheets (or breakdown chart for the short method), scene by scene — one sheet for each scene (or group of scenes that you'll film together). I find it useful to make these as complete as reasonably possible. How complete you make them may also depend on how much responsibility you want to delegate to other people. Do you want to list every prop or let the prop person read the script and figure it out and hope they are right? Fill the forms out as completely as you want to, down to the level of detail you decide is important. I find it useful to list things that might not be obvious, such as specific kitchen implements. Do you want a toaster? A Cuisinart?

Put down things that are implied in the script even though they haven't been stated explicitly. For example, if scenes 14-16 are in the same room and "John" is specifically mentioned in scene 14 but not in the other two, although we don't see him leave, then mark him down for scenes 15-16 as well. Same for props.

BREAKDOWN SHEET

Film: _Child Abuse: The People Next Door_   scene(s) _12_

scene	hours	pages	int/ext	D/N	location	description of scene
12	7	4¾	I	D	Parents Center	waiting room

PRIMARY CAST
Angie, Mary, all kids

SECONDARY CAST
Rosalia

SPECIAL EXTRAS

EXTRAS
4 (counsellor, client couple, receptionist)

VEHICLES

ANIMALS

WARDROBE
jackets, purses

PROPS   wall chart on child abuse
kids toy corner

SPECIAL EQUIPMENT

SPECIAL EFFECTS

NOTES   Parents Center available Sat. only

83

Breakdown sheet details. Breakdown sheets are only useful if you take care to fill them out completely and accurately. The following are some things to consider as you fill in the forms.

A) **Scene number.** Group scenes together here only if you are sure they will be shot together.

B) **Location.**

C) **Scene description.** This can be just a brief catchword to let you know what the scene is if you have several scenes in the same location.

D) **Interior or exterior.** This will be important in knowing the type of lighting and perhaps the type of film required.

E) **Day or night.** Also note if the scene is a night scene that can be shot during the day (day for night — D/N). If you have scenes with people going out a door, you can sometimes tent in a small area outside the door and still shoot during the day. Night shooting is usually more difficult and so any scenes you can shoot during the day will give you more flexibility.

F) **Estimated shooting time** (hours). This section is difficult to determine but critical. Your schedule is only as good as your estimates of shooting time. If these are inaccurate, your whole schedule will be off.

To some extent your budget will determine your estimates. High budget features may take 3-4 months to shoot perhaps 100-120 pages. A lower budget TV movie may have to shoot the same number of pages in less than a month. Arbitrary time limits may be a necessary way to estimate — but that is also very dangerous. You need to know what your director, DP (director of photography), and actors can do. If your director can't work that fast and/or your DP can't light that fast, you're in deep trouble. If you have unlimited money (and therefore time), you can base your estimates solely on the time your director and DP think they need. But if your money and time are limited, you need to make absolutely sure that your director and DP (and actors and crew in general) can work within the schedule dictated by your budget.

Once you've determined the average number of pages you'll need to shoot each day, decide which scenes will take longer and which will take less time than average and indicate your estimated shooting time on the breakdown sheet. I often know in my head (and sometimes indicate on the chart) whether my estimate is likely to be accurate, whether it's even a little generous, or whether it's a difficult scene to predict and I may run into trouble and go over (in which case I make sure to allow for that).

G) **Pages.** In addition to shooting time estimates, I find this helpful as a kind of double check. If the estimated shooting time seems much higher or lower than the average per page (for your film), you might want to re-check the estimates.

H) **Cast.** You may want to list all cast here, or separate out main cast and bit players.

I) **Extras.** The type and number of extras ("4 mothers with babies," "2 truck drivers," "7 miscellaneous passers-by") are probably all you'll need here unless some of them work more than one time in which case you'll want to indicate that. There are no rules on how detailed to get, just decide how accessible you need to have certain details.

J) **Props.** Decide how much detail you want in this section. You might want to separate out things like cars into another section. You might also want to make some distinction between background props and "working props" that will actually be used in the scene and that may therefore be more important.

K) **Special information.** This can be anything that will affect scheduling, such as time restrictions for locations, actors, equipment, or props; weather or seasons; feeding or sleeping schedules for children or animals.

Other lists. For a complicated film you might want to make some specific lists that either take their information from the breakdown sheets or are more detailed than the sheets. You might want a prop list, vehicle list, extras list, location list. This step can be very helpful for budgeting if you add a cost column next to every item. These separate lists are also useful to keep track of what you have and don't have. As you find a prop, or location, you (or the person in charge of that department) can write it down.

Short-cut. For the short method, you can skip the breakdown sheets and just put this same information (or as much of it as will fit) directly on the breakdown chart.

5) MAKE PRODUCTION BOARD STRIPS. You already have all the information you need for these on the breakdown sheets — just transfer it (or as much as will fit) onto the strips, using colored strips if you want.

Short-cut. For the short method, all you have to do is cut up the breakdown chart into strips. These can now be used just like production board strips.

6) ORGANIZE THE STRIPS. When you finish this step you'll have a complete production board or chart that will show the schedule for the film. Your task is to take all the strips and arrange them in the very best order to create a shooting schedule that is efficient and maximizes savings of time and money. Obviously there are many possible combinations — the more strips you have, the more possible combinations. You also have restrictions to work with. Spread out on a big table (the bigger the film, the bigger the table, or move to the floor).

A) Sort your strips into groups. You might begin by putting all the same locations together, since that's usually the main criteria in scheduling. If you will be filming in several rooms of a house, put each room in a separate pile.

B) Divide these groups into day-long piles. Each strip should list how may hours it will take to film that scene. You then need to know how long your shooting days will be. Are you working with a standard day or are you flexible enough to shoot 7 hours one day and 13 the next, depending on the needs of each scene or group of scenes? The standard film day is 10 hours and the standard Screen Actors Guild day is 8 hours. In some cases you'll have to pay overtime after that, sometimes not, depending upon the arrangements you make with your crew and cast. Plan for set-up (lighting) time and lunch and then decide how many hours you actually want to schedule each day. Some of that will depend on how much set up time you built into your shooting time estimates for each scene. You might, for example, need a half-day to pre-light a certain location, or extra time to move to a new location or an extra hour to load or unload equipment at a location — or your estimates might already include that.

BREAKDOWN CHART

film: **Child Abuse: The People Next Door**

scene	location	day or night / int. or ext.	pages	time (hours)	Mary	Angie	Bill	Larry	Martha	Peter	Rosalia	extras	props	misc.
1	Angie's apt.	I/D	5/8	5	✓	✓	✓						cat, toys, baby bottles	
2	Angie's apt.	I/D	2 3/8	3		✓	✓	✓	✓	✓			toys, TV	
3	laundromat	I/D	3 2/8	6	✓	✓						1-2	laundry, bouncer chair	
4	Angie's apt.	I/D	7/8	1	✓	✓							TV, diapers	
5	Angie's apt.	I/D	1 1/8	4		✓								
6	supermarket	I/D	3/8	4		✓		✓	✓	✓		3-4	poster (Parents Center)	before 10 a.m.
7	outside apts.	I/D	3/8	2			✓	✓	✓	✓			car	
8	Mary's apt.	I/D	2 1/8	4	✓							1-2	blood	next to Angie's
9	outside apts	I/D	2 1/8	4	✓	✓		✓	✓	✓			tricycle, throw rug, bandage	
10	Angie's apt.	I/D	4/8	4	✓	✓		✓	✓	✓			coffee pot, cups, coffee	
11	Parents Center ext.	I/D	1 7/8	7	✓	✓		✓	✓	✓	✓	4	jackets, purses	
12	Parents Center	I/D	1	1	✓	✓		✓	✓	✓			wall chart, toy corner, jackets	Sat. only
13	Parents Center ext.	I/D	1	—	✓	✓		✓	✓	✓			jackets, purses	new Parents Center
14	ice cream shop - ext	I/D	1 1/2	—	✓	✓		✓	✓	✓		2	ice cream	

If one scene will take more that one day to shoot, make up another strip ("scene x continued") and under "hours" list only the number of hours you'll have to shoot on the second day.

At this stage you should also think in terms of weeks. Will you be working 5 or 6-day weeks, or another schedule entirely?

C) Put strips in order. After you have divided up your strips by days, you can begin to put them on the production board in some logical order, using dividing strips to separate days and weeks. You can buy strips that are white at the top and black below as daily dividers. I color the top part red for weekly dividers — that makes it easy to use the production board.

When you're planning to shoot odd hours (night or very early morning), remember that the crew needs "turn-around time." This is a certain period, usually 10 hours, of time off between hours you'll be shooting. That's a requirement if you're dealing with unions but it's also common sense when dealing with people. If the crew works until 1 a.m. one night, don't expect them to be on the set cheerful and ready to go at 6 a.m. the next day. If you need to film at night, try to ease in and out of it (working a little later each day before and starting a little earlier each day after) or schedule night work next to a day off.

As you plan your schedule, keep in mind when you plan to view dailies and allow time for that.

D) Juggle the filming order. And re-juggle. And juggle some more. This is the hard part. There are so many combinations and permutations of the strips that you have to figure out what's most important for your film. Do this process in peace. Close the door and give yourself a while — don't set it up so you'll have to stop half way through. The more you play with the strips, the more familiar you are with them (and therefor with the film, broken down into its component parts), the easier this task will be and the better you'll do it. The strips are moveable, so shuffle them around. Try different orders. You might want to keep track of some combinations that seem to work especially well, either for the whole film or for some sections that seem pretty solid. Feel free to take notes. The more you play around with the strips, the more options you may discover.

Priorities. What's most important for your film? What's important to schedule around—locations, cast, shooting sequence? The ideal would be for none of these to conflict, but the reality is that they all probably will and so you'll need to select priorities. Some of these priorities will be preferences, and some things will be necessary. It might be nice to shoot in sequence — that's usually easier for the director and actors (although it becomes less important the more experienced they are). But if one of your main actors has other commitments and is only available for part of the time, you have to shoot all his scenes then. If an actor shaves off his beard in the film, it's essential to shoot all the scenes with the beard before the ones without it. Unless you use a fake beard, which means you need a good make-up person and time to put the beard on each day, although it does give you more schedule flexibility.

Guidelines. Here are some guidelines you can use to help plan your schedule.

1) Minimize movement — of people and equipment to locations and within locations. Moving takes time. This is the logic for shooting all the scenes which take place at one location together.

2) Don't shoot the hardest or most important scenes first or last. This includes the opening and closing shots of the film. Start with an easy scene or two that will not stand out if the acting is a little sloppy because the actors haven't gotten totally into the film yet. Start with a scene that's also easy for the crew because they'll take a while to warm up too. At the very end of the shoot, you may all feel rushed and that pressure may not produce your best acting or technical work. Try not to rush days with critical or very difficult scenes.

3) Plan around the weather. In California, this can be fairly easy — you're almost guaranteed of no rain for certain months of the year (although you may have fog or clouds). Or you may want rain (real rain rather than what you can create). Then you might want to schedule the shoot so you hit the beginning or end of the rainy season, and schedule the rainy scenes in consultation with the local weatherman. Wherever you are, if you need real rain (or snow), you'll need to allow for flexibility in the schedule.

4) Plan around inflexibility. Discover where you are locked in and where you aren't. Look at the restrictions you have. Are there limits on cast or location availability? Are there things you need to shoot in a certain order. What is inflexible in your film? Don't forget special needs and problems. If an actor needs a 3-day beard growth for one scene (and you want to have it be real), plan for that.

5) Give yourself as much flexibility as possible. For example, if the script calls for different hair lengths and you can use wigs, do. If you can shoot some night scenes during the day, so much the better. If you have some short, easy scenes that pretty much stand alone and can be shot at any time, you're in luck. Use those as cushions wherever you need them. Know which scenes will probably go smoothly and which may not. Where are you most likely to have problems? As you make up the schedule, remember these places and allow for flexibility.

6) Shoot wide shots first and outside shots first. It's easier to match indoor shots and tight shots to outside shots and wider shots than vice versa. If you have bright sunshine for an outdoor shot, you can create sunshine for the matching indoor shot more easily than you can create sunshine outside on a rainy day to match you indoor shot. You can control lights more easily indoors and in tighter shots.

7) Shoot in sequence when you can. This will help both the director and actors.

8) Separate out scenes that can be shot with a smaller crew and limited or no cast. These might be scheduled together, at the end of the shoot or some other time — or even shot by a second unit crew. For "Peter and the Wolf" we shot most of the animal footage (without actors) with a smaller crew at the end of the shoot.

9) Plan for crises. They will happen. Give yourself some leeway to switch days around in case of rain or other problems. If there are days that are tightly scheduled and you might go over your scheduled time, know ahead of time how you will deal with that. This might be a place to put a short ("moveable") scene that can simply be taken out and re-scheduled elsewhere if you go overtime. That will probably be easier than moving the whole schedule down a half day. You might want to have some easy, moveable scenes planned for the end that can be moved up in case of rain or in case you go faster than anticipated.

Thinking out potential crises might help you plan for them better and deal with them more quickly when they do occur. You might have the wrong weather, lose a location or an actor, or a key crew member or actor might get sick. Plain old catastrophes can also happen, although those are harder to plan for. You'll stand a better chance of coping if you're not already pushed to the limit.

The juggling process didn't take much time to write down here but it may take you a lot of time to get the best possible schedule. For a small film, with limited variables, it can be very simple. But for a big film, with many conflicting variables, you're never sure you have the *best* way. You may wake up in the middle of the night with a new idea of how to arrange things. This juggling process may also let you fine-tune things enough to be able to cut a few days off the schedule simply by tight planning. That's an easy way to cut costs.

When I have the sequence of my schedule figured out, I add the shooting dates. For a production board, I put a strip of 1/4" tape across the top and write the days and dates in there. If the schedule changes, I adjust the tape. (You could also have a space on the production strips for this information.)

PRODUCTION CHART

film: Child Abuse: The People Next Door

scene	location	day or night / int. or ext.	pages	time (hours)	Mary	Angie	Bill	Larry	Martha	Peter	Rosalia	extras	props	misc.
1	Angie's apt.	I/D	2/3	5	✓	✓	✓						cats, toys, baby bottles	
2	Angie's apt.	I/D	2/3	3	✓	✓	✓						toys, TV	
7	outside apts.	X/D	3/8	2	✓	✓				✓			car	
5	Angie's apt.	I/D	1/2	4	✓	✓		✓	✓				TV, diapers	
4	Angie's apt.	I/D	7/8	1		✓	✓							
10	Angie's apt.	I/D	1/8	4		✓		✓	✓				coffee and cups, coffee	
9	outside apts.	X/D	2/4	4	✓	✓		✓	✓			1-2	tricycle, throw rug, bandage	
3	laundromat	I/D	3 3/4	6	✓	✓				✓		3-4	laundry, bouncer chair	
6	supermarket	I/D	3/4	4	✓	✓							poster (Parents Center)	before 10 am
8	Mary's apt	I/D	2 1/4	4	✓			✓	✓		✓		blood	next to Angie's
12	Parents Center	I/D	4 3/4	7	✓	✓		✓	✓	✓	✓	4	well chart, toy corner, jackets	Sat only
11	" ext	X/D	9/1	1	✓	✓		✓	✓				jackets, purses	
13	"	X/D	9/1	1	✓	✓		✓	✓				jackets, purses	
14	ice cream shop	X/D	1/2	1	✓	✓		✓	✓			2	ice cream	near Parents Ctr.

PRODUCTION BOARD

Film: Child Abuse:

Breakdown page															
Day or night	D	D	D	D	D	D	D	D	D	D/N	D	D	D	D	
Number of pages	2 3/8	2 3/4	3/8	1 1/2	7/8	1 1/8	2 1/4	3 3/4	3/4	2 1/2	4 3/4	1/8	1	1/2	
Hours	5	3	2	4	1	4	4	6	4	4	7	1	1	1	
Scene	1	2	7	5	4	10	9	3	6	8	12	11	13	14	
Location	Angie's apt.	Angie's apt.	outside apts.	Angie's apt.	Angie's apt.	Angie's apt.	outside apts.	laundromat	supermarket	Mary's apt.	Parents Center	" ext	" "	ice cream shop	
Character															
Mary					✓	✓	✓	✓		✓	✓	✓	✓	✓	
Angie	✓	✓	✓	✓	✓	✓	✓	✓	✓		✓	✓	✓	✓	
Bill	✓	✓	✓	✓					✓						
Larry							✓	✓		✓	✓	✓	✓	✓	
Martha						✓	✓	✓			✓	✓	✓	✓	
Peter		✓					✓	✓	✓		✓	✓	✓	✓	
Rosalia											✓				
extras								1-2	3-4		4			2	

Short-cut. If you're using the short method, you'll end up with a lot of floppy strips taped or glued together. I xerox this to make it neater, using black strips to separate days (or laying it all out on a sheet of black paper, leaving spaces where appropriate). This then becomes your production chart (see p. 92).

7) EVALUATE AND ADJUST. Now that you have your ideal schedule, does it work? Is it practical? What if your schedule comes out to 42 days but you know you don't have enough money for that? Then you have to go back and somehow find a way to cut down the schedule. (I'm assuming here that you've already looked for other ways to cut the budget or raise more money.)

If you have to cut the schedule down, you can shave off a little bit here and there, or eliminate entire scenes, until you arrive at your goal.

The more you know about the technical side of filmmaking, the greater advantage you'll have. If you use a higher speed film stock, will that let you cut down on lighting enough to save significant time in some locations? Can you shoot certain scenes day for night? You probably won't know the answer to some of these questions until you've selected your locations. Or you can begin at the other end and look for a location where you can shoot day for night.

Some of these adjustments involve artistic decisions and will involve working with the director. You can leave less time for scenes (some or all), cut out scenes, condense. Be creative. Can you shoot two scenes that are theoretically in different locations in the same place (for example, shoot "Mary's kitchen" and "John's living room" in the same house)? That will save the time of moving to another location. If you have a sequence that takes place in the living room and continues as the actors go out into the hallway, can you simplify that and have it all take place in one room (so you don't have to light two rooms)? If this was planned as a dolly shot, can you cut that out and save a little more time? Can the director shoot a certain scene in 4 hours rather than 6? Come on, it's not really that complicated a scene. What if you use fewer shots, or simplify or eliminate a complicated dolly move? Would it help to add one or two people to the lighting/grip department, either for the whole shoot or just for certain days? Or just push people to work a little faster? Or do you need to re-

WEEKLY CALL SHEET

date	time	location	scenes	cast	misc.
Tues 5/20	9:00	Angie's apt. & outside (address)	1,2,7	Angie, Bill, Peter	car
Wed 5/21	8:00	Angie's apt. (address)	5	Angie, Bill, Peter	
	12:00	"	4,10	Angie, Mary, Martha	
Thurs 5/22	8:00	outside apartments (address)	9	Angie, Mary, Larry Martha	tricycle
	11:00	laundromat	3	Angie, Mary, all kids	
Fri 5/23	6:00 crew 6:30 cast	supermarket (address)	6	Angie, Bill, Peter	
	10-4:00 4:00	BREAK Mary's apartment (address)	8	Mary, Larry	
Sat 5/24	8:00 crew 8:30 cast	Parents Center (address	11,13,12	Angie, Mary, all kids, Rosalia	
	3:00	Ice Cream store	14	Angie, Mary, all kids	

think your whole lighting plan (with the DP) and go with a simpler lighting style for certain scenes or the whole film? Narrowing the scope of a scene may cut down lighting time by decreasing the area you have to light.

There are, however, limits that you need to recognize. You can't simply say, "We'll do this scene in 5 hours," if that can't be done without compromising lighting, directing, camera work, or acting (or any of the many other pieces that go into a well-shot scene). Maybe another scene can be tightened without compromise and you can leave this scene alone. Or maybe you *have* to begin to think about compromises — and where and how to make them. If the scene just can't be shot in 5 hours without compromises that you're unwilling to make, you might as well face that now and re-schedule accordingly. Not facing it will only leave you exceptionally frustrated and angry on the day of the shoot. You might as well make rational decisions on how to deal with the problems rather than just ignoring them now and having to face them later.

Now that you have all this information organized and handy, what do you do with it? Probably the first thing will be to make up a budget. You may already have made up a vague budget, but you'll need this schedule to be more exact. And when you have a budget that is too high, you'll have to come back to the schedule to attempt to lower it.

You'll also use this production board or chart throughout the shoot — to make call sheets (see p. 95), to find out what's happening the next day or next week, and to be able to make adjustments in the schedule.

A side benefit of the production board is that it may also be useful to show people when you're raising money for your project — it gives both a good sense of what's involved in making a film, and also of how well you understand the process.

HOW TO KEEP COSTS DOWN

Although costs depend on many factors — and some costs can't be cut without also cutting quality — there are many things you can do to keep costs down without affecting quality.

GIVE YOURSELF ENOUGH TIME. To some extent there is truth to the equation that money equals quality. But there is an even more important equation for low budget films: time can equal money. With time you can often do things (like find the right cast, the right props) that might otherwise cost a lot of money. Props and costumes are good examples of this. You can rent or buy most anything, for a price. But with time and ingenuity you can often find what you need for a fraction of the cost. Time also lets you accomplish tasks that you'd otherwise have to hire other people to do (such as casting, location scouting, or any production task). You may not want to do all this, but you can.

HIRE PEOPLE WHO CARE. Hire people to work on the project (at every level) who really care about it. The above equation should really read: *time* and *love* can equal money. Caring can give you a level of quality that money can't buy.

BE FLEXIBLE. Hollywood works with a very strict system of job categories that defines who does what on a film. While this system usually works pretty well, it's not cost-effective for a film with a limited budget. You can save a lot of money by not limiting yourself to those categories and by using people in a way that works for your particular situation. Having flexibility in the script and in how things are shot will also help control costs.

BE CREATIVE. I've already discussed some aspects of this, such as different ways to write scenes. But there are also creative methods of handling money. For example, you can sometimes buy and re-sell things (everything from props and costumes to editing equipment and vehicles) for less money than it would cost to rent them. Bartering and borrowing save money. There are other ways to compensate people for their services, such as by giving them screen credit, providing them an opportunity to work in a higher job category than they usually do, offering them a role that is a challenge or a showcase for their talent, or giving them "points" (a percentage of income or profits from the film). You can also save money by using people part-time when that's appropriate. You may be able to hire a wardrobe or makeup person or extra grip or electrical people only for difficult days or only part of a day.

FIX PROBLEMS EARLY. It's much cheaper and easier to fix problems at the conceptual or script stage than during shooting. It's cheaper to adjust the length of the script than to overshoot or have to do additional filming. After the script stage, it's cheaper to stop and work out a problem during rehearsal than to shoot repeated bad takes (wasting film and crew time). It's usually cheaper to work out sound problems and get clean sound on location than to have to loop the film later and it's usually cheaper to stop and record some wild sound while filming than to have to go back and get it or create it later.

HAVE A GOOD, WELL-PREPARED DIRECTOR. The director needs to know what he or she wants and be able to move quickly on the set. Make sure the director has enough time to work with the actors and plan shots. Storyboarding ahead of time might help some directors (and can also reduce wasted shots).

SC. 1

HAVE A GOOD PRODUCER-DIRECTOR RELATIONSHIP. Establish a good relationship between the producer and director that is based on mutual trust and respect. This will probably mean agreeing on shared goals for the film. Have a clear understanding of your division of labor and of basic decisions about the film. You need the cooperation of the director to stay on schedule and on budget — you can't do it without that. Have an agreement on how you will deal with major problems that arise, especially ones that affect costs. Will you tackle them together or be at odds about how to handle them?

KEEP THINGS IN BALANCE. Maintain perspective. Know the level of quality you want and need for your film and keep that consistent. Don't go overboard in one area when it's not necessary.

A fantastic sound track for an educational film may be a waste of time and money. On the other hand, one area of your film that is much lower in quality than the rest will greatly hurt the entire film. Again, sound is a good example — a beautiful film can be ruined by an unclear sound track.

MOBILIZE YOUR RESOURCES. First you need to discover your resources. You probably have more than you think. Tell your friends and acquaintances what you're doing and what you need — and ask for their assistance. Many will be glad to help, if you simply tell them what to do.

ASK FOR ADVICE. Some people may not have the time, but you'll be surprised at how many people will share what they've learned. And hopefully you'll be as generous with others who follow you. Seek out filmmakers who have done projects similar to yours. Work with your lab and seek out friendly technicians. Ask them at each stage of production if there are any ways they can suggest to save money or improve the film. You may learn about specific savings — and you'll also let people know you're serious about saving money, which may make them more inclined to help you do so.

LEARN as much as you can. The more you know about each aspect of filmmaking, the better you'll do your job, the better able you'll be to oversee others, and the more ways you'll discover to cut costs. There is no one way to do things; learn as much as possible about alternatives. Ask lots of people — everyone has their own way of doing things and their own special tricks.

TEACH. The more knowledge you can pass on to others, the more help they'll be to you. This becomes especially important if you use less skilled people. Encourage people to learn more about aspects of filmmaking outside their particular area of expertise. You can teach specific skills, but also ways of thinking, such as how to anticipate and how to be frugal.

QUESTION EVERY COST. Don't make assumptions. Check out every cost carefully. Get estimates of both money and time. It's not enough to ask the rate for something — also ask how long it will take (at that rate). It's your total that counts, not the hourly rate. Question whether every cost is necessary. Don't *assume* you need anything. Get second opinions. People routinely obtain several cost estimates before buying a television or refrigerator, yet film costs will far exceed those. Compare costs carefully.

LEARN THE ART OF NEGOTIATION. Most film expenses are negotiable — though some more than others. This is especially true for low budget films or those with redeeming qualities. Think of reasons why people should give you reduced rates — your film is worthwhile, your budget is limited, you can offer non-monetary rewards, or their cost to provide the material or service is low. If their actual costs are low (for example, for the use of existing stock or archival footage or music, or use of equipment that otherwise might just sit around) maybe they'll even absorb that cost for a worthy cause. Talk to a person who is authorized to negotiate, not just a clerk in the order or billing department. Negotiate prices and terms *before* you make any commitments.

TIE COSTS DOWN IN ADVANCE whenever possible. Don't just say, "Do the job and bill me." Instead say, "I'm on a low budget and need to know all my costs ahead of time. Please tell me what this will cost." If the estimate is too high, ask about ways you might cut costs or get an estimate from someone else. Be clear with people about your budget for a particular area, and emphasize that you intend to stay within it. If there is no alternative to going over budget in some areas, figure out where the extra money will come from before going on.

DON'T DO WHAT IS NOT NECESSARY. In Hollywood, many things are done "just in case." I suspect that the practice comes from a desire to do a good job in a system where the decision-makers often aren't easily accessible. Rather than bother a decision-maker, crew members prepare for different possibilities. They get alternate props, just in case the director doesn't like their first selection; they build extra sound tracks, in case they're needed. Some directors want extra shots or extra takes, "just in case." On a low-budget film, all this can be very expensive. Encourage production people to ask if they have questions about what's wanted or needed and not to over-prepare. You can help by being accessible and making sure those questions are answered.

Don't overshoot. If your script is too long, cut it down before filming. Work with the director (and editor if necessary) to make sure you have sufficient coverage but not excessive coverage. A detailed script (including shots) or storyboard can help prevent shooting unnecessary footage.

CUT WASTE. Obvious? Great. But look hard and you may find even more places to cut. Waste need not only be limousines — it can be anything that doesn't really add to the quality of the film. Is every person on the crew necessary? Is every piece of equipment necessary? Is every shot necessary? Is every technical process necessary? Is every bit of paperwork necessary? If not, cut!

SET A GOOD EXAMPLE. If others see you wasting money, they'll be less motivated to be frugal, no matter what you tell them. If you don't seem to care, they won't either. No one is perfect but try to practice what you preach. If others see you being helpful and considerate, maybe they'll be inspired to follow.

ALWAYS WATCH YOUR BUDGET. Fill in actual costs as they occur and keep comparing actual costs to your original budget. Make sure you are staying within the budget. If you go over in one area, find someplace else to cut, *now*.

BEWARE OF FALSE SAVINGS. Saving money is wonderful — but there are times when cuts may be false savings. People have different levels of experience and expertise; know when that's important and when it isn't. Two cheap but less experienced grips may sometimes more than make up for one experienced but expensive one — unless you need smooth dolly moves. A camera assistant who is slow or, worse yet, blows takes, is no bargain. People work at vastly different speeds so only paying attention to rates can be deceptive. Someone who charges slightly more but works twice as fast is obviously a bargain, unless speed isn't all that important for a particular job. Time estimates can vary greatly, depending sometimes on the skill of the technician and/or on the equipment or process being used. Other false savings can include promising screen credit for the loan of props or equipment or locations. Check out the cost of making your titles — it might be cheaper to pay cash. And "free" help takes up space and has to be fed and may take up a lot of time with questions or mistakes — all of which may end up costing more than the value of the help you receive.

THE BUDGET

Once you've figured out your basic schedule, you're ready to make up a fairly accurate budget. You can estimate budgets roughly, and with experience you might be able to do this pretty accurately. But I find that a detailed budget, especially for a bigger film, is valuable in keeping costs down and making sure you don't go over budget. If you budget carefully — and watch your costs as you make the film — you should not go over budget.

BASIC DECISIONS

Before you can fill out the budget form, you'll need to make some basic decisions. Some of these will be very specific — such as whether to shoot in film or video; 16mm, 35mm, Betacam, VHS, or Hi-8; mono or stereo sound. Some will be more general — such as what quality you are aiming for and therefore what caliber people, equipment, and processes you'll need along the way. Think these out carefully before you begin — or try budgeting alternate ways.

FILM OR VIDEO. You may want to shoot in video or shoot in film and then transfer to video for all or part of the editing process. You can also shoot and edit in video and then transfer to film at the end. While this will depend some on personal preferences and skills, other factors will be involved.

1) Cost. This will depend on what video format (Betacam, 1", 3/4", VHS, or Hi-8) or film size (8mm, 16mm, super 16mm, 35mm) you will use, access to equipment, and the type and amount of footage you expect to shoot. Video tape is cheaper than film stock (and processing), which can be important if you'll shoot a lot of footage. Also check the costs of camera, sound, and editing equipment. Sometimes what seems like a big saving may not be when all is considered for your particular film. Check if any crew people you're using have their own equipment — and what kind.

2) Intended markets. Will the film eventually be shown in theaters (almost always 35mm film) or only on television (video) or in the educational film market (now primarily video and sometimes 16mm film).

3) Quality desired for both picture and sound. Film quality is superior to video, but for some purposes video can be perfectly adequate.

4) Current technology — which will influence all three above factors. As technology improves, including video resolution and transfer technology, it may matter less in what format the film is originally shot. That day has not yet arrived, however.

FILM: 16MM or 35MM. This decision will probably be based on factors that are similar to those for the film vs video decision.

1) Cost. Check this out carefully — there are many hidden extra costs for 35mm. Film stock and processing is cheaper for 16mm, which becomes more important the more film footage you intend to shoot (for example, documentaries or any films with a high shooting ratio). Don't forget that you'll use more feet of film for 35mm (because each frame of 35mm is larger, there are fewer frames per foot) as well as paying more per foot (because the film is wider). Camera equipment for 16mm is also smaller, lighter, easier to use, and cheaper than 35mm — which means it takes up less space, requires fewer people to operate and move around, and is much more suited for hand-held work, quick moves, or working in tight quarters. Editing equipment for 16mm is usually cheaper and more available, and there are differences in editing procedures that will affect costs. Magnetic sound stock for 16mm is also cheaper, although working with 35mm sound tracks will give you better quality. It's possible to work with 16mm picture and 35mm sound tracks but that involves having special equipment and you are more likely to have sync problems.

If your 16mm film will eventually be shown in commercial theaters, then you'll need to blow it up to 35mm (in a lab) which is an expensive process. Some people hope to sell their film quickly and let the distributor pay for the blow-up, but don't count on this. The blow-up affects quality and you'll need to light more carefully to get the best possible quality, which takes time and perhaps more lights.

"Super 16" is another alternative. Modified 16mm cameras use a 16mm film stock with sprocket holes on only one side. This allows for a slightly larger frame size and reduces the amount of enlargement necessary for a blow-up (which, in turn, will lead to less loss in quality). Super 16 is fairly uncommon and equipment is not as easily available as for regular 16mm.

Add up all your costs carefully — 16mm may not be that much cheaper (relative to the total cost of your film) when everything is considered, especially if you include a blow-up to 35mm, although shooting in 16mm lets you defer a large cost until the very end. The calculations I made for "Hard Traveling" led us to shoot in 35mm, although we seriously considered 16mm.

2) Market. The only market for which it really makes much sense to use 35mm is the theatrical market. Educational films are now distributed primarily in video and sometimes in 16mm and you can transfer to video (for television or home video) from 16mm as easily as from 35mm.

3) Quality. The quality you get with 35mm is hard to beat.

4) Technology. New technology, especially "super 16" is narrowing the quality gap for the theatrical market. Du Art Labs (245 W. 55 St., New York, NY 10019) does a lot of blow-ups — ask them for information and advice, including about "super 16."

VIDEO FORMATS: These include Betacam, Betacam SP, 1", 3/4", VHS, Hi-8, and more. Look at the key factors very carefully, especially since this is a changing field with new technology affecting all the other factors.

1) Cost. As with film, check out the cost of equipment, tape, and lab processes for the various formats.

2) Market. Betacam SP is now commonly used for television (although 1" is fine). Because of changing technology, check current preferences, especially for the market you have in mind.

3) Quality. 1" and Betacam SP are best (1" is used less now); 3/4" is usually acceptable; VHS and Hi-8 aren't professional quality but can pass. Remember this is a changing field.

4) Technology. Since video technology is constantly changing, check current information — and make sure it won't be outdated before you shoot your film. Be especially careful if buying equipment.

SOUND: ANALOG OR DIGITAL. Analog is the traditional system where sound is recorded on tape. Digital technology is spreading fast; much post-production work is now digital, and you can also record digital sound with either a DAT recorder, digital Nagra or digital Betacam.

1) Cost. Digital recording equipment is still less common (and thus more expensive) but post-production digital is becoming standard with comparable prices.

2) Market. Digital sound is so new that tape is still totally acceptable. You can easily change to digital in post-production if you want.

3) Quality. Digital is better but analog is still fine.

4) Technology. It's new and changing fast — check it out.

SOUND: MONO OR STEREO. This is a decision you probably won't need to make immediately. As long as you record your music on at least two tracks (which you're likely to do anyway), you don't have to make this decision until the mixing stage.

1) Cost. Stereo is not very much more expensive than mono, unless you use one of the special systems (such as Dolby) where there is an extra charge. Check costs out with a sound studio.

2) Intended market. This is an area that is currently changing. Video cassettes (home video) are eager to have stereo sound and most movie theaters are now equipped for that, as are foreign television networks. Television in this country is primarily still mono but that is changing. Talk to distributors about current preferences for your type of film.

3) Quality desired. Think about your particular film and the music you'll use. For some types of music, stereo may not be an advantage. For "Hard Traveling," we decided not to use stereo, although we had originally intended to do so, because we ended up using only a guitar and harmonica and stereo didn't seem warranted. Although we originally released both "Peter and the Wolf" and "The Ugly Duckling" in mono, we later went back and re-mixed both in stereo for foreign television and home video

106

sales. We had recorded the music for these films with orchestras of about 20 and 10 members respectively and each had been recorded on enough tracks so that we were able to re-mix fairly easily.

4) Current technology. Check with local studios on state of the art technology, including Dolby and other systems. Find out about all alternatives (and relative costs).

SIZE OF CREW. This is really a complicated decision that depends a lot on the quality you want, what equipment you'll be using, and your budget. But it also has to do with personal preference. Do you like the feeling of working with a smaller crew? Would you rather take longer with a smaller crew than less time with a larger one? Bigger is not necessarily better!

STARS. This is a tricky one. The common wisdom is that stars sell films, although I maintain that they are neither necessary nor sufficient. There are many examples of films where stars don't seem to have helped — and also films that have done very well without big names. Stars, combined with good acting and a good story, will certainly help sell a film, but stars won't save a film with bad acting and a poor story. On the other hand, a successful film with an unknown actor can create a star. Some people who are considered stars for one market (such as television) may not be stars for another market (theatrical).

RATES

You'll need to get some basic information on rates. There are various sources for this. Labs, production facilities, equipment rental houses, and supply companies all have rate cards or price lists — ask for them, and make sure you have current ones since rates can change frequently. Ask about any special low rates.

Another good source for some basic rates is called the *Brooks Standard Rate Book*. It has rates for most union categories — both cast and crew. As you talk to people and obtain estimates, write them down, including details as well as prices. If a camera person quotes you a rate, note if it's for a 10-hour day or a flat rate. Also note provisions for overtime and any other details. Try asking what rate they'd like and what rate they'll work for if necessary. If you don't know sources for things (equipment or people) ask around. Use the experience of other filmmakers, and ask about both price and quality.

If you are trying to come up with a fairly exact budget, you'll have to ask around to find the cheapest sources and begin making decisions about what particular suppliers you'll use. If I have time before I need to make these decisions, I begin by using almost any reasonable estimate as a guide. Then later I refine the budget, knowing I can probably shave a little off various costs. I make my budget in pencil and I can always erase figures and replace them as I get better estimates.

Above and below the line. Budgets are often divided into "above-the-line" and "below-the-line" expenses. This refers to an imaginary line that serves to separate the more fixed "below-the-line" expenses (for crew, equipment, production services, etc.) from the more variable and negotiable "above-the-line" expenses (where high priced stars, directors, and/or producers can greatly increase the cost of a film) (see p. 267).

CONTINGENCY

I always leave some "slush" or padding in my budgets in a variety of places rather than having a separate "contingency" category. That's my personal preference, but make sure you have a contingency somewhere. I estimate generously in a variety of places — and I usually know which of my estimates are exact, which are pretty tight, and which are padded. If in doubt, I estimate high. Later I can fine-tune my budget as I make deals and choose specific suppliers, but for the first round on a big film, I don't worry too much about that. For small films, I tend to budget much more quickly, but that's also an area where I've had more experience and where there are fewer categories and variables so I'm more sure of my estimates from the beginning. The more unknowns and unpredictable factors in your film (everything from the weather to actors and the director), the bigger contingency you should have.

COMPUTER BUDGETS

Those of you using computer budgeting programs will have the advantage that, once you fill out the basic information sections, the computer will automatically add it up for you. And readjust totals every time you change any information. That's certainly nice if you have access to a computer budgeting program, but you still have to enter the basic information correctly — so read on.

BASIC INFORMATION

Now pull out your production board or chart and any other lists you've made up with your basic information. You'll need to know the number of shooting days, the size of the cast and crew, and the length in time and footage of your finished film. (To find footage, multiply the number of minutes in your finished film by the number of feet per minute — 36'/min for 16mm, 90'/min for 35mm.) You'll also need to estimate your shooting ratio to know how much film or video you'll shoot.

Shooting ratio is the ratio of how much film you'll shoot to the length of your finished film — for example 8:1 means you'll shoot 8 times as much as you'll use in your finished film. This figure will vary with both the experience of the director, actors, etc., and also the level of quality desired for the finished product. If the first take is always perfect, great. Additional takes mean a higher shooting ratio. But even with just one take you'll have waste, for example at the beginning and end of the shot. And then there will usually be duplicate coverage on scenes — different angles and close-ups. Good planning by the director can help minimize unnecessary extra coverage.

BUDGET FORM

The first step in figuring out your budget is to decide on a budget form that you'll use. I would suggest making one up to fit your particular needs. Take a fairly complete sample budget and adapt it. Add things that are particular to your film or your style of shooting. Leave out things that don't apply. I begin with a fairly complete budget form because I use that as a checklist. One common cause of budget errors is to simply forget certain items or even whole categories.

The sample budget is just that — you'll probably need to adjust it for your film. The one on p. 267 is appropriate for feature films. It's more elaborate than you'll need for shorter films, but use it as a guide and eliminate what you don't need. I use the budget on page 279 for shorter films. To obtain 8 1/2" x 11" copies of the budget or other forms in this book, increase them by 150% (or see p. 297). You might want to arrange the categories differently — some of this is purely arbitrary. For example, meals that are listed under location expenses might be listed separately under cast, extras, and crew. You might want to create whole sections for things now lumped under another category, such as "publicity" or "transportation." You might want to consolidate some sections or, depending on your film, you might need a special section for "animation" or "special effects" (the complex kind as opposed to simply a gunshot or fog).

CAUSES OF ERRORS

Before you fill in the blanks, you should know some of the main reasons for errors.

The principle causes of budget errors are: 1) omissions, 2) incorrect time estimates, 3) unrealistic estimates, 4) not understanding processes or technology, 5) budgeting for the wrong thing, and 6) inflation.

1) Omissions can be minimized if you begin with a very complete budget form and go over the steps of your film carefully to see if you've left anything out. Make sure you don't leave out needed equipment, processes, or people. Ask others for advice, especially your technical people. Ask another producer (of the same type of film) to go over your budget and see if you've left anything out.

This will be especially important if you're inexperienced, or even just inexperienced with this particular type of film.

2) Incorrect time estimates. Obtain flat rates whenever you can, for example for crew and editing. Where you can't obtain flat rates, ask technical people to help you with estimates. Ask more than one person because speed and methods of work can vary greatly. Know the abilities and limits of your director and crew — not knowing them can be a major source of mistakes.

3) Unrealistic estimates. Some people base estimates more on wishful thinking than on reality. Don't simply assume you'll find a camera person for $50 a day and equipment you can borrow for free. Don't assume you can make your film with a crew of five if that's not realistic. Wishful thinking may be pleasant, but it's not helpful when making up an accurate budget.

4) Not understanding the processes or technology — and all they require. If you don't understand all the processes involved, you won't be able to budget accurately. This can lead to very expensive mistakes. If you choose to edit on a non-linear video system, for example, you'll need to budget to digitize your material. If you think that's a minor expense that won't affect your budget, check out the costs quickly. If you'll have a dolly that needs to run on a track, be sure to budget for sufficient track as well as the dolly.

5) Budgeting for the wrong thing. Be clear on exactly what you need and make sure you understand the technical terms you're dealing with. It's like buying a car. If you want a car and you call only one car dealer and assume you'll have to pay the price he quotes, you may be in trouble. What kind of car? Suppose you call a VW dealer for the estimate when you really need a Cadillac or a cheap used car. Different Cadillac dealers may also give you different prices, and may have different models and different features on the car, or different warranties or financial terms. And if the guy who gave you the best quote has no cars in stock and you need one now, the estimate is useless. There's almost as much variety in film services so it's important to know exactly what you need. If you'll be renting camera equipment, for example, know not only what camera you need, but also what lenses, filters, tripods, and other accessories you'll want. If you

111

talk to a lab or sound studio, know exactly what services you need from them.

6) Inflation. If you'll shoot the film the day after you obtain your estimates, you're probably safe (except, perhaps, for post-production costs). But film budgets are often made up months, even years, before any film is shot. Don't expect prices to remain the same. When you obtain your estimates it might be wise to ask if they expect any increases in the coming months. If you have a 10% contingency in your budget, that seems like enough to cover a lot of things, right? But if inflation causes a 10% rise in prices, you've just used up every penny of your contingency.

FILL IN THE BLANKS

Armed with your basic information and your calculator, go through the budget line by line and fill in the blanks. In the "detail" column, show how you arrive at your figures ("30/hr x 10 x 42" means you are paying someone $30 an hour for a 10-hour day for 42 days). The detail column will be very useful in trying to pare down your budget, if you have to do that later. What's important in your budget is the totals — and the totals can be lowered by lowering any of the components. So, with the above example, you can save money by lowering the rate — but also by decreasing the number of days or the hours per day or getting a flat rate. If you shorten your shoot, or decide you'll somehow manage with a lower shooting ratio, take your calculator and re-figure your totals. List both cash payments and deferments (in parentheses). Keep track of deferments as part of your total costs.

Now I'll go through the different budget categories, using the budget form on p. 267 as a guide, and I'll point out some things to think about and watch out for in each category as you make up your budget. Referring often to the sample budget will be useful.

SCRIPT AND RIGHTS. Do you have to pay for the rights to the story or book on which the film is based? Will you need research before the script is written? Will you need a secretary to type the script? How many revisions do you expect to have (which will effect typing and copying costs)? Will you need technical consultants? Will the writer have expenses (such as travel, hotel, meals)? Will the writer be on the set during the filming (paid or just fed and housed)? Will you perhaps need to bring in another writer (or writers) for re-writes?

PRODUCER'S UNIT. How many people will you have in this category? Will you have expenses such as travel, hotel, or meals?

DIRECTOR'S UNIT. Will you have expenses (travel, hotel, meals)? What other people do you want in this category (choreographer, casting director, dialogue coach)?

TALENT. You might want to make up a separate page in the budget (see p. 287), or a list elsewhere, detailing the expenses for each cast member — salary, days worked, transportation, hotel, meals. Then you can enter the totals in your budget. Separating out stars, supporting cast, and day players gives you a better picture of where your costs are than if you lump them all together. If you have stunts, you'll need that category. If you have kids in the film, you'll probably need a social worker and/or teacher. Each state has laws governing this, so check the requirements locally. Will this person be on the set full-time or only part-time? You might have someone who serves that function (and is properly qualified) but also has other tasks. The looping listed here is the cost for the cast only, not the technical parts such as studio rental. Don't forget to include rehearsal time, if paid.

Fringes and overtime. I won't mention these in each category, but don't overlook them if they apply (for both cast and crew). If you'll be billed for overtime, don't assume you won't ever go overtime — you probably will sometime and those amounts add up fast. Budget something here, even if you hope not to use it. "Fringes" includes all the legal and union requirements governing extra payments you'll have to make for employees. Most of this will be taxes and pension and welfare costs. If your film is made under SAG or other union contracts, you'll have a pension and welfare fund fee (a percentage of salary). Check union regulations for amounts and payment schedules. They have very particular and strict rules, and fines if you don't follow them.

The tax area (both federal and state) is one you should research carefully, especially concerning the distinction between an "employee" (for whom you will have to withhold taxes) and an "independent contractor" (responsible for his or her own taxes, see p. 140). Check with tax authorities, a lawyer, accountant, and/or other filmmakers. Federal taxes will include social security tax (part of which is deducted from the employees salary and part of which is paid directly by the employer) and withholding the employees' income taxes. For independent contractors, you don't have to withhold anything but you do have to report what you paid them to the IRS at the end of the year. On the state level, you'll have disability/unemployment insurance and withholding for employees' state income taxes. If you are doing your own payroll, study this area carefully. If you have an accountant or book-keeping service doing it for you, ask them what to budget for. Be sure you have all the appropriate forms before the shoot — and know all the deadlines. Fringes can amount to as much as 1/3 of your actual wages, so this is not an area to ignore.

EXTRA TALENT. How many extras will you have? How will you pay them? Will you pay them in cash or put them on the payroll and take deductions? Will you pay people for a full day or have special provision for partial payments for people who only work a few hours (I often use a half-day rate as well as a full-day one)? Will you need to have extras come for costume fittings or rehearsals for which you'll pay them? Will you have any expenses such as travel costs? Will you need a welfare worker for kids? Will you pay drivers of prop cars separately or will you include that in the car payment (under "props")? Will you use any union extras (Screen Extras Guild) and therefore have union payments?

TALENT EXPENSES. The meals I list in this section refer only to what is paid directly to actors as cash "per diem" (for meals not provided on the set, such as dinner or meals on non-working days for out of town actors). I prefer to lump all on set meals for cast, crew, and extras together, since that is how you'll pay for them, and I list those under "location expenses." An alternative would be to list all the cast meals (on and off set) here and then list meals for crew and extras elsewhere.

Will you pay for phones (long distance calls?), laundry, parking tickets, other expenses? Will you provide any cast members with cars? If so, list that here (or put cars under a separate "transportation" section if you prefer — just make sure you list them somewhere).

CASTING AND REHEARSAL. How will you do your casting? Will you use a casting director? Will you need to rent casting space? Will there be any expenses connected with casting — such as mailings or advertisements, video taping of casting sessions (which I highly recommend) or screening of video cassettes? Will the director and/or producer travel to do casting (probably listed under their travel expenses) or will you bring any potential cast to you (listed here)?

Will you have paid rehearsal time? If so, will it be right before the shoot (in which case you can more easily budget it as one piece) or will it entail separate arrangements?

PRODUCTION STAFF. Who will this include? Some production people might also serve other functions (and be listed elsewhere). Production people might, for example, also help with props and set decoration, food, wardrobe, or even grip or electrical tasks. Will you have a production office? If so, who will run it? Our office for "Hard Traveling" (as well as all our other films) was our house and during the shoot we had only an answering machine (with remote beeper to be able to receive messages).

Who will watch continuity and take script notes? Will you need research on production details or technical advice? Will you have an accountant, book-keeper, or auditor? Will you have a publicist (full or part-time)? This is a function that's easy to ignore — but it may be important for some films, such as features.

115

The production department is an area where you can really save money, if necessary. It's also an area where the formula of "time equals money" is especially true. With enough time, one person can fill many of these roles.

ART DEPARTMENT, SETS, PROPS, WARDROBE. What are the needs of your film? A period film with many locations and a short prep time will obviously need more people and money than a simple modern-day film. This is an area where time and creativity can save you a lot of money. Can you buy things from thrift stores or borrow them rather than renting, making, or buying them? Another way to save money on props is to have good communication with the prop person. I've often seen prop people cover themselves by getting many extra things, unsure of what the director will want. If they can simply ask when they have questions, you can save time and money. Some props are crucial and some are insignificant. Details are important for some, while others will barely be seen or could easily be replaced by another item. The more a prop person knows, the easier their job will be and the more money you'll save. Loss and damage costs will stay low if you (and the crew) are careful.

SPECIAL EFFECTS. This refers to location special effects, not the "Star Wars" kind, and can be anything from working guns to rain, fog, or fires. Be aware that some things will require permits and licensed operators or special services like police and firemen. Check local regulations.

HAIR AND MAKE-UP. What are the needs of your film? Perhaps all you need is a hairbrush and a some face powder to dull shiny noses. For more complicated hair and make-up needs you might want someone full-time or you might be able to manage with a part-time person (perhaps to come in first thing in the morning). Is there a local beauty school that might like a chance to work on a film? Be creative. You might need someone only on certain days. You want to avoid having under-employed people standing around on the set all day.

STILL PHOTOGRAPHY. Don't ignore this one. You may not need a full-time photographer but you will almost always need stills for distribution. Check with the people you know or hope will distribute your film and find out what they'll require. You'll need some black and white stills and possible some color photos

116

(probably slides) as well. Find out for sure what you'll need, and how many "good" shots. We have never used a full-time photographer, even on "Hard Traveling." Usually someone on the crew (often a production assistant) who has some free time (and can take good photos) will take on that role. For "Hard Traveling" I wanted to be sure we had good photos so we hired a professional photographer to come on a few days for certain scenes that would make good publicity shots. Since many scenes won't be appropriate for publicity shots and you don't need a huge variety of photos, it's useless to have a photographer standing around when not needed (or wasting film shooting film things you won't use). Will you want the photographer to take photos for continuity? We usually have a Polaroid camera on the set for the script or make-up person's use for continuity photos when necessary (although we try to minimize that).

CAMERA DEPARTMENT. What people and equipment will you have? What level of quality do you want? Whether you use film or video, and what type of film or video (see p. 103), will make a difference — both in equipment and crew needed, and also in time needed (to move and service the equipment — and in lighting). Don't forget to allow for prep time (to test equipment, scout locations, etc.).

Will you have a second camera (operator, assistant, and equipment) or a whole second unit? More than two? For how much time? Will you bring in extra people for this second unit or will some of the existing crew do double duty? Does the second camera need to be a sound camera? Second cameras are sometimes efficient and valuable (for example, for getting difficult footage such as animals, a mass scene, or a dangerous stunt). But it also means lighting for more than one angle, and planning the scene to be shot from different angles and that takes time (unless your second camera is simply a close-up from a similar angle). Think out the needs of your film.

If you're shooting in film, will you use video-assist or a video tap? Again, there is no pat advice for this — it will depend on your needs. Video assist is expensive and tends to slow you down (there's extra equipment to set up and it takes time to look at the video, if you do that between takes). But you can also see exactly what you have without waiting for dailies to be developed. If you have a confident and eagle-eyed director and/or camera operator, DP, producer, or whatever, this may be superfluous. On the other hand, it may save you re-shooting a scene because you aren't sure you have what you want (which will save time and film). Figure it out for your film and your crew. Get advice from people who've worked both ways.

Will you need a camera truck to transport the camera equipment or will it fit in another truck or a car (16mm or 35mm can make a difference here)?

With all crew people, you'll need to decide whether they will be independent contractors or on payroll (which means adding money for fringes, see p. 113)

SOUND DEPARTMENT. (Note: this is production sound — post-production sound is listed later.) How many people do you need? Hollywood still uses a third person ("cable man") to hold and re-coil the cable. I don't even list that function for budget purposes but in some tricky situations you might want to have a production assistant help out. What equipment do you need? Do you need lavalier ("lav") or radio mikes? Remember that good mikes and good production sound can save you money in post-production. Talk out your sound needs with your sound person.

I'm not enamored of walkie-talkies and prefer to use them as little as possible, but you might like them and sometimes they are necessary (for crew communication or traffic control). Fancy ones are expensive to rent. You might consider buying cheap discount store models (and you'll have them for your next shoot). Be clear on what you need and what the walkie-talkies can do. Don't forget to budget adequately for batteries.

LIGHTING DEPARTMENT. Again, this will depend on how many people and what equipment you need. To make accurate estimates you'll need to have a pretty clear idea of what your locations will be like (especially how big and how dark) and what your shots will be (how wide and what angles), as well as what quality of lighting you expect. The more information you can give the DP and the gaffer, the better their estimates will be of what lights you'll need and how long they'll take to set up. Tell them if you really need to keep costs down and ask for their help and suggestions. Perhaps altering a few shots can result in big savings on equipment. Don't forget to allow for prep time.

Are your locations distant enough from electric power to require a generator? Could you get the electric company to give you a "power drop" (temporary power line) if there's electricity nearby but no place to plug in? Check the costs and how long it would take to hook up. If you need a generator, do you need the special low-noise ("blimped") variety generally used for film or can you get by with a regular generator (cheaper and more readily available outside major filming areas) and then build your own sound-proofing around it (if it will remain in one place)? Do you need to hire an operator with the generator? Don't forget to budget for gas and oil for the generator, and transportation costs to get it to you.

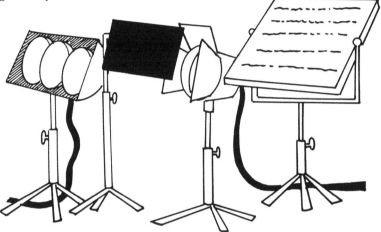

GRIP DEPARTMENT. What equipment and how many people? What are your shots likely to be? Do you need a dolly, crane, car mounts, or other equipment? Can you get by with a wheelchair, shopping cart, or homemade dolly? Will you use the dolly on smooth floors or on bumpy ground where you will need to lay track (or plywood or boards)? If you need a dolly or crane, you'll need someone who knows how to operate them (and smoothly!). An inexperienced dolly grip will cost you dearly in blown takes. Don't forget to budget time to prepare the grip truck and collect all the needed equipment — and also to return equipment and clean up the truck after the shoot.

TRANSPORTATION. What vehicles will you need and where will you get them? Will you need drivers? Teamsters? (See p. 138.)

CREW EXPENSES. As with cast, meals I list here are only meals paid to the crew as "per diem." Meals provided on the set are listed under "location expenses" (although you might prefer to do it differently). Will you be on location and therefore responsible for housing and "per diems?" Before you hire people, make sure you are clear about what they expect you to provide. Will you be responsible for phone calls, laundry, parking tickets? Does the crew expect a specific type of accommodations? Lodging can be anything from a sleeping bag on someone's floor to a shared room in a dingy motel, a shared apartment, or a luxury hotel with swimming pool and jacuzzi. What agreements have you made or will you make?

LOCATION EXPENSES. This is the category where all the meals you provide are listed. Will you have catered lunches or find another alternative? Will you go overtime and need to provide any dinners? What will you provide for breakfast and snacks? Don't forget to budget money for beer for the crew at wrap time (if they expect that and you want to provide it) and for snacks and drinks during the day (more if it's hot) and for a wrap party if you'll have one. Little things — but they can add up.

How many people will you be feeding? Make sure you count accurately here. If you have children, will their parents be on the set? How about the writer or editor? Will you have unpaid interns and production assistants you'll be feeding? Do you have investors who want to come and watch, or press, or friends, wives, husbands, girlfriends, sisters, great-aunts, third cousins...? What policy will you have about feeding these people?

Merchandising (getting items donated in exchange for exposure in the film) can cut costs if you want to do that. For example, a soft drink company might provide drinks if their product is featured in the film. Or an auto dealer might loan a car.

What will you have to pay for the locations you need? Will there be extra expenses, such as electricity, or phones, or improvements to the location? Find out what official permits you'll need. Will you have to pay auxiliary people such as janitors, watchmen (to guard equipment overnight), police, or firemen? Do you need a location office or can you do without, or simply use someone's apartment or hotel room? What vehicles will you need and where will you get them?

FILM AND LAB. These figures are easy to obtain from the suppliers and labs. Figures in this section will depend on how much footage you'll shoot, so you'll need to know both the length of your finished film and your anticipated shooting ratio. Make sure you read the rate cards correctly and that you understand the technical terms being used. If in doubt, ask. See if you can make deals, especially on longer films or if you're a regular customer.

You can sometimes save on film stock by using someone else's leftovers. If you do this, be sure to have the film tested by a lab before using it (unless you know its history and trust the seller) but you can often get perfectly good film at much lower rates. There are companies that specialize in buying and selling leftover stock (look for ads in film magazines). You can also ask around about people in your film community who are just finishing a film and who might have some leftover stock. When you budget for audio tape transfers, don't forget to add extra footage for wild sound.

If you need a video transfer (either to edit on video or to use to compose or record music or effects) decide what format and quality you need. Prices for this can vary greatly. You might even be able to make a rough transfer with a home video camera from a projected image. It'll be very rough, but it'll be cheap and might be adequate for some needs. If you're transferring for editing purposes, you'll need to include a time code "window dub." If you're doing non-linear video editing, you'll need to digitize material to computer disk.

EDITING: FILM. These budget categories assume you'll edit on film. If you're unfamiliar with post-production processes or terminology, see page 225. If you're unsure whether to edit on film or video (linear or non-linear), and money is a consideration, budget both ways carefully before deciding.

Editing is another area where costs can vary greatly — and where a thrifty producer can save a lot of money. How fast does your editor work? How many editors will you have, and for how long? How many sound tracks do you envision for your film? (And how many do you really need?) How complicated is the sound?

What equipment will you need? Will your editor work on a flatbed or an upright Moviola (or something else)? Costs of editing machines vary greatly. Will you rent or buy equipment?

Will you rent an editing room or will you have one rent-free (in your, or your editor's, office or home)? How is your editor used to working? Some editors are used to working alone and doing everything while others are used to having several assistants, plus a sound editor, music editor, and/or dialogue editor. An editor who has never had to worry about a budget may end up being very expensive, while an editor used to working on low budgets may do only what is absolutely necessary and know how to cut corners. Talk with the editor about the budget and his or her needs beforehand and watch the budget carefully as you go through post-production. When in doubt, ask what is necessary and what isn't.

Will your editor (or assistant) be syncing the dailies or will you have a specialized company do that? Will you be edge-coding your film? Footage for edge-coding will be twice what you shoot because you have to edge code both picture and sound.

What editing supplies will you need? If you're renting a fully-equipped editing room, you'll only have to add expendables. But if you're setting up an editing room from scratch, add up all the equipment you'll need carefully — every splicer, reel, and gang synchronizer. It can add up. Talk to your editor.

What other equipment, facilities, or processes will you need? Will you have to pay for projecting the film, either to view dailies or at any of the various editing stages (less likely if you're working in 16mm or on a flatbed)? Will you be making a trailer to advertise the film (for a feature film)? Do you need to budget for that now or will you leave that to the distributor?

The editing process can be simple or complicated. And some filmmakers make it more complicated (and therefore more costly) than necessary. We edited "Hard Traveling," a relatively straightforward 35mm feature film, in 4 months. The editor worked as we filmed and we had a fairly polished rough-cut 2 weeks after the end of the shoot. We then spent about a month fine-tuning the final cut and another month building all the sound tracks. We had one editor and one assistant, plus a dialogue editor who worked for about 5 days to split and clean up the dialogue tracks. We used an upright Moviola (with a second one for the last month of building tracks) set up in a room in our house.

We ended up with 9-12 sound tracks (depending on the reel). We had a very low editing budget — but a professional quality film.

VIDEO EDITING. If you're unfamiliar with either the processes or the terminology, see page 241. What off-line equipment will you use? Linear or non-linear (costs vary greatly)? Will you rent an editing room or suite, or edit in someone's house? How fast will your editor work with the equipment you'll have. Will you need extra technical support (a computer technician) for the equipment or can you or the editor fix minor technical problems?

Will your off-line system produce a computerized edit decision list? If not, will you use a computor program to create one before the on-line or just work from a hand-written list? What on-line equipment will you need? Will the on-line equipment price include everything or will you need to add special options (for titles or special effects)? Ask about flat rates.

TITLES. How elaborate will your titles be (see p. 239)? What quality do you need? Are you using 16mm or 35mm or video (it can make a difference for titles)? And then, simply, how many words will you have to set in type, how many cards to shoot (or titles to generate on video)? Will your titles be on cards or over the film? Will they be separate cards or a roll-up? Will they be black and white or color? All these questions will affect the processes and costs. If you will be showing your film abroad, especially in festivals, you may need to think about foreign sub-titles, although distributors (and some festivals) may pay for that.

Ask professionals to help you save money. Ask what your alternatives are. Remember, as you talk to different people, that different companies will be especially knowledgeable about what their equipment can do and they may not know (and therefore be unable to tell you) all the alternatives.

MUSIC. This is another area where there is room for a lot of variation, depending on what kind of music you want or need for your film (see p. 231). You can: 1) record music with your film sound crew during the making of the film (not in a recording studio); 2) buy "library" music that has been especially recorded for this purpose and for which you pay a set fee for the use of the music (which depends on the type of film, quantity of music, and which markets you want the rights for); 3) have music composed, arranged, and recorded specifically for your film; or 4) buy rights to existing music by known or unknown people. Your costs will vary greatly depending on which route you choose.

If you're having music composed for musicians, don't forget that it may have to be arranged for the instruments you want, then copied onto separate sheets of paper so each musician can have a part, then recorded in a studio, good takes selected and edited together, and then mixed down to the number of tracks (mono or stereo) you need. If you're dealing with unions, find out all their regulations, including residuals and fringes. If it's appropriate for your film, check out the possibility and costs of composing music electronically or using a composer/musician.

POST-PRODUCTION SOUND. (See p. 229 for more on the processes involved at this stage.) How many sound effects tracks will you have and where will you obtain your sound effects? Unless you have a very simple film, you'll need some sound effects. Even if you recorded effects while filming, you may still need to budget for additional transfers and mag stock.

Will you need a foley track (see p. 235) for your film? Ask recording studios that have foley stages about their rates, and ask foley walkers as well — and ask both for estimates of how long it will take. Be prepared to have the estimates vary greatly. An experienced person can save you a lot of money here.

Looping, also known as ADR (automatic dialogue replacement, see p. 230) works in a similar way. Will you need looping? Do you have many locations where you'll have a difficult time recording good sound while filming (for example, a scene at an airport or a location near a noisy airport or a busy intersection)? How good is your sound person (and equipment) — a good sound person may save you the necessity (and expense) of looping, unless you have very difficult locations.

Mag (magnetic) stock is expensive, but you can often use much cheaper recycled stock for your sound effects (including foley). You'll need enough mag stock and slug (used film to fill blank spaces) to build all your tracks. How many tracks will you have? How many total feet of mag stock (new and used) and slug?

When you have all your sound tracks assembled, you're ready for the mix. How long your mix will take will vary with the number of sound tracks, the quality of your sound (how hard the mixers have to work to fix bad sound), the clarity of your cue sheets, and the competence and speed of the mixer(s). You'll need more than one mixer if you have more than a few tracks. If you have more tracks than the studio can handle at one time, you'll need to pre-mix some of the tracks. Tell the studio how many tracks you expect to have and how complex the film is likely to be and ask them for an estimate of how much time they think it will take and how many mixers. Again, estimates may vary greatly. Try several sound studios. If your film will be in stereo, ask about extra costs. Will you need a separate music and effects (M&E) track (to be able to dub foreign versions, see p. 237)?

FILM AND LAB POST-PRODUCTION. Will you be using any stock footage (see p. 239)? If so, make sure you can find what you need and check rates. Will you be using opticals (see p. 238)? Even if you don't plan to use opticals for cinematic reasons (such as special effects), you may need to use them to fix mistakes (such as a boom visible in a particular shot or a poorly framed shot). In 35mm dissolves and fades must be done as opticals. Some of this will depend on the type of film you're making, the quality you want for the finished film, and the experience of your crew. Title opticals are listed under "titles".

Will your editor cut the negative or will you use a separate "negative cutter"? Get an estimate (which will usually be based on the number of cuts to be made).

The lab can give you an estimate for an answer print based on footage, whether it's 16mm or 35mm. Find out what the lab's rate includes. Some labs charge for a second (corrected) answer print if one is needed. Others say their rate is for an "acceptable" answer print, which means that if you aren't satisfied with the first one, they'll make another one for free. Take this into consideration when comparing rates. The lab can provide reels and cans for your film or you might want to get them elsewhere (perhaps used ones, especially for 35mm). If you are doing a feature film, or do a lot of business with the lab, try negotiating a lower rate.

An electroprint is a cheaper method of obtaining a sound track for an answer print, although the quality is lower than an optical track. Ask the lab for costs for both. How will you use your answer print? Can you get by with an electroprint?

INSURANCE. Talk to an insurance agent to find out what coverage is necessary or advisable for your film — and how much it will cost. The main types of insurance you'll need are liability (many people will want it before letting you shoot on their property) and Workers' Compensation (required by law to protect employees in case of accident or injury on the job).

You might also want negative insurance so that you are covered if anything happens to your negative (camera scratch, lab error) and you have to re-shoot some scenes. There will be a deductible and the rates are high and may not be worth it for some simple films.

For longer films, you'll probably want more complete coverage — and an agent who is used to dealing with films. You may want cast insurance to cover you if one of your cast members should die or get sick, causing you to have to re-shoot or postpone filming. This isn't important for small films or minor actors but it's a good idea for the major actors (and perhaps the director and producer) on a feature film.

Equipment companies may require you to have insurance that covers their equipment while you're renting it, although you may be able to simply pay extra to the rental company to be added to their insurance policy. Find out which is cheaper.

An errors and omissions (E & O) policy may be required at the distribution stage, depending on what markets your film is aimed at (probably needed for theatrical and television but not for educational films). This is to protect you (and the distributors) from lawsuits. You can usually obtain E & O coverage after production but it's a good idea to at least obtain the information before production so that if you have to make any script modifications for legal reasons you can do that before you shoot. (You can check with a lawyer about this.)

Will you need a "completion bond"? A completion bond is a type of insurance where a company guarantees funds to complete the picture if you go over budget and run out of money. They charge high rates for this and usually require various protections (such as a certain amount allocated in the budget for contingency, approval of key crew, and/or perhaps one or more persons on the set to oversee the operation). They are not fools — they know films often go over budget. The question of whether to use a completion bond is a complex one and will depend on the nature of your film and on your sources of funding. Investors may prefer or require it — to protect their investments — but for low budget films they are proportionately very expensive and difficult to obtain.

Don't be foolish and don't take chances — but if you can avoid a completion bond, do so. The money you save can be added to your "contingency" fund. Just be sure you don't get stuck without money to pay bills if you go over budget. Budget very carefully — and know where you can obtain additional funding if necessary. Then you need to convince your investors that you're being responsible and that their investment is secure without a completion bond. A good track record obviously helps. Perhaps you (if you have the resources) or one of your investors will serve as a completion guarantor, promising to provide extra money if needed.

Most insurance rates will depend on your budget (and on your payroll for Workers' Compensation) so be prepared with some general figures in order to obtain estimates from a broker.

LEGAL AND ACCOUNTING. Will you have any legal fees, either in relation to a limited partnership for an independently financed film or to write contracts with actors, crew, or distributors? Will you need legal advice about potential lawsuits or help in securing rights? What are your needs for accounting, book-keeping, and tax preparation? This will depend a lot on the complexity of your film and your willingness or ability to do some or all of the work yourself. If lawyers or accountants quote you hourly rates, get them to help you estimate total costs. Doing some of the work yourself can cut costs.

FUND-RAISING. You may not need this section at all if your film is funded by someone (for example, a distributor or your rich uncle) and you had no expenses to make that deal. Otherwise decide on a fund-raising strategy and budget accordingly. Will you have to travel, take people out to dinner, hold parties or film screenings? Will you need to print up publicity materials and send out mailings? Will you pay other people commissions or finder's fees to help you with fund-raising?

GENERAL OFFICE EXPENSES. You'll need to know for how long a period you'll have to pay for a phone and office rental. Do you have to set up an office from scratch or just cover your normal office expenses (in which case an "overhead fee" might be appropriate)? What special equipment and supplies will you need?

CONTINGENCY. Some people simply add on 10% here. I prefer to make up my budget very carefully, building in little contingencies in a variety of places but not putting anything here. You may also plan to use all or part of your salary (if you have one in the budget) as a contingency reserve. If the film goes over budget — you get paid less (or not at all).

If you're very careful in budgeting, you shouldn't need a big contingency. But don't omit it unless you're absolutely sure you won't need it — and most people seem to need it. It's no fun going over budget and running out of money. You need to have extra money somewhere in your budget because nothing will ever go exactly as planned and some things are simply beyond your control. Hopefully, you'll come in under budget in some categories which will compensate for the areas that go over budget.

I prefer to put contingency money where I think I may need it rather than at the end. That's more useful to me. If I seem to be going over budget someplace, I know I have to find another place to cut in order to balance that excess. With a contingency category at the end it may be too easy to say, "Oh, we have a contingency," every time something goes over budget and to lose track of the total. But again, this is personal preference — what I really want to do is urge you to budget adequately. Don't budget low and pray — it doesn't work.

DISTRIBUTION. This section will vary depending on whether you'll have 1) no distribution expenses at all (if you immediately turn your completed film over to a distributor), 2) expenses geared to obtaining a distributor, 3) partial distribution costs (if you put up some money for prints and advertising in conjunction with a distributor), or 4) complete distribution expenses (if you will distribute the film yourself).

EVALUATION

Once you've filled in the budget carefully, line by line, add it up and take stock. Is the total one that you can live with? Does it fit the amount of money you have available or think you can raise? Another very important question if you're financing the film independently is whether the total cost of the film fits with what it's "worth". Will you or the investors be able to get your money back by selling the finished film (to whatever markets)?

Another thing to consider at this time is whether the budget is balanced. Do all parts of the budget have the same degree of extravagance or leanness? Will the expenses in the various areas result in a similar quality level at all stages? If not, try to achieve a better balance. Being stingy in one area while being much more generous in another may create resentment among those people working on the film who are being asked to cut corners. A film is only as good as its weakest link so, for example, if you have a good script and gorgeous cinematography don't bring down the overall quality of the film with poor acting.

Once you've compiled your basic budget, you can refine it. As more of the details of your film become known, you can solidify estimates. If you need to cut costs, check to see where you can do that. Creativity is often motivated by necessity. I find it useful to have a base budget to refer to if I'm going to make a lot of adjustments. I may xerox and keep my original budget for comparison. Rather than add up all the figures again after each adjustment, I keep track of changes with a plus/minus system. I'll write +400 or -700 in the margin and add those up to find out how my budget has changed. When I've finished adjusting, I make out a clean budget. I use the same +/- system during production to help stay on budget (see p. 207). If you're using a computer, it will automatically re-calculate totals as you make changes.

PAYMENT SCHEDULE

Once I have my budget, I make one other financial chart — a rough schedule of payments. What will need to be paid when? This information may be necessary when you negotiate deals. I make several columns, representing the major payments periods: 1) pre-production, 2) start of the shoot (money you'll need through the shoot), 3) end of the shoot (to pay all the bills incurred during the shoot but not paid until after, plus cash for the basic editing period), 4) rough cut (to pay most of the post-production costs, except final mix and lab costs), and 5) answer print (to pay final mix and lab costs and anything else you've succeeded in putting off until now).

If your payment schedule doesn't match the timing of your income, make credit arrangements with all whose who will be affected beforehand. Don't wait until the bills are overdue to make excuses, especially if you ever want to make another film.

You might also have a deferred column, even several different levels of deferments. Exactly what gets put in which column will depend on how much credit you have with various suppliers and what kind of payment deals you're able to arrange. Make sure your totals in this area coincide with when you expect to have cash available. If they don't, take steps to correct that now. You don't want to run out of cash in the middle of a shoot. And remember to have a contingency at all times.

CREW AND EQUIPMENT

DETERMINING CREW NEEDS

Thinking about the crew should have started when you began making up your master plan. The basic question is how big a crew you need — and want. This decision should be based on the needs of your film, the amount of money you have available, and your (and the director's) personal preference. The type of equipment you will be using, the specific logistics of your film, and the quality you want for your film will also be important in determining your crew needs. For example, if you use many lights, you'll need people to set them up and move them about (or fewer people and more time, which is also an option). Using a dolly or crane necessitates someone skilled enough to handle it. Using make-up on actors means someone to apply it (or actors who can apply their own). Moving around to many (or difficult) locations means more people to help move equipment.

More people means you can usually do any given task faster — at least up to a point. Too large a crew can become unwieldy and it might be better to spend a little more time than add more crew people. You need enough people to manage the equipment you have and not too many so as to be unwieldy or waste money. You need enough people to do all the tasks — but you should organize the tasks so the minimum number of people are required.

You can be creative. The Hollywood system (which may mean a crew of over 100 people for a feature film) assigns each crew member very specific tasks. At the other extreme, a small 16mm film may be produced with 2-3 people. Most likely, you'll be somewhere in between. For educational films we often work with 4-10 people, while for "Hard Traveling" we had a total of 22-25, depending on the needs of the day. We always double up on many tasks. Because the Hollywood system usually doesn't let the

131

make-up person carry grip equipment doesn't mean that *you* can't combine those tasks.

Think not only about the tasks you need done but also about how much time they require, and when that time is needed. Some tasks happen mainly while the camera is rolling, while others happen in between takes — and some occur infrequently enough that it might be worth wasting a little time occasionally rather than hiring an extra person to do them. Some tasks can even be done in the evening or before or after the shoot.

On "Hard Traveling" we had one person who bought food in the evening and set up breakfast in the morning before each day began, but during the day she was a grip/electrician. On smaller films we seldom have a wardrobe or make-up person on the set full-time (and usually not at all unless it's a period film). Even for "The Ugly Duckling," a 30-minute film set in the 1920's with a fairly large cast and many extras, we had a wardrobe person who collected and made the clothes but who was only on the set for an hour or so each morning (except for several big scenes where she stayed the whole time). For make-up, we usually just keep a compact and hairbrush on the set — and assign a production assistant to watch for shiny noses and messy hair. On small films we often combine tasks and have a production manager and one or more production assistants who do everything from set dressing to food, make-up, script notes (a very simplified version), wardrobe, and often help with grip and electric.

You can arrange to have some people work only on certain days or at certain hours. This may be obvious for a second camera crew on days you need two cameras but it can also apply to other departments. For "Hard Traveling" we had only one wardrobe person and one make-up person, who also did hair when that was necessary. Setting the basic hair styles for the main actors was done before the shoot by someone who was not on the set at all. This was a period film and we had several days with 40-50 costumed extras. On those days we brought in a couple of extra helpers, and carefully staggered arrival times for the cast and extras. Those days were hectic, but we managed. One hint — some of the extras had experience with wardrobe and/or make-up and were cast in those scenes specifically to be able to help out.

When one person does more than one job it's very important to make sure the job requirements don't conflict — and everyone is clear about which tasks have priority.

Interns, often unpaid, who want to learn more about filmmaking can be very useful, depending on the level of training they have — or how much training you give them. We use interns on most of our productions. We like teaching and it's an excellent way of discovering potential crew people for future films. The more training an intern has, the more useful they're likely to be. My classes in film production began as training workshops for our interns. I would get interns together before a shoot and talk about the different aspects of film production and the tasks that needed doing. I gave very specific information geared to the tasks they would do and also an overview of the production because of my belief that the more each person knows about the entire process, the better they'll be at any given task. It was also a way to repay people for working very hard for a few days on our film.

You can also help interns set up a "buddy system," where an intern is essentially an apprentice to a particular crew member. You can also make and post a chart showing the basic grip and lighting equipment you'll be using so that when someone yells, "Get me a pancake," interns will know what to bring.

Interns and production assistants often get stuck with all the menial tasks that are part of filmmaking — but this doesn't have to be. The work has to get done, but it can also be spread around (directors and producers are perfectly capable of carrying apple boxes and they are not always too busy). There are ways to combine unexciting tasks with some that are more challenging. When someone needs to be sent on an errand off the set or needs to stand outside to guard the grip truck, you can rotate that so it's not always the same person.

How many people will you have on your crew? Go through a list of potential crew categories (see the budget, p. 267) and decide what people you think you'll need for your film. You might also want to note whether each job is absolutely necessary or simply desirable and whether it's full or part-time. At the same time, keep in mind how many people you can afford. Remember that film production is a juggling act. If the number of people you can afford and the number of people you need match perfectly, you're all set. If they don't (most likely!) then you begin the juggling. What jobs can you simply eliminate? What jobs can you combine? Perhaps you can find some interns who will work in exchange for training and experience. Remember, you haven't made any money deals yet so you can decide to hire 5 people for $200 per day or 10 people for $100 per day. Creativity and flexibility are the key.

What are the skills of the particular people you're considering? And how do they like to work? Does your favorite sound person also need a boom operator or will he or she do both? Do you want him or her to do both? Remember the quality level you are aiming for. Does the DP also like to be the camera operator? For a small film you're not even likely to ask that question but for a larger film it's important. A DP who is great at lighting and setting up shots may not be a very smooth operator. Or an operator who is great with a tripod may be very shaky for hand held work. If you have a lot of crane or helicopter shots, make sure your camera person isn't afraid of heights. All this seems obvious, but don't take anything for granted. The best person for one job may not be the best person for the next one. Part of the challenge and excitement of filmmaking (for me, anyway) is that no two films are ever the same.

If you'll have a large crew, check out your crew decisions with your department heads. Making arbitrary decisions about how many people you can afford or how many you think you'll need is senseless if the people you hire as department heads don't agree with your decisions. You want to work with your department heads, not against them (even though you have to worry about the budget more than they do).

Another issue that's important for morale is to make sure you have an overall balance on your crew. If some departments are well-staffed and others are under-staffed, you're likely to create resentment. I'm a firm believer in equalizing things as much as possible, in people helping each other, and everyone pitching in at wrap time. You won't be able to please everyone all the time, but you can pay attention to these things.

SELECTING CREW

Once you've made your basic decisions about crew size, you have to decide who the people will be. There are two ways to begin doing this. You can start with how much you can afford and look for people who will work for that rate — or you can begin by deciding who you want and ask their rate (or if they'd be willing to work for what your budget allows). Begin by trying to get both — the people you want for the price you can afford. Don't assume you can't afford someone until you ask.

As you begin to talk about money remember that you may have more to offer than just cash. You might be able to offer a worthwhile project, decent working conditions, or working in a particular location (some might prefer to work close to home while others might enjoy going to a distant location). A chance to learn may also be important. Someone working as a production assistant might appreciate being invited to go along on location scouting trips, casting sessions, or rehearsals. And don't forget screen credit or a chance to work in a higher job category than the person usually works at. If you make films regularly, people may be willing to work for less on a film with a very tight budget if they know they'll be hired again (and perhaps for a higher rate next time).

Ask potential crew members about their familiarity with the equipment you'll be using. If you'll be shooting on film, make sure your DP and lighting people are experienced (and good) at that. If you're editing on video, make sure your editor can work (quickly) on the equipment you'll have. Make sure crew people can work within the budget limits of your film. You may want to tailor some equipment to the crew. For example, the editor we chose for "Hard Traveling" was very accustomed to working on upright Moviolas, which allowed us to use that rather than a more expensive flatbed.

It's ideal to work with people you know and have worked with and whom you love, trust, and respect. But the ideal isn't always possible. You may be just starting out, or hiring people for location work in another city, or need a different level of quality than your previous films, or your favorite person may simply not be available (or willing to work for the amount of money you can afford).

Hiring people without having worked with them will always be problematical. You can look at someone's work, when that's appropriate (for example, a DP, camera operator, sound, editor, director). But there are real limits to that. Suppose you are looking for an editor and you view one of his or her films and it's great. What this doesn't tell you is who is really responsible for that greatness. You don't know who really decided on each cut, how long the editor took, what footage there was to work with, and how the editing process worked.

Was the editor's first cut 90% right and done with lightning speed or did he or she take forever to get a version of the film that was very rough (in terms of sequence, how the shots flowed together, and on exactly what frame the cut was made) and very different from the final cut that you so admired? Or did the director or producer really cut the film, either by standing in the editing room the whole time giving directions or by totally re-cutting the film? Or was the editor's first cut such a disaster that they brought in another editor to re-cut the film? Some editors know instinctively where to make a cut while others find the right place only after much time-consuming trial and error. And some simply don't understand where to make the cut at all even though they call themselves editors and know how to use a splicer. In addition, editing is often largely subjective taste and not objective at all. Will that editor be right for your film?

What footage did the editor have to work with? With endless good footage and enough time, anyone should be able to put together a film. Some editors, however, can work miracles fixing footage that doesn't really work. If the director (or DP) didn't understand editing enough to give the editor adequate material to work with (so shots didn't cut together well, or at all), then poor editing may not be the editor's fault. Or perhaps the picture was all right but the sound was bad, limiting what the editor could do. Or the acting was bad on takes where the camera work was decent. And on it goes.

How long did the editor take to complete the film? Did he or she have a generous time frame and budget? Did he or she stay within both? How many assistants did he or she have?

You can discover some behind the scenes information by getting references from other people who worked with that person (the director and/or producer are obvious places to begin). And you have to hope that you'll get honest references. I could have avoided more than one problem if other producers or directors had been more honest with me about potential crew members. We need to help each other by sharing accurate information about our experiences (trying also to assess and admit *our* responsibility when there were problems with a particular person).

The questions I suggest about an editor can apply to any crew member. Great sound is not nearly as hard to obtain on a sound stage as in difficult locations with little time and inadequate money for the right equipment. Judging a cinematographer's work is hard if you don't know the time and money constraints — or perhaps the director chose every shot and the gaffer did all the lighting. In that case the footage really tells you very little about the cinematographer's skills. Ironically, out-takes may often give you more information than the finished film. You can find out how many tries it took to get the finished product, and why.

So, if you look at someone's work, also ask other people about the shoot. Ask who really did what, don't rely on titles or credits. And ask what the person is like to work with, as well as about his or her technical ability and artistic taste. Or observe the person at work on another film, if that's possible.

Lastly, try to hire people who really care about working on your film. The care will show up in the finished product.

UNIONS

The whole question of the relationship of the unions to independent filmmakers is a tricky one. While unions were created to protect their members, many union regulations that were designed for the major studios are difficult and often prohibitive for low-budget films (especially rules requiring a certain number of people to be hired). Many unions are realizing that their rigid regulations are simply making it difficult for their members to work on independent productions, at a time when there are more and more independent productions looking for high quality crews. Some unions have created new relaxed regulations (and rates) for independent producers of low-budget films and some simply overlook violations. Each union is different and each locale is different — investigate what the situation is in your area.

The principal unions that have jurisdiction in the film industry are:

IATSE (International Alliance of Theatrical and Stage Employees), often simply referred to as the "IA." The IA is an umbrella organization that has numerous locals for all types of technicians from cameramen to editors, set designers, electricians, grips, hairdressers, etc..

NABET (National Association of Broadcast Employees and Technicians), which covers many of the same technical categories as the IA. NABET originated in the television industry, mostly in New York, but now includes film as well. It's often more flexible than the IA.

International Brotherhood of Teamsters covers primarily drivers for equipment trucks. They are a powerful union that is often totally superfluous for independent filmmaking, although they usually try to insist that you hire some of their members even if you don't have any trucks for them to drive (for example, if you are using only a small grip truck that is driven by its owner, your grip or gaffer).

WGA (Writers Guild of America) — for writers.

DGA (Directors Guild of America) — for directors, assistant directors, and production managers.

Producers Guild of America — for producers.

American Federation of Musicians — for musicians.

There are also several actors' unions (**SAG, SEG, AFTRA**), see page 156.

To obtain union information, you can begin by getting rates and contract information from the current *Brooks Standard Rate Book*. You might then want to contact the unions directly or you might first want to talk with other producers or sympathetic union members. Gather all the information before deciding whether to work with a particular union. You can often sign a SAG (Screen Actors Guild) contract without using the technical craft unions or the Teamsters. However, it's sometimes difficult to use the IA without having them also contact the Teamsters. If you are making a film in the heart of Los Angeles or New York, you'll have greater problems with unions than if you're shooting far from a major film center.

Unions not only set rates for all categories of technicians, but also have very strict regulations governing working conditions. Many of those rules came out of a need to protect workers in a crazy industry that tends to overwork people. Some of the regulations are complicated, but you should learn them thoroughly — violations can result in expensive penalties.

When investigating union rates, check out the provisions for health and welfare benefits and residuals (for sales to other markets or re-runs). At a time when prices paid for films (by television, for example) vary greatly, SAG and some other unions have very inflexible rules about residuals, usually stated as a percentage of the original fee regardless of the sale price of the show. This means that residuals for actors alone can be higher that the price you'll be paid for the entire show from a subsidiary sale. Someday this may all get straightened out, but until then, if you work with unions find out what all their regulations are. Residuals that you don't have to pay until later are easy to ignore now — but they can come back to haunt you later. Don't assume that the union will be reasonable and understanding.

At some point, after you've checked rates and regulations, you'll have to decide whether you'll work with any of the film related unions — and if so, which ones. One factor is whether you want to hire particular people who are union members (as many good crafts people are — although most film unions have historically been very exclusive and kept out many qualified people including, but not limited to, women and minorities). Be aware that unions often have stiff penalties for members who work on non-union productions (although these are not always applied). Be careful to protect union members who want to work with you.

The smaller your film, the fewer problems you're likely to have with unions. If you want to go non-union, ask advice from other filmmakers as well as crew people you'd like to work with. They'll be able to give you advice that's appropriate for your area and your type of film.

TECHNICAL DETAILS

When you hire people, you'll have to determine whether they are employees or independent contractors. This is a complicated and delicate issue and you should investigate carefully before deciding which category the people you hire fall into. Check IRS (Internal Revenue Service) regulations. The basic distinction is that employees are people whose work you control in terms of what will be done and how it will be done. You are responsible for withholding income tax for them as well as paying other taxes. Independent contractors are hired by you to perform a task (largely under their own direction) and they are responsible for their own taxes. In some professions, the distinctions are very simple, with people being clearly classified as one or the other. Film, however, has some grey areas. Although independent contractors are responsible for their own taxes, you must report payments they receive to the IRS, if they are over a certain amount (on a 1099 MISC form, over $600). Check with a lawyer or tax consultant about this and/or read relevant IRS regulations. If you hire independent contractors, make this very explicit and make sure they understand the legal and tax implications.

What written agreements do you need with the people you hire? Do you need a lengthy contract, an informal "deal memo", or simply a handshake? This will depend on your style and perhaps the size of your film. A deal memo, while simple and informal, might be very useful to get everything down in writing. This can clear up any misunderstandings before the shoot and aid you if misunderstandings arise later. The deal memo should include at least the rate, the hours the rate includes, the provision for overtime (if there is one), any equipment that is included, any fringes (such as per diems, housing, meals, laundry, phone), whether the person is an employee or an independent contractor, and their social security number (or tax ID number).

There are a number of issues you will want to discuss with crew members at the time of hiring. What happens if the shoot goes over schedule? Can they work longer or do they have other commitments right after your film? What happens of you don't get along and a person quits or is fired? Are there limits to what you can ask of the crew (for example, how much overtime there will be, even if paid)? Some of these are things you might not want to think about before the shoot, when you assume that everything will go smoothly — but it's better to be prepared. I'm not in favor of complicated contracts but I think it helps to have a basic agreement on paper, especially for a larger shoot or when working with people you don't know well. "An ounce of prevention is worth..."

BEING A BOSS

You can't talk about the crew without also talking about the boss. Whether or not you like the word, or even the concept, someone has to both make decisions and convey them to other people. Someone has to be the boss.

Making decisions. When decisions need to be made, they will be made — whether you make them neatly and rationally (perhaps specifically delegating others to make subsidiary decisions) or whether you allow them to be made by default (and perhaps by people who you don't want to have make them). For example, you can sit down and decide what kind of lighting style you want for the film (with whomever you want to have make that decision) — or you can never discuss it, which will essentially leave the decision to the DP or the gaffer. I favor making decisions neatly and cleanly — and I hope this book will help you to do that.

Giving orders. Once you've made decisions, the next step is to convey them to the crew and to see that they are carried out accurately, on time, and within the budget. This, in turn, depends on you giving clear instructions — and on the people responsible for carrying out your instructions being able to do what is needed. You have control over both parts. Select capable crew and give clear instructions. Let people know that if they don't understand something, or if they're having difficulties, they can (and should) come back to you.

If you're uncomfortable being a boss, deal with that before the shoot. You can talk out your style of working with the crew, simply grit your teeth, or delegate some of the bossing tasks.

Delegating responsibility. This means letting other people make some subsidiary decisions on the film. It also means giving them adequate guidelines to make those decisions — and also letting go to some extent. Decisions that you delegate may not be made exactly as you would make them. That's an inherent danger in delegating responsibility — but the reality is that on most larger films you simply can't do everything yourself. You have to trust the people you hire, even if you want to maintain a large amount of personal control over the production. Trying to do everything will only exhaust you. In addition, requiring that you approve everything is very inefficient. Hire good people, and give them some responsibility and power — but be clear on the extent and the limits of the authority you are delegating. What can the other person decide and what must they check out with you?

One advantage of delegating responsibility is that you can avoid some of the more obvious bossing tasks by assigning those to a production manager or assistant director.

Making sure things get done. Once decisions are made and responsibilities assigned, you need to make sure that things are in fact being done as they should. Don't just assume that once you make a decision or assign a task it will be carried out correctly. You need a mechanism for checking up — before a problem becomes a crisis.

Personnel problems. Dealing with personnel problems is generally an unpleasant task — but it's part of the job. Members of the crew (or cast) may simply not be doing their job adequately or you may have intra-personal conflicts. This is much less of a problem on a small shoot that will only last a few days or a week, but working with people for a month or two is another story. I don't have a simple solution for this — but I do want to suggest that you consider ahead of time what you will do if problems arise.

You should at least consider the fact that you might have to fire people. Firing people isn't pleasant, but it may sometimes be the only alternative, or the lesser of evils. The first time I had to face the possibility of firing people was very difficult for me and I didn't fire a couple people who, with hindsight, I should have fired. I thought that since I had made the mistake of hiring them, I should live with my decision, but I didn't realize until after the shoot how great a price I paid for not firing them.

PRODUCER-DIRECTOR RELATIONS

One major thing you'll need to determine early on is the relationship between producer and director — both in terms of creative decisions and also the chain of command during various stages of production. To some extent this will be determined by who had the original idea for the film and how each of you like to work. There are no laws here about who does what — but both you and the crew need to be clear, otherwise you'll have confusion on the set. And you need to be clear about who will keep the film on schedule and on budget. Sometimes, of course, the producer and director are one and the same. This may ease some problems but that person then has to be able to focus on the creative side — and stay on schedule and on budget (or delegate that responsibility to someone else).

A good producer-director relationship (with good communication and trust) is important for another reason. You'll need each other's cooperation at all stages in order to keep the film on schedule and on budget — and get the best possible film.

CASTING

Casting is one of the key ingredients of a film — and one to which you should pay a lot of attention. How you cast will vary with the type of film you're making, the level of acting you want, and where you're making (and casting) the film.

Leave yourself enough time to cast leisurely. Don't get into a bind where you're scheduled to begin filming next week and therefore have to take the first decent person you see. Casting is a key part of your film — give it the time and care it deserves.

There are four parts to the casting process: 1) getting the word out that you are casting, 2) the audition itself, 3) the selection, and 4) the formalities.

GETTING THE WORD OUT

How you publicize your auditions will depend on where you are and who you want to reach. Are you looking for professional actors or are you open (for financial, geographic, or other reasons) to non-professionals? Are you casting in a major film center or a small town? Do you want to cast a wide net and audition lots of people or do you want to be very selective about whom you try out? Do you simply want to put out the word that you are casting and wait and see who comes or do you want to actively encourage appropriate people to try out, or even seek out specific people?

Casting professionals in large cities, either through casting agencies or through open auditions is a fairly straight-forward process. In addition to casting agencies, you can contact theater groups and place ads announcing auditions. Some large cities have specialized audition newsletters.

Casting non-professionals may necessitate a different approach. Actors, by definition, are people who can create a variety of roles. But in your film, you will have certain specific roles to fill and

SHIRE FILMS
CASTING INFORMATION

If you have never worked in films before, there are a few things you might want to know.

The pace is slow. Before a scene is shot, the scene and props have to be arranged, the action planned out, the camera moves planned, and the lights set up. It may take an hour to set up lights for one scene. Often a "master shot" is done of the whole scene and that is repeated as many times as necessary until there is a good "take" (which means that the acting was good, the lines correct, no dogs barked in the middle, and the camera and sound people didn't make any mistakes). If anything was not right, that means another take. When the master shot is completed, the same scene may be filmed again for close-ups and other angles (other angles may require new lighting). So it's a slow process. It takes 4-6 days to shoot a 20 minute film. And because there are so many things that can go wrong, it's important to minimize problems.

There will be a lot of people around (we'll have a crew of 5 plus the director and production people). This may be distracting so it's important to learn your lines well enough so you won't be distracted by the commotion.

If you are chosen for the film, we expect you to come prepared:

— Be there on time.

— Come with proper clothing (we'll let you know ahead of time what to bring). Make sure that everything fits together, that socks and shoes go with what you're wearing. The camera sees details!

— Know your lines well. We'll have some rehearsals before filming.

— Pay attention to continuity. We'll sometimes shoot scenes on different days that in the film take place on the same day. This means you need to look exactly the same — same socks, same jewelry, same hairstyle, as well as obvious clothes. Don't get a haircut in the middle of a film, or even right before unless you check with us first.

We'll be shooting the film from _____ to _____ at various locations around town. Some people will work only 1-2 days, some will work 4-5. We work long days, generally 9-10 hours, although you may not be in all the scenes on a given day. We'll have an exact schedule later. We hope to not go overtime, but you should be prepared to stay later on the days you work.

We will let you know by _____ if you have been selected for a part. If you do not hear from us, it means you haven't been selected for this film. But that doesn't necessarily mean we didn't like you or your acting. Each film calls for a distinctly different kind of person or talent — and if you don't fit into this film you may fit for another. We'll keep your card on file for future reference.

If you have any questions about this, please ask us. And thanks for coming!

SAMPLE FLYER FOR NON-PROFESSIONAL CAST

146

each actor has to play only one. You can choose an actor to play a part — or you can find a person who may not be able to "act" at all, but who may in real life be very close to the character you want. In other words, you can "type-cast." To find these people you might need to be more creative than simply putting out notices to the acting community. We sometimes look for people in areas suggested by the subject of the film. For example, for "Physical Fitness" we sent flyers to local health and sports clubs; for "The Ugly Duckling" we contacted all local dance groups and dance classes; for teen-oriented films we notify local high schools.

Being on camera does require certain talents — primarily the ability to take direction, to speak clearly, and to appear natural. Look for people who are used to performing or speaking in public, even though they may not be actors. Such people are likely to be more confident and less upset by the presence of the camera and the commotion of filmmaking. Consider performers of all kinds (musicians, dancers, athletes) and others who deal with the public (such as teachers, social workers, or sales people).

Non-professionals usually don't know the demands of film acting and it may be useful to make these clear from the very beginning. For most films I hand out a printed sheet to everyone who comes to the audition explaining what will be required in terms of a commitment (time and energy) and asking people to make sure they understand this before trying out.

In deciding what kind of people to cast, think of the needs of your film — and also what resources you have. Do you have a director who is very good with actors and can help an actor deliver a good performance? Do you have a lot of time to rehearse and work on acting quality? Do you have a good make-up person who can alter people's physical appearance? Affirmative answers to those questions give you more leeway in casting.

THE CASTING SESSION

Casting sessions can be run in many different ways. Think about the needs of your particular film. How your session will be run will depend on whom you expect to have attend. Did you cast a wide net so that your first audition is really just to eliminate people and get down to serious contenders — or can you skip that and go straight to a serious audition?

One of the things I like about the audition process is that I generally learn a lot from it. As clear as I think I am about the characters at the script stage, I inevitably become clearer, or even change my mind drastically, during the audition process. What this has taught me is to stay fairly open about the type of person I'm looking for, and to not make up my mind ahead of time about specific people. I also learn a lot about the script by having people read it aloud.

I like to begin the casting session by giving people a little written or verbal information about the film and about our film company, including a brief summary of the film, shooting dates and time (and how much work will be required of actors), and expectations we have of actors (see p. 146). This shouldn't be necessary for professionals — but it's especially important for those not used to working in film. I let people know what our casting process will be and when they'll be notified if they are selected.

The audition process is meant to help you find the right people for your film. Help the actors show you what they can do. If they need to be made comfortable and relaxed, try to do that. You want them at their best. Tell them about the character. If you don't like what they do, explain what you don't like and give them a chance to change. Some actors are excellent at cold readings (but don't improve much after that) while others may be very poor at a cold reading even though they might eventually give you exactly the performance you want. You may have to take some risks. Work with the actors. If someone wants time to work with the script before reading for you, let them. If your film requires a range of emotion, test that in the audition. Some actors may be great in a loud, brash scene but unable to do a quiet, tender one (or vice versa).

Don't assume anyone who calls himself an actor can act, including big name stars. If you cast anyone for your film without testing him or her first, you're taking a big chance. Some known actors may be reluctant to read for a part, and some may be insulted if you ask. But it's your film and if you want to have an actor read for a part before casting him, be firm (but be aware of the politics involved and ask politely).

Video. Video taping can be very helpful for casting sessions. First of all, it lets you relax because you don't have to remember everything. You can replay the auditions as often as you want later — and discuss them with whomever you want. Secondly, people often look different on camera than in person and since they will eventually be seen on film (or video), it's useful to test that early on. Video also lets you get close and focus on faces more than you might normally in a casting session. Lastly, the video camera gives the actors a taste of what the actual filming will be like and you can sometimes discover who won't be able to ignore the camera (and will steal looks at it) and who will be nervous because of it (although you might also be able to desensitize them before the actual shooting). We also use video cassettes to look at known actors in other movies they've been in.

You can run casting sessions in many ways. Let me give you some examples of different kinds we've held.

For "Peter and the Wolf" we were looking for a young boy. The film would be narrated by someone else, which meant we didn't care about the boy's speaking ability. But the film was mostly music, so we did care about his sense of timing. We were looking for a fairly special boy, but we cast a wide net to find him. We interviewed boys in groups. We had them walk and skip to Prokofiev's music. I'm very conscious of the way people move and always pay attention to that in casting, but we thought it would be especially important in this film. Some kids kept time to the music and seemed to love it, while others were completely stiff and their walking and skipping bore no relation to the beats.

149

That was one test. We also set up an obstacle course of tables and chairs and had the kids climb over and under them to see how agile and coordinated they were. That was test two.

Because the film would be narrated, we would be able to talk and give direction to the boy while filming. So we talked during the audition, asking the kids to follow instructions without looking at the director. We had them pretend they were walking in the woods, then a bird flew overhead, then landed on their shoulder. We asked them to put it on their finger and talk to it, and then let it fly away. Some were very stiff, some couldn't do it at all, some didn't really understand the directions, and others got totally into the fantasy. Some kids did only what was required, while others added wonderful little touches. That was test three.

Until this time, we tried to make the kids feel relaxed and at ease, but for our last test, to see how self-conscious the boys might be with a camera, we had a production assistant follow the kids around at close range, pretending to be filming with a camera. (Now we routinely videotape sessions but this audition was before we had video equipment.) Some kids were very easily distracted and nervous while others weren't at all. Although we began with over 40 boys, these tests enabled us to narrow our choices down very quickly during the casting session.

For some films we begin with just an interview, especially if we have some prior knowledge of the actor's ability. This was our first step for "Hard Traveling." We began with actors who had been recommended either by casting agencies, by friends and colleagues, or whose work we had seen. We assumed they could act but wanted to see their physical appearance (not made up for another role) and get a sense of them as people. The second step was to have them read from the script because we needed to see how they would work as the characters we wanted them to play. For the lead actors this step didn't come until a second interview, generally after they had a chance to look over the script.

Of course, the best way to learn about an actor's ability is to see him or her act. We regularly go to theater performances, casting in our minds all the time. And we make a special point of going to even more plays when we are casting for a film. For "Hard Traveling" we spent months looking at video tapes and scouring television listings to look at any films that might include actors we were interested in. Although we considered numerous known Hollywood actors for our male lead, we finally selected a San Francisco stage actor who had impressed us during a performance in a play.

A word of caution. Be careful about ruling out people based on seeing them in other films or plays. They'll be playing other characters, and although that may give you a good idea of their acting ability, you may not know how they'll work for the character in your film. Don't eliminate them simply because you don't like the part they're playing or even their interpretation of that character.

I often like to audition people in groups for several reasons. One is that it simply allows you to have more time with each person. In situations where you cast a wide net, it allows you to eliminate certain members of the group in your mind while spending more time watching others. Other advantages are that you can see how the actors relate to one another, the group situation often lessens the pressure on each individual actor, and the actors can learn from each other.

For "The Birth Control Movie" we had about 20 kids that we called back for a second audition for 10 parts. First we had them read from the script and then we did improvisations based on situations in the script, round-robin style, with the kids taking turns at various roles. They came up with new lines and bits of business that I later incorporated into a revised script. They could see which interpretations of characters worked and which didn't work as well as I could (and that was much more effective than me telling them what I wanted). Actors who were technically good or who had a nice look but who were unimaginative in creating characters would learn from the other kids and sometimes incorporate someone else's ideas into their own acting when their turn came around. We also had a chance to mix and match people and try the kids in different combinations, as well as try each person for many roles. The group session helped relax the kids and the whole session began to feel much more like a party than an audition. The end result was that everyone learned a lot from the experience, even those who ultimately weren't cast. And I found that we cast differently than if we had not had the round-robin.

Physical appearance is often important for a film, but people may be able to look very different than how they look at an audition. Don't be misled. Some actors are aware of this and come to an audition dressed as they think you want them to look, which may or may not be what you want.

Composite photos are sometimes useful in helping you imagine an actor as a different character and you can also ask the actor for assistance. For "The Ugly Duckling" we were looking for a grandmother. During the audition we asked a younger woman who was trying out for another role to help us out by reading the role of the grandmother with another actor. She did such a wonderful job that we began to consider her for the role — only she didn't look like a grandmother (and we knew we wouldn't have a make-up person or hairdresser on the set). We decided to call her and explain our dilemma — that we couldn't imagine her as a grandmother although we loved her acting. She informed us that she'd just finished playing an 80-year old in a play we hadn't seen. I asked if she could do her hair and make-up and come over and let us see her. We were skeptical about whether she could do an adequate job (since film make-up needs are more demanding than theater requirements) but as soon as she walked in we knew she had the part.

Going into the audition, you may or you may not have a clear idea of the character you want. I've been influenced by auditions so often that I now consciously try to be more open-minded going into the session. For example, in "Teenage Pregnancy: No Easy Answers," we had a part for an older female drama teacher. No one at the auditions really impressed us, but a younger man trying out for another part did. We decided to change the script a little and we gave him the part (and, actually, the more we thought about it, the more we liked the idea of a younger male teacher).

For "Peter and the Wolf" our image of the grandfather was very definitely of a slight, somewhat frail old man. One of the people who tried out was very rotund, but used his weight well when he moved and created such a great character that he got the part. Now I can't imagine the grandfather any other way.

SELECTION

How do you make your decision? What's important? The main criteria for casting should be: 1) image (physical appearance and personality), 2) acting ability, 3) directability, 4) chemistry (how the actors work together), and 5) what the actor is like to work with.

1) Image. What is the physical look you want for the film? Is that important? Personality is as important to the image of a character as physical appearance. Do you want the character to be warm, strong, gentle, cocky, vulnerable, cold, withdrawn, aggressive, confident...? To a large extent, the lines in the script will define the character but image can also be very important. The way someone walks can say as much about them as any words they may utter.

When dealing with images, think about stereotypes. Do you want to follow them or go against them? I'm generally very conscious of stereotypes and often like to counter them. For example, for "Child Abuse: The People Next Door" we were looking for a young woman to play the "abuser." Most of the women we auditioned fit the stereotype of a quick-tempered woman who got angry easily and who carried so much tension inside that you expected the outbursts. One woman, however, went totally against the stereotype. She was soft and gentle, with long flowing hair and a sweet southern accent. She was the last person you would imagine striking a child. All of a sudden I realized that we had been looking in the wrong direction. The whole point of the film was that *anyone* could abuse their kids. We began directing the actors differently. We eliminated all of the loud and strong actresses who had been such believable child abusers (none of whom was able to be soft and sweet enough when we requested that). The woman who had originally jarred our thinking wasn't a strong enough actress to play the role so we began a new search, specifically for a very soft and gentle person. The film is very different because of that decision.

Voice. Pay attention to a person's voice as well as to their physical appearance. Often a voice that sounds perfectly natural when you see the person saying the words takes on a totally different quality when you don't see the speaker. This becomes especially important in any film that uses voice-over narration or where the speaker is off camera a lot. Close your eyes during the audition (or later while watching a tape) and listen to the voice. Is the voice dull or even irritating? Does the voice go with the character? (I have a pet peeve about women who sound like little girls and will not cast a grown woman who sounds like a child.)

2) Acting ability. How well does the person act? Can they create the character you envision (or one you like even better)? How skilled are they as an actor — do they just do the job adequately or do they add nuances that make the difference between average acting and good acting? How consistent are they? How many takes will they need to get it right? Pay attention to an actor's presence when he isn't speaking. Some actors just stand there looking out of place unless they're speaking, while others know how to keep busy and "listen actively."

Casting stage actors is complicated because of the differences between acting for theater and for film. You need to be sure the actors can adapt to the needs of film. When actors aren't used to film acting, it might be useful to talk to them about the differences. The loud voice projection and large gestures needed to be seen in the last row of a theater are usually too broad for film. Film requires more subtlety. The concept of continuity, of doing things the same way for each take and matching shots, is often foreign to stage actors where variety is welcomed with each new performance. Make sure a stage actor can adapt — or you'll waste a lot of time and money.

Non-professionals also need to understand how to hit a mark (without looking at the ground), how to cheat looks, and how to ignore the camera and director. Explain these concepts to them and see how well they do.

3) Directability. When you cast, you either have to find actors who are absolutely perfect as they are — or you have to direct them to be different. If you want someone to change even 1%, make sure they can do that. Some people may naturally be very close to what you want but may not be able to change that last 1%. Even if they seem perfect at the audition you might want to see if they can respond to direction and alter their performance because you never know when you might need that later. See if they can understand when you want them to do something differently. Ask them to speed up the pace, for example, or slow it down, or to add more or less emotion. In general, see if the actor can do the kinds of things you'll need to have him do in the film.

4) Chemistry. Even though you'll generally interview actors separately, they'll work with other actors in the film so it's important to know how well they'll work together. What do your main actors look like together? This may be especially important if there is supposed to be a family relationship between some of the actors. How well do they work together? What is the chemistry between them? And, simply, do they like and respect each other? You might want to audition certain actors together before making your decisions.

5) What is the actor like to work with? How well you can work with an actor may be as important as his or her acting skill. For a small film this isn't nearly as important as for a major role in a feature film where you'll be living and working with someone for a month or more. How do you get along? How well do the actor and director communicate? Does the actor get stubborn or have temper tantrums? Do they expect star treatment? Can they do their own hair and make-up if that will be necessary? Find out all of this beforehand. Ask other people with whom the actor has worked. Keep in mind that their experiences may not be the same as yours, but do get that information.

FORMALITIES

Once you've selected your actors, you have to deal with the formalities — what you will give them (primarily money) and what you expect from them.

Money. When dealing with payments for cast, as with crew, remember that everything is usually negotiable and that you have other bargaining chips besides money. Unions have minimum rates that vary with the type of film and the market for which it's intended. Pay close attention here — if you use a lower rate originally because you intend to use the film for public television or the educational market and your film then sells to another market (for example theatrical or commercial television), you may be liable for high residuals (higher than if you had originally paid the theatrical or commercial television rate to begin with). Think out carefully beforehand what rate you want to use — a short-run saving might be very costly in the long run.

Unions. A word about the actors' unions. In places where there is a professional film industry, most good actors (although not all) will be members of SAG (Screen Actors Guild). If you decide to use at least some SAG actors and work with SAG, you'll have to deal with paperwork and bureaucracy as well as fixed rates and regulations (much more for a feature film than for a shorter one — find out what's involved for your type of film). If you work under a SAG contract, you can still use actors who aren't members of SAG under what is known as the Taft-Hartley clause (although you must still pay them union rates). This provision gives those actors the right to join SAG if they want to (and are willing to pay the fees involved). Some actors will be delighted to have this opportunity while others won't care. If an actor has worked under the Taft-Hartley clause once before, however, he or she is required to join the union the second time (which means paying the high fees). Make sure your potential actors understand these regulations if they apply. If you want to use actors under this provision, you must notify SAG (they have a special form for this) and justify why you chose this particular actor over union members. If you haven't worked with unions before, talk to filmmakers who have — before you contact SAG.

There are two other film actor's unions: AFTRA (American Federation of Television and Radio Artists) and SEG (Screen Extras Guild). SEG is the union for extras, although they cover only certain geographic areas. Find out whether you are within one of their areas of jurisdiction.

Expectations. After you have selected your cast, go over exactly what you expect of them, especially if you are working with non-professionals. This should include dates and work times (for filming and for any rehearsals — and don't forget to warn them about possible overtime and/or an extended or altered shooting schedule so they don't make plans for immediately after the shoot), what you want them to wear (especially if it's their own clothes), how you want their hair, and that you expect them to be on time (and with clean fingernails and socks that match). All this sounds obvious but there are many things we take for granted that are not obvious to those who have not worked in film ("Does the camera really see my fingernails?"). If we didn't give out a printed information sheet at the casting session (see p. 146), we generally do so at this point. For larger films you might want to confirm casting with a letter, a deal memo, or a contract, specifying dates, conditions, and pay scale.

REHEARSAL

Once you've selected your cast, think about how to obtain the best possible performance. This is largely the role of the director — but you can aid that process. Rehearsal time will generally help any performance. Plan for a rehearsal period (paid or unpaid) if you possibly can. You might even want to schedule the rehearsal time well in advance of filming (instead of immediately preceding it as is common practice). That lets the actors get a sense of what you and the director want from them early on. They can then practice that rather than arriving with ingrained interpretations that are contrary to what the director wants and are sometimes difficult to change at that point. Of course, this will only work if the actors are willing to spend time preparing for their roles — some actors begin to work only when they arrive on the set. Know this when you hire them.

We used an advance rehearsal period very successfully for "Hard Traveling." A large part of the film is a love story and we felt that the relationship of the two principals was crucial to the success of the film. We wanted them to get to know each other and build rapport early on (they had only met briefly before we made our casting selections). We scheduled several days of rehearsal with the two main actors about a month before we began filming (in addition to another couple days right before filming).

During the first rehearsal period we also introduced the lead actors to the two boys (ages 5 and 8) who would play their children in the film. Although we had confidence in the kids' abilities, they had no acting experience and were somewhat nervous. We thought that the best way to put them at ease was to have them all become friends beforehand. We wanted them to really *feel* like a family. We also wanted the boys to not be intimidated by the professional actors they'd be working with.

We did very little actual rehearsal with the boys during the first rehearsal period but we all went to see the house that was to be our main location and the director blocked out a few scenes to give them a sense of what the process would be like. Then we sent the actors, the "family" in the film, out for ice cream — just the four of them. They would be a family unit in the film and we wanted to begin to create that. In addition, we suggested to the boys' parents that the kids spend as much time together as possible. They did and by the time we shot the film the boys were fast friends and totally believable as brothers. During the shoot, in an attempt to deal with the boys' tendency to look at the director for instructions or approval, the director gave most of his instructions through one of the "parents" (the actors, not the real parents) so that the film "parents" actually took on some real parental roles. That worked very well.

LOCATION SCOUTING

On the surface, location scouting seems simple — you find a place you like and that's it. But underneath the surface, it's not that easy. Paying attention to all the factors involved in selecting a location can make your shoot a lot smoother.

The first thing to remember is that film is often illusion — and you can use imagination and creativity to find locations. Take a step back from reality. For example, someplace that is meant to be one location in the script can, in reality, be several different locations. The outside and the inside of a home or the kitchen and bedroom may not really have to be filmed at the same house. Or conversely, several totally different places in the script might actually be shot at the same location. Places can pass for things they are not in reality. In "Hard Traveling" we used a school principal's office for one police station and a theater basement for another. (A Spanish director friend used a religious school for a prison and an old folks home for a hospital psychiatric ward. Interesting substitutions.)

THE SEARCH

There are many ways to find locations. One is to simply wander, either at random or in an organized way. This can work if you can see what you need from the outside, but that isn't always possible. Think of specific people who might know the type of location you need. Think of types of people who might have reason to know about houses and offices — repairmen, interior decorators, painters, realtors. Friends (and sometimes even your actors) can also be a great source of leads. For "Hard Traveling" we printed up a flyer about the hard-to-find main location we were seeking, giving as many specific requirements as we could. We gave the flyer to friends and acquaintances, including several real estate people and old time residents who knew the county well.

In some cases you can also use publicity. We made a special effort to place an article in the local newspaper mentioning our need for a farmhouse (and listing our phone number). And, of course, you can use pre-existing location lists if they exist. Some film commissions and location scouts keep files of potential locations. Begin your own file. Keep a record of rejected locations as well as the ones you use (and contact names and phone numbers) and save them for future use.

When you're looking at locations, pay attention to the particular shots you'll need. This is another place to use creativity and imagination — and where good communication with the director is helpful. If the shots are limited, you might have much more leeway in choosing locations. For example, suppose your scene is New York's Grand Central Station, but you just have a few quick shots. Maybe you don't even need to go to New York, or don't need a railroad station at all but could get by with a few props, a crowd, a section of wall, and some train station sound effects. If necessary, add an establishing stock shot of the real thing.

Think about whether to use a real location at all. Hollywood used to film everything on sound stages. Although stages are used much less these days, shooting on a stage may still make a lot of sense for some scenes. Sets are usually expensive and you have to find a place to build them (although not necessarily a Hollywood sound stage — a vacant warehouse might do just fine), but you have more control on a stage than in many real locations. The time saved by having that control might be worth it.

HOW TO APPROACH OWNERS

Tell people clearly who you are, what you are doing, what you are looking for, and what you can afford to pay (at least in general terms such as, "This is a low budget film and we will only be able to give you a token payment" or "Of course we will be glad to compensate you for the use of your house"). Some people might want to be reassured that you are legitimate — bring along a brochure, business card, or any publicity you may have about your company or project. Some people care about money, while others don't.

Be sure to explain to the owners (and tenants) as clearly as you can what filming at their place will involve. They may think it will be fun to have a few actors come into their house to make a movie. They may have no idea it may mean twenty (or more) people taking over their home, perhaps moving furniture around, setting up lights and equipment, tapping into their electrical system — and staying long hours. Some scenes can be shot with a minimum of disruption, others can't. Explain what you will do. Give them a sense of the filmmaking process. And reassure them that when you're done, you'll put everything back exactly as it was (and then make sure you do that!). If your crew will staple up sound blankets, use tape that will peel paint off the walls, or put nails in the walls — warn the owners and arrange to repair the damage or pay for it. If your crew won't do that, reassure the owners. The last thing you want is to have the property owner evict you in the middle of filming because you misled him or her about what you were going to do.

If you plan to take all their furniture out of the living room, remember that you'll have to put it someplace else. Don't tell them, "We'll just be using the living room" if they'll later discover that you are not only filming in the living room, but also that the dining room and hallway are full of furniture and props, you're making lunch in the kitchen, actors are changing in the bedroom, and twenty people are traipsing to the bathroom (and the toilet paper just ran out). This may be far more disruption than they bargained for. Consult with them ahead of time. Maybe they'd like to go away for the day. You might phrase your financial offer in terms of, "We'd like to give you money so you can all go out and enjoy a nice dinner after work because we'll be here late" or so they can go away for a few days vacation while you're filming. Perhaps they'd prefer that you only use certain rooms or serve lunch outside. Some people are generous and flexible, others aren't. Don't make assumptions. If you are clear ahead of time, your hosts will be less likely to be upset. And, if you behave well, they'll be more likely to invite you back again!

SELECTING A LOCATION

There are many things — both aesthetic and practical — to consider in selecting a location.

AESTHETIC CONSIDERATIONS. The aesthetic considerations are fairly obvious. What look do you want? What time period? What social class? What geographic locale? Do you want a generic look, that could be most anyplace and that many people will identify with — or do you want to portray a particular geographic area? Red tile roofs and palm trees are commonplace in southern California but don't exist in Iowa so avoid them if you want the location to be able to pass for a typical mid-western town.

What are the particulars of your script? For example, if you're shooting in a classroom, what kind of classroom? What age students? Do you want a classroom that's neat and clean or do you want one that's warm and looks lived in? For "The Birth Control Movie" we chose a classroom in an older school that had painted yellow woodwork, which gave the room a very warm look. There was a big oak desk for the teacher. To that we added several bright film posters (it was supposed to be a film classroom) and film editing equipment. Another location we had considered was in a much newer church-run private school, with metal desks, green blackboards, and venetian blinds on metal windows. The whole room had a very cold greenish tone. We could have brightened up the room with posters but it still would have had a very different feel to it than the room we chose.

What subtle messages do you want to convey? Do you want a house to look neat or messy, in top shape or run down? For a film on teenage pregnancy we wanted the apartment of a young single mother to appear unkempt and poorly furnished (with dirty dishes and dirty laundry). We wanted to imply that life is not easy under those circumstances. If, however, the teenager lives with her parents, you might want to counter the stereotype that only the poor get pregnant and show an average middle-class home. People's surroundings say a lot about them — what do *you* want them to say?

How close is the location in terms of its overall look to what you want? How many furnishings or props will you have to bring in? We once needed to recreate Mark Twain's billiard parlor. The main criteria were a big room in an old house and a billiard table. Since billiard tables are big and heavy, we decided to begin by trying to find a room with a billiard table. We asked stores that sold billiard tables if they knew of such a place. Although they gave us some wonderful leads, none worked out and we finally ended up renting the billiard table — but finding a room with a table would have been much easier.

Is accuracy a criteria? Do you need to recreate a particular place or a historical period? If so, you need to begin with research. And you have to decide how important exact accuracy is. Maybe you just want to create an impression. Sometimes what is totally accurate doesn't seem quite as real.

PRACTICAL CONSIDERATIONS. Once you're clear on your aesthetic requirements, it's time to think about the practical ones.

Sound. How much noise is there near the location? Are there low background noises (such as machinery)? Traffic? Airplanes? What other noises might there be in the neighborhood? Does the neighbor have a barking dog? Do the neighbors mow their lawn often? Is a new house being built down the block? Are any street repairs scheduled?

Listen to the "noises" of nature. We tend to think of nature as quiet but in reality it isn't at all. And some of those noises can be very annoying on film, especially if not identified. Sometimes birds we take for granted when we're sitting outside can be very obtrusive on a sound track. The noise of a babbling brook in the country is totally appropriate and you might not notice it. You know what the sound is. But if you don't see the stream in the shot, it may sound like just plain noise or static and be very annoying. If you must shoot near a stream, you might want to include a shot of the stream to establish its presence. Then the audience, like you, will know what the sound is and may forget about it.

You can always add sound to a film but it is sometimes very difficult to take it out. Anyone who has labored over editing a sound track, removing bits of extraneous sound (sometimes including subtle things like breaths or clothes rustling) will tell you that taking out sound is time-consuming, frustrating, expensive, and sometimes impossible. You can remove a sound between words, but you can't take out a sound that overlaps a word. All you can do then is re-record the words (unless you can find that particular word clean in another take and it matches well enough to substitute it).

Sometimes it's extremely difficult to obtain clean sound — for example if you're trying to record intimate dialogue at an airport or a busy intersection. Even if you'll want airplane or traffic sounds in the film, you'll probably want them at a lower level than in the real scene so you can hear your characters' dialogue. Discuss the problem with your sound person, but you may have to resign yourself to re-recording (looping) the actors' dialogue. If lip sync is not important, you can record the sound clean at some other time during the shoot and avoid a looping session. Plan this in advance.

For sound, as with the physical look of the place, it's important to know the content of the scene. Will the shots be wide or close? For close shots (or ones where you can use lavaliere mikes attached to the actors), the microphone can be closer to the speakers and you'll hear less outside noise. Will there be loud music laid over the scene in the editing stage or will every sound in the room (or the nearby street) be heard?

Noise levels are different at different times of day and on different days. A peaceful street may not be quite as peaceful at rush hour. Near some small airports with a large number of recreational fliers there is a great upsurge of flying activity around 5 p.m. after work (and on weekends), which is often just when you're trying to rush through your last shots of the day.

Nature also has time schedules. We filmed a scene for "Peter and the Wolf" at a lovely peaceful pond — or so we thought when we went to look at it before the shoot. But when we arrived to film, in the early morning, we discovered that the pond had thousands of bullfrogs, who had been totally silent when we scouted the location. And down the hill and out of sight (but not out of hearing) was a turkey ranch with hundreds of loud gobblers, who had also been silent during our previous visit. Luckily we were shooting very little sound at that location and we were able to obtain it while the frogs and turkeys were napping.

Check to see if there are any events or street repairs scheduled that might present sound problems. In "Hard Traveling" we filmed on a Saturday in a building across from a small town square. What we didn't know was that there was a concert scheduled in the park all afternoon. As soon as we got the room set up and the lights adjusted properly, the band began to warm up. There was nothing we could do — the band had waited months for the opportunity to play there. We finally reached a compromise — they would take a short break between each song and we'd have time for one take. Then another song, then another take. We stationed a production assistant with a walkie-talkie next to the band all afternoon. Luckily the band was cooperative and our excellent actors didn't require many takes so we were able to use the band's playing periods to set up for the next shot. We got through the afternoon but not without a lot of stress.

Before the shoot, keep your eyes peeled around the locations you'll be using for any signs of upcoming work. Ask the owners specifically if they know of any planned work nearby — they won't usually think to volunteer that information. At our most difficult location on "Hard Traveling," workers all of a sudden began setting up scaffolding on the next building for a several month sand blasting operation. It took some negotiation to have them not interfere with us. Make sure someone on your crew is a good negotiator. Watch out for neighborhood construction — power tool sounds carry for long distances.

Acoustics inside the location can be as important as unwanted sound around it. Bare walls and floors will echo a lot. This can often be fixed with sound blankets on the walls, floors, and/or ceiling (unless they interfere with shots). Sound blankets are standard equipment on a professional shoot but if it's just you and your buddy shooting, you need to pay more attention to acoustics. How will you hang the sound blankets? You can staple them into the wall but that will leave marks. Hanging them from stands takes time (and it also means having sufficient stands). These aren't big problems, just things to think about before the shoot.

Sound blankets can also be used to deal with unwanted outside noise at a location. Before rejecting a location because of excessive noise, see if you can cut down the noise. Sometimes this is simple, sometimes not. Think creatively. Sound travels in straight lines and bounces off hard surfaces but is absorbed by soft ones. Can you block the sound?

For "Hard Traveling" we had great difficulty finding an appropriate 1930's style courtroom. The only one we liked was a room with big windows on a main street of town with a lot of loud traffic. Since we really liked the room, we tried to deal with the sound problem. We explored putting thick panes of glass over the windows, but the windows were very big and our budget was very small. We could easily have covered the windows with fairly inexpensive sound-board, but we wanted to be able to see the windows in certain shots. To complicate matters the DP was talking about lighting through the windows, which would have meant building scaffolding up to our second floor room. One solution might have been to close the street but since it was a main street that wasn't possible.

Our eventual solution was to plan the shots very carefully. Most of the courtroom action was intense drama that would be filmed close. We placed the actors so that key people wouldn't be in front of windows. We filmed some wide establishing shots of the courtroom with the windows clearly visible, at a time when there was the least traffic. Then we blocked up the windows completely (with cheap sound-board) for the rest of the time. We set up the courtroom so that we could move everything over and create a five foot corridor along the windows which we used to set up lights so it would look like the natural light coming through the windows. The finished scene had enough shots with windows to provide an open feeling — and we were able to shoot most of the action without sound problems with the windows boarded up. The main disadvantage was that we roasted for four days because there was no ventilation!

Lighting. Another major practical consideration is lighting. Know in general what kind of lighting you'll need. Is the power supply to the location adequate? Although Hollywood productions usually bring their own generators, small productions usually don't and so must rely on available electricity. You'll usually need 220 amp wiring, which is now standard for new homes but wasn't in the past. Ask a gaffer or electrician to give you a short course on how to recognize 220 wiring. (A hint — electric stoves require 220 wiring so if the house has one you're set.) If you're using minimal lighting you may be able to manage without 220 wiring, using either a few small lights and/or bouncing sunlight in from outside with reflectors. If the location doesn't have 220 wiring, perhaps the neighbors do and wouldn't mind letting you plug into their electricity (you won't use much but you can offer to pay them for it).

If the location has enough power, where is the power source (usually where the main electrical line comes in)? How close is that to the spot you'll be using? For most houses this won't be a problem but for a large building it may, since you'll have to run cable from that source to your filming location (and electrical cable is expensive to rent and heavy and bulky). When filming in a school, we chose a first floor classroom close to the main power box rather than a nicer room on the third floor on the opposite side of the building. You'll need to be able to get to the power source at the time of shooting (some are kept locked) and have a cable running to your filming area. This may sometimes present a safety or security problem. Check it out.

Large rooms are harder to light than small ones (and need more lights which means more money). Windows can create a problem because outside light has a different color temperature than inside light and the two need to be balanced (which can be done with gels on either the windows or the lights, but find out what that involves in terms of time and expense). If the sun comes in directly through the windows and you'll be shooting over a long period of time, the sun's position will shift and you'll have a continuity problem. Some of these problems are very minor, but some can be major. On all these lighting problems, consult with your DP or gaffer — or better yet, learn enough about lighting so that *you* understand your options and the potential problems and possible solutions. This is an example of what I mean by the more you know about other areas of filmmaking the better you'll be at any one part.

If you'll use natural lighting, do you need to shoot at a certain time of day to get the right lighting? Remember that the lighting when you scout the location probably won't remain the same all day. If you'll be at the location only a short time, correct scheduling may be important. If you'll be there all day, you'll want to avoid constantly changing lighting.

Security. If you'll be at the location for more than one day, can your equipment be left safely overnight (at least the lighting and grip equipment — you'd be unlikely to leave the camera)? Can you leave the lights in place and leave the room in disarray until the next day — or are there people living in the house who want to retain some semblance of normalcy after hours? Are you filming in a location that will be used in the evening when you won't be there? If you have to take down all your equipment every night, either to store it neatly or pack it up in the truck, you'll lose precious time. Whether you can leave the lighting in place or not may affect the lighting style you close. Lights rigged from the ceiling usually take longer to put up, but once in place they are more out of the way. Does someone need to stay with the equipment overnight? For "Beware the Jabberwock" we filmed for several days in a secluded but not totally private wooded area. We had many lights and a generator and props carefully set up in a redwood grove. Instead of packing up every night, we had someone camp there to watch the equipment.

Logistics. There are other practical things to consider. Is the room big enough to work in comfortably (to fit all the cast, crew, and equipment)? How available are the miscellaneous amenities you'll need for the cast and crew, such as bathrooms and eating, changing, and rest areas? A crew of 4 is obviously easier to accommodate than a crew of 30. Think of these things as you scout locations.

Are there any other important details that you need to know? For example, is there a pre-determined schedule for mowing or watering the lawn that will interfere with your filming? Is there an automatic sprinkler system that might be set off by hot lights? Is there a loud air conditioner or heating system that can't easily be turned off?

Figure out ahead of time how you will keep the phones from ringing during filming. This may be a special problem if you're shooting in a business location where they need to be able to receive calls or where there are many phone lines to incapacitate.

Be very clear with the owner or manager about exactly what you'll need ahead of time. This might help prevent problems. We once filmed in a supermarket that normally opened at 9 am. We had arranged to come at 7 and be finished by 9. But when we arrived, we discovered that their overhead lights, which we had counted on using, were controlled by a central computer 100 miles away and absolutely could not go on before 8:45. No one had thought to mention this to us before. The manager was very sympathetic, but nothing could be done. So we improvised and altered our filming order. We brought in some additional lights and shot a few close-ups without their overhead lights. We then set up for the wider shots, rehearsed, and waited. When the overhead lights went on at 8:45 we swung into action, got the last shots quickly, and left only a little behind schedule.

Related locations. Are there any other places (buildings or signs) that you need to check out because they will be seen in the background from this location? Ask the owners if there are any uncooperative or unfriendly neighbors who might cause a problem? Sometimes neighbors will turn on the lawn mower, stereo, or power saw just to antagonize you — or in the hope of being paid to keep quiet. Can the neighbor be neutralized beforehand?

MONEY

Suppose you found the ideal place but they want to charge more than you can afford. First, make sure there is no way to get them to lower their rate. If they remain firm, you may need to find another location. Cost becomes another criteria for an acceptable location. We always let people know early on what we can spend so we don't waste time on a place we can't afford — and so the owners don't build unrealistic expectations.

170

How much should you pay? There are no set rules here. You can offer what you think is fair or what you think you can get away with. The owner may ask for what is fair or whatever he thinks he can get. Make an offer and negotiate. If fairness is your criteria, think about what it will cost the owners, if anything, to let you film there. Will a store lose business? Will people be put out of their home and need to eat in a restaurant? Will they need to hire a janitor or take time off from work to be there with you? Will you cause any damage that will need to be repaired? Remember to include all incidental costs (such as janitors or security guards) in your budget.

APPROVAL

Once you've selected your preferred location, you'll need to obtain approval to use it. Who is authorized to let you use the place? If you make an agreement with a tenant, the landlord may evict you if you don't have his or her permission. Ask whose approval you need to obtain. And think about who else you should consult even if legally they don't have a say. For example, in "Child Abuse: The People Next Door" we had a scene in a laundromat that would take half a day to film. We had lined up a nice laundromat in a mobile home park and had obtained a signed release from the owner of the park, who was very friendly and excited about our making a film on his premises. But the night before we were to shoot he called to say that we couldn't come the next morning — his tenants had rebelled. It turned out that he hadn't consulted his tenants (nor had we) and when he posted a notice on the laundromat door announcing the closure, his tenants became very upset. I suspect that the tenants would have been as excited as the owner if we had simply consulted them ahead of time. But once the owner put up his notice (at the last minute), the tenants resented his lack of consideration in not consulting them and the lack of advance notice, and they didn't want us to film there. So we scurried around late at night trying to find another laundromat (at the same time making contingency plans to alter the schedule if we couldn't find one in time). We did find another laundromat — but we had several very tired people the next day.

Get your approval in writing (see p. 76). This won't give you total protection (we had written approval for the laundromat) but it is

171

good protection. Get your releases signed early, in case the piece of paper causes the owner to hesitate or back down. Find out if they'll want to see your insurance or require you to obtain a special insurance "rider" covering them (which will cost extra, consult your insurance broker).

Get all the names and phone numbers you'll need. If the janitor is supposed to meet you at 7 am to unlock the door, get his home number in case he oversleeps. In fact, better get a back-up number as well. Make sure you'll have access at that hour to all the areas you'll need, including the power supply.

Permits. Will you need any permits to use the location? Some cities require many and complicated permits, while others don't. Know the regulations where you'll be filming. And remember that bureaucracy takes time — apply for your permits early. If you'll need to notify neighbors or put up any special signs (such as "No Parking" signs), make all those arrangements ahead of time.

If you have to clear a street of cars (for a period film, for example) notify people well in advance and remind them again closer to the shoot. Personal contact will probably win you more cooperation that a printed notice. Make sure there are no non-functioning cars on the street or cars with owners on vacation. If you'll be posting "No Parking" signs, make sure no one takes them down. The last thing you want is to have someone's car towed, even if you legally have that right.

There are a lot of things to pay attention to while location scouting. And each time you'll probably make a few mistakes and learn a few new things to watch out for. You'll slowly build up a bank of experience and a list of mistakes not to repeat. I hope that by mentioning some of ours I can help you avoid those particular ones — and hopefully give you enough idea of the kinds of problems that can arise that you'll be able to spot potential problems more easily.

WARDROBE AND PROPS

Aesthetic and practical considerations are both important in selecting wardrobe and props.

AESTHETIC CONSIDERATIONS

You'll need to consider many of the same things as for locations. What look do you want? Whose tastes do you have to please? Think about the period, class, and occupations of the people, as well as the story. You'll need to coordinate props, wardrobe, and set design closely with the overall art direction of the film. Clothes are a key part of art direction. They can brighten up a dull room or set a tone — or distract. Do you want muted earth tones, only blues and browns, bright primary colors, or a mixture? In a documentary, clothes and props can make talking heads much more interesting.

Props and costumes can suggest subtle messages as much as locations can — so be clear about what messages you want to convey. Do you want the clothes to appear fresh off the rack or worn (slightly used or completely threadbare)? Do you want them neatly pressed or wrinkled? If you need dishes in a kitchen, should they be matching sets or odd pieces, clean or dirty? Is the person a neat housekeeper or not?

Details can add nice touches to your film. For "Hard Traveling," a 1930's depression-era story, we used old, worn clothes — altered to fit, but not custom-made. On one dress, our costumer lengthened the skirt but didn't press out the old hemline (hemlines that have been in a long time are hard to get out). We purposely allowed the actress's slip to show some of the time. Those things were noticed and added to the texture and reality of the film.

Details can also ruin a scene, if they aren't consistent with the main wardrobe or props. Pay attention to accessories such as belts, earrings, socks, shoes, rings (especially wedding rings), and watches. We had one shot in "Physical Fitness" where an actor bent down to touch his toes. As the camera followed, his pants hiked up to reveal garish socks and old shoes that didn't fit with his neat clothing. We were under great time pressure for that scene so he quickly traded socks with someone. No one had feet as large as his so we were stuck with the shoes, although we did polish them. Some very simple items are hard to find on a moment's notice or on out-of-the-way locations.

Be aware that a camera sees much more than a theater audience. If your actors or crew are used to stage work they may not think about this. Even sewing stitches might be seen. Our "jabberwock" creature in "Beware the Jabberwock" had big purple polka dots sewn on with large stitches (by a costume person with stage but not film experience). Although the stitches would never have been seen on stage, they were quite visible to the camera, so at the last minute we had to unstitch every dot and glue it down (we had no time left for small, careful stitches). Preparing all costumes and props well ahead of time can let you catch mistakes early.

PRACTICAL CONSIDERATIONS

You need to know how a prop or set will be used. Will a prop only be seen briefly in the background or will it be seen up close or even handled? If it's seen up close you'll have to pay more attention to detail. If you need a teapot, does it just have to look right or will it have to hold water or be heated on a stove? Will someone have to be able to sit on a porch railing? Will a door or window have to open? Laundry that will only be seen going around in a dryer is less critical than laundry that will be seen hanging on a clothesline. Do you need clean or dirty laundry? If the laundry begins dry but gets washed in the scene, how many takes will you shoot? If the laundry will be seen in another shot, you'll have to have matching laundry for each take. Let the prop and wardrobe people know these things early on.

Will the prop be used to demonstrate something? For "The Birth Control Movie" we needed to show specific types of birth control devices up close. Planned Parenthood loaned us a demonstration set they used for school lectures — but when we inspected the kit, we discovered that the diaphragm had a tear in it that would show if seen up close. Luckily, a crew member was able to loan us her diaphragm.

Know the context for clothes too. Will the wearer be seen clearly or will he be seated behind someone so that he'll only be seen above the waist? "Hard Traveling" had a 1940's courtroom scene in which people in the front row and those who had to walk in were fully dressed in period costumes while many others were only partially in costume. That saved us a lot of time and money and simplified the costumer's life tremendously (which let her concentrate on other scenes). This worked both ways — we told her which people had to be seen fully and she told us which others could be seen fully because she had complete outfits for them. We selected the rest of our "visible" people from that group. This kind of communication and coordination can stretch limited budgets.

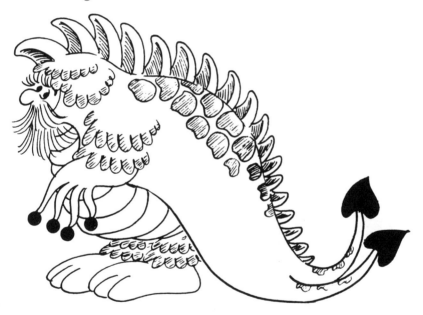

How much will a costume be used? If it will be worn for many hours, make it comfortable and sturdy. Our fantasy Jabberwock was a very large, dinosaur-like creature. The design looked great on paper but the costume turned out to be very impractical. Always insist that props and costumes be ready well before filming. The Jabberwock costume was finished too late to discover (and fix) problems before the shoot. Once the costume was finished, our first problem was simply to get it from the costume designer's workshop to the location. The costume, built on a rigid chicken wire frame which was attached to a back-pack frame (to be worn by the actor) wouldn't fit into any of our cars, not even a station wagon. To get it to the set, I had to wear it, standing up in the back of a pick-up truck that was driven very slowly to minimize wind damage. A producer does many jobs!

After a short time on the set we realized the costume left no way for the actor to sit down and rest — and it took too long to get the costume on for him to be able to take it off, except for lunch. We finally discovered how to wedge a tall stool under the costume for him to half sit and half lean on, but he was basically trapped inside the costume.

Is accuracy important for your film? Will you need to do research in order to prepare authentic costumes or obtain appropriate props for any given period? Accuracy can also apply to simple things. For example, laundry for an elderly bachelor should not include bras and lace slips (if there's any chance they'll be seen — or unless...).

The director or DP may have additional practical needs. They may need a picture on the wall, or a plant or knickknack, for composition purposes. The DP or gaffer may have lighting considerations, such as wanting glass removed from picture frames (to eliminate reflections), having an actor wear a light-colored shirt to bounce more light on his face, or asking for less contrasting clothing on the actors. Black and white are generally difficult colors for lighting purposes. Pure white glares on camera unless dipped in a weak tea solution beforehand.

HOW TO PROCEED

1) Make your prop and wardrobe lists. The lists can come from the breakdown sheets, if those are accurate and complete, or directly from the script. In any case, the script should be used to learn the context and use of props and clothes. The director should add any additional information or clarify anything that's not explicit in the script. Annotate lists — add any additional information about context, details, priorities, or possible sources. Don't forget accessories such as purses, watches, or jewelry, and also implied items such as a helmet and pants clips for a bicyclist, knee and elbow pads for a skateboarder, a stethoscope for a doctor, and wedding rings.

2) Estimate costs. You might want to make these detailed lists early and add estimated costs for each (see p. 288) — to both guide you in making up your budget and to help stick to it later. When you begin pre-production you'll know the total budget allotment for each department. This will largely determine how you proceed after you have your lists. If money is no problem, you can arrange to buy or rent most anything. But money usually is a problem so you'll need to be creative or compromise (or both).

3) Set priorities. Make your priorities clear. Circle key props on your lists. If you have a long prop list, it's likely that some will be used purely as background, while some will be critical. This should be obvious to the prop person if it's clear in the script, and if he or she reads the script carefully. But it may not *be* in the script. The director may envision some specific piece of business using a prop that was perhaps mentioned casually but not singled out. In the rush of pre-production, the prop person may ignore or forget a hard-to-find item, not realizing its importance. Good communication between the director and producer and department heads can prevent many such problems.

Be realistic. If you have limited resources (low budget and/or limited time), don't expect miracles. It may be wiser to compromise on unimportant items so that you can concentrate on getting the important ones right. Find out what will be seen. If you know how wide a shot will be, you may not need to dress the entire room. If you know that some extras will never be seen fully, you can cut corners (and costs) on their costumes.

4) Compromise. Not all compromise is bad. You might look from the very beginning for places to compromise that won't matter at all. You might be able to substitute an easy-to-find item for a difficult one without hurting the story at all. For example, if the script calls for a girl to eat an ice cream cone, you'll need lots of cones for all the angles and takes (especially on a hot day) and an ice chest to keep them cold and a production person full-time on ice cream duty. If a big lollipop will do just as well you can save money and free up an ice chest and a production person. That money and energy can then be used elsewhere.

Props can sometimes be re-used in another scene. Even big items such as cars can be used more than once. Think of how the prop was used in the original scene (close up or way in the background).

How much time will separate the scenes in the finished film? Can a prop or costume be altered to make it less recognizable?

Fit people (especially extras) to available clothing when that seems appropriate. If you have some hard-to-find clothes (such as special uniforms or period clothes) you might want to find people who fit the clothes you have. Or you might want to look for people who already have the clothes or props you need. Hire a real policeman, nurse, clown, surfer, or recent bride.

5) **Collect everything in advance** — and have the person whose decision counts (director, producer, art director) look it over. That way you can see if things are right and you'll have time to make changes if they aren't. Many props that are easy to find given enough time may be impossible on ten minutes notice. Advance planning saves wear and tear on people, as well as money.

6) **Always have extra things.** Always have a selection of extra props and clothing readily available on the set at all times. This will be helpful for last minute problems that need to be solved. You may need props (pictures, knickknacks, plants) for the composition of a shot or to hide things you don't want seen. A box of extra clothes (especially for a period film) can come in handy if you suddenly find yourself needing a couple more extras. We had a street scene once in which we had planned to park an old car to hide a parking meter. But the car didn't arrive on time and rather than wait we quickly dressed a production assistant and had him stand in front of the meter.

WHERE TO GET PROPS AND COSTUMES

Creativity can help you stretch meager budgets. You don't need to buy new things or rent them from film rental houses — both of which are usually expensive propositions.

1) **Thrift stores and flea markets** are the first obvious solutions, although they won't always have what you need. Time can really help here, since their stock changes constantly. A prop or wardrobe person familiar with local thrift stores can be invaluable. When selecting production people, pay attention to whether they enjoy scrounging and being creative — and whether they can do it at all. If not, you may have problems if you're on a tight budget. After the film you can have a garage sale and sell

props and costumes you don't want to keep (and recoup some of your costs). Don't forget you can dye and alter costumes.

2) Borrow from friends. Let people know what you need. For "Hard Traveling" (and other films requiring numerous difficult props) I made up a "treasure list" of things we needed, including props, costumes, cars, and locations. We received many calls (including three offers of old wooden wheelchairs, one item on our list!). We had a very low budget for "Hard Traveling" but we also had lots of pre-production time and many contacts in the community so we were able to borrow everything from clothes to furniture, old magazines, kitchen implements, and toys.

If you borrow things, make sure you catalogue them very carefully (set up a procedure with the prop person) and take care to return them in good condition.

3) Have actors bring their own props and costumes. You might even cast with that in mind. When I cast extras for a large Clint Eastwood feature that required 450 extras (many needing props), I specifically looked for people who already had dogs, surfboards, bicycles, skates, or whatever. Sometimes actors didn't have the needed items but were willing to take responsibility for finding them and coming prepared for their role. One woman came as a "bag lady" complete with a shopping cart loaded with junk and a bride came complete with her own wedding dress (used only once!). For contemporary films you may routinely use an actor's clothes but don't assume that won't work for period films as well. Ask actors if they have anything appropriate. If they think they do, look it over (always look it over because their idea of "appropriate" may differ greatly from yours).

Check all clothing out ahead of time. When we made "The Birth Control Movie" purple was the most popular color that season and when the kids showed up for wardrobe selection (wearing their choice outfit and bringing others) most had on some shade of purple. Ask people to bring a selection of clothing to the set (even if you've tentatively decided on their wardrobe) so that if the shirt you selected for one actor clashes with someone else's dress (perhaps selected on another day) or with the room decor, you can switch things around. Make sure the actors bring accessories to match the back-up clothes as well. If people bring their own clothes you'll have to pay extra attention to continuity to ensure that they wear the exact same clothes (and accessories) for matching scenes.

4) Borrow from stores — or offer to rent an item. We work in a small town where this is easier to do than in Los Angeles or New York, but try anyhow. Tell the store what you are doing and what you need. Bring literature about your film company and your project. Offer to leave a deposit. It never hurts to try — the worst they can do is say "no."

5) Merchandising. Companies will sometimes loan or donate an item in exchange for their brand name appearing in a film. We borrowed a hard-to-find original 1940s Wheaties box from the company. And you may be able to obtain more than just props this way; beverage company may provide free drinks for your cast and crew, or an auto dealer may loan you a car.

6) Other creative methods. What are the special needs of your film? For "Hard Traveling" we needed a lot of old cars — some looking new and some very dilapidated. We contacted old car clubs and garages that specialized in repairing old cars. We also drew up a flyer explaining what we were doing and what we needed and we left a flyer on the windshield anytime we saw an old car parked around town. I once saw a great car going down the road in the opposite direction so I turned around and chased it down back country roads until I caught up with it. The owner agreed to loan us the car, as well as an old truck he had at home.

Think about appropriate organizations or clubs that might help. You might be able to make a donation to the association if the members help you (which may be less expensive than paying each person individually).

7) Rental houses. There are also costume and (in some cities) prop rental houses. They're convenient (if you're near one) because of their wide selection. Although they're usually expensive, don't rule them out for low-budget films because for some items they may be your best bet. There are specialty printers (such as Earl Hays Press, 10707 Sherman Way, Sun Valley, Ca 91352) where you can purchase things like old fashioned cigarette wrappers, Cracker Jack boxes, and police car decals. You can also have most anything printed to order.

LOGISTICS

There are many logistical details you'll need to arrange before the shoot — lodging, food, transportation, equipment, supplies, paperwork, money, and publicity. There are many ways to arrange all these details — but the main thing to remember is that creativity can save you money. Plan your logistics well in advance — as the shoot nears you'll have plenty of other things to worry about.

LODGING

You can rent hotel rooms (plain or fancy) or ask cast and crew to camp in sleeping bags on your floor — or anything in between, such as renting or borrowing apartments for everyone.

Pay attention not only to out front costs but also to hidden ones. A hotel near the set may be cheaper in the long run than a less expensive but more distant hotel or scattered apartments. Think about transportation (how people will get to the set and around town when not working), eating (meals when not on the set), and communication (phones). What quality of housing do you want to provide — and what do the cast and crew expect? A disgruntled cast and crew won't make for a happy film shoot. An actor who didn't sleep well or who has a sore back from sleeping on a bumpy couch won't give you his best performance. What amenities do you need or want to provide (television, phones, refrigerators, kitchens, swimming pool)? Do you need food (markets or restaurants) nearby? Do you need easy access to public transportation (think about days off as well as shooting days)?

See what deals you can make with hotels if you'll be housing a number of people over a period of time. Ask around. And don't forget to mention that it's a film crew and cast (but specify if it's a low-budget film so they don't think that you're Hollywood millionaires).

FOOD

Will you have a professional caterer do everything or will you have a production assistant pick up pre-ordered lunches from a local deli, pizza parlor, Chinese restaurant, fast-food place, or caterer? You might also make an arrangement with a good cook who doesn't normally do catering to provide the food you need. If you're filming near a restaurant you might be able to pre-arrange a special lunch (for a set price). Vary your food, especially on a long shoot. You can be creative here and save money. Buy drinks, condiments, fruit, plates and utensils from a supermarket.

Do you need tables and chairs and everything set up or can you make do with a couple of card tables to set the food on and let everyone find their own place to sit? Does anyone have any special dietary needs or restrictions? Plan for that ahead of time.

How many people will you need to feed? Add up your cast and crew (and don't forget mothers or fathers of kids, friends, or investors who may drop by at lunch time — or be prepared to turn them away). You may want to have a clearly stated policy about who will be fed. If we have an open set we make clear that visitors are welcome but should bring their own lunch. Remember that cast and crew work hard and will be hungry — and thirsty. Good varied food helps morale. Good food doesn't have to be expensive — but don't skimp on it.

Pay attention to the health of your cast and crew. Traditional Hollywood fare often includes a lot of food we now know isn't very healthy. Caffeine and sugar are especially common. I'm not advocating employing a full-time nutritionist, but do pay attention to providing healthy food — for meals, snacks, and drinks.

TRANSPORTATION

This includes getting people to the town in which you're filming as well as to the set every day. Will people have their own cars, rented cars, or have to be picked up by a production assistant? When arranging for airline tickets, remember that you can often save money by making reservations in advance.

EQUIPMENT AND SUPPLIES

You have to plan for their purchase (or rental), delivery (and return), transportation during the shoot, and secure storage. This applies both to equipment used every day (such as cameras, lights, props, and costumes) and to special equipment used only on occasion (such as car rigging, a crane, or a generator). Also plan for supplies such as film, tape, and light bulbs. How will the exposed film get to the lab? In some locations this is simple, but for others it may require a lot of planning and coordination. Be creative. A courier (perhaps a local student) might be cheaper than a professional delivery service. It may be less expensive to buy a used truck or van at the beginning of a long shoot and re-sell it afterwards than to rent one.

Security is obvious for expensive camera and lighting equipment but it's also important for props and wardrobe. You don't want to lose a key prop or article of clothing in the middle of the shoot. Depending on where you park your grip truck during the day, you may need to have someone guard it, especially if the doors will need to remain open.

Before the shoot, make sure all vehicles (including yours) are in good working order. The last thing you need to deal with in the middle of a shoot is a broken car.

PAPERWORK

What paperwork will you need — for yourself, cast, crew, unions, the IRS, and any other bureaucracies (see p. 73)? I hate paperwork and try to make do with the bare minimum. Make sure that cast and crew get the information they need, especially a phone number to contact you at all times in case of emergency (flat tire, sore throat, etc.) — but try to do it simply and efficiently. A portable cellular phone might be handy for the shoot.

As much as you try to minimize it, you'll still have paperwork. When do you need to do it? If you're short on crew, do as much as possible before or after the shoot (if necessary, make special arrangements with unions, etc.). Make or obtain the forms you need in plenty of time. Figure out who will do what paperwork and make sure that all your systems are set up before the shoot. Paperwork is a silly thing to spend precious time on during a shoot.

MONEY

Handling money will, of course, be more complex for a longer film and you'll have to do more of this during the actual shoot rather than before or after it. But in either case you'll need to figure out payment schedules, perhaps obtain and fill out credit applications, set up a book-keeping system, a payroll system, and a petty cash system (see p. 70). Depending on the size of your payroll, you may be required by the IRS (see their circular E) to deposit taxes during the shoot.

Who will do all this? Will you hire an outside book-keeper or payroll service or hire someone specifically to do that (full or part-time or in conjunction with other tasks)?

Who will handle petty cash on the set? Make sure you have a good system to keep track of all money spent, either on receipt slips, on a master list, or on the petty cash envelope itself. Have people sign for any money they receive and save all receipts. On a small film this is fairly easy to keep track of but for a feature film it may be more difficult. Set up a system (and a person) to approve all expenditures over a certain amount. This will help control costs. Careful planning and organization before the shoot can save you a lot of time trying to sort things out afterwards.

Who will go to the bank when necessary? Who is authorized to sign checks? Plan this before the shoot so you don't get stuck sending a key person to the bank in the middle of an important scene. Who will hand out (or mail) paychecks?

Make sure your book-keeping is set up in such a way that you'll be able to keep track of expenses as the shoot progresses — and to see how they compare with your original budget (see p. 207).

PUBLICITY AND PUBLIC RELATIONS

For some films much of this section may not be important (for example, for an educational film where you already have a distribution deal). But for many films, especially features, it can be critical. Yet, since publicity isn't really "filmmaking," it's often overlooked or forgotten. Don't ignore it — selling you film is, unfortunately, part of filmmaking. You should begin to think about publicity when you make up your master plan.

What kind of publicity do you want or need? Aimed at whom? For what purpose? All this will affect when you want the

186

publicity and what type you want. Are you aiming your publicity at distributors or buyers (to sell your film), or to the film community (to enhance your reputation and perhaps to obtain future work), or to the general public (to build interest in your project), or to a specific community (to help raise funds or obtain other resources to help in the making of your film)? Although most publicity will usually be done after the film is completed, you need to think about it during the shoot and begin to collect the material you'll need later (especially publicity stills and photos or interviews with cast or crew at work).

Think also about publicity you don't want. For "Hard Traveling" we wanted to avoid a lot of local publicity right before or during the shoot — to minimize interference and distractions on the set. But the local press had helped us a lot during the early stages of our project and we felt an obligation to be as accessible as possible. Although some press people did come to watch us film, I asked them not to publicize our shooting locations until we were finished filming there and to call us in the evening with questions rather than interrupting work on the set. They were very cooperative — and we received more good publicity.

Will you have friends coming by — or investors, or friends of the cast and crew? Will you have an open or closed set (or some days of each)? What restrictions do you want for visitors? I always feel that the film takes top priority — but I also like to make as much room as possible for people to watch as long as it doesn't interfere with our work. Take the needs of the cast and crew and location owners into account. I sometimes try to use people I know want to watch as extras, if that is appropriate, or ask them to help in other ways. I also explain clearly that cast and crew have work to do and they shouldn't be interrupted.

Stills. During the shoot you'll need to concentrate on getting some good stills for future publicity. Stills will be important in the distribution of almost any film. How many and what kind of stills will you or the distributor need? Black and white and/or color (slides are usually better than prints) or both?

The most useful shots for publicity purposes are usually representative shots from the film featuring the principal actors. These shots should be fairly close-up, with no extraneous equipment or crew people visible. Think of what shots you want to have be representative of your film. What aspects of the film do you want to stress? What parts do you not want to give away?

How will you obtain those stills? Getting the publicity shots may mean stopping the action before or after takes to let the photographer get his or her shots, although a good photographer should be able to get most shots during rehearsals right before a take. But if you must interrupt the filming, do so. Shutter clicks can easily ruin a sound take so you don't want to shoot stills during filming. If you need to pose specific shots, do so. Make sure you get all the stills you need, since you can't get them after you've left the location and the cast has gone home. Production stills of cast and crew at work are easier to obtain since they generally don't involve interrupting the process.

SETTING THE SCENE FOR THE SHOOT

The last thing you want to do before filming is to set the scene for the shoot. There are several parts to this: a tour of locations, a meeting with the crew, and perhaps a meeting with the cast.

A tour of at least the principal locations should include the main crew people. The farther ahead of the shoot this is done, the more time they all have to prepare for any special needs, to discover potential problems, to think about solutions, and to plan how they'll do their job during the shoot. This may be unnecessary for a short, simple film but very useful (even essential) for a more complex one. This is also the time for the director to go over the basic scenario at each location and for the DP and gaffer to decide for sure what equipment they'll need. It's also a time to specify any restrictions so that crew can keep them in mind.

You might also want to visit the main locations with the principal cast to let them see the physical layout and get a sense of the mood of the location if that seems important for the film.

A crew meeting with everyone in attendance if possible, perhaps on the eve of the shoot or even the first morning, is a time to go over all the basic ground rules. What do you expect from the crew? What are the lines of communication and command? Be clear at this time about how much input you or the director want from the crew — and how you'd like them to give it.

There are traditional ways of working and non-traditional ways — and everyone has his or her own style. It may help to explain your style clearly in the beginning, especially if you are using less traditional systems (which I advocate, and which are almost necessary on a low-budget shoot). That first meeting is a good time to begin the communication process that will be of vital importance on the shoot. Leave time for questions or suggestions. This meeting is also a time to let the crew know any rules or policies you may have that they should know about.

A cast meeting may depend on what kind of cast you'll have (how many and whether they all work at the same time). If such a meeting is appropriate for your film, it can be a time to talk things out, raise questions, hear suggestions — and simply begin the communication process and get to know each other.

Now you're ready to begin the shoot!

PRODUCTION

THE SHOOT

The shoot itself can be an exhilarating experience when everything runs smoothly — and if you like the results when you see the dailies. But it can also be excruciating when things don't work right.

Good planning certainly helps, but with so many people and processes involved, crises seem to be part of the nature of filmmaking and you can always expect to have some problems. Good planning will help minimize crises and will prepare you to handle them more smoothly when they inevitably do occur.

SHORT SHOOTS — LONG SHOOTS

There are really two very different kinds of shoots — short shoots and long ones. With a long shoot (say over about one or two weeks) you just can't have everything completely worked out ahead of time. It's much easier to handle a short shoot single-handed and to take care of planning and paperwork before or after filming. On a long shoot some of this will have to be done during the shoot — but working six-day weeks and/or long hours gives you almost no time to catch up or do advance work as you go. All this means you'll need to delegate more work to others.

Personnel problems, which might be a minor annoyance on a short shoot (I can put up with most anything for a few days) can become more serious and threatening on a long one. Problems have more time to develop, everyone is likely to be under greater pressure, and it's simply harder to just tough it out.

Finally, on a long shoot you are more likely to run out of clean socks and underwear, or cat food. And you have to think about paying your phone bill, rent, car payments, or whatever. In other words, your life has to continue even though you have almost no free time. If you're away from home on location, this becomes even more complicated.

HINTS FOR A SUCCESSFUL SHOOT

The following are some general things to keep in mind during the shoot.

1) Keep your eyes on the prize — keep track of your vision, your goals, and your priorities. Are you getting what you want from actors, camera, sound, the director — and everyone else?

2) Watch for problems. Keep your eyes and ears open for existing or potential problems. The better communication system you have established and the better rapport with cast and crew, the easier this will be.

3) Be clear on the division of labor within the crew. Who makes decisions and who gives what orders? Make sure everyone understands this.

4) Anticipate and think. This is very important for filmmaking. You want to catch problems *before* they develop. Teach others to anticipate as well.

5) Re-evaluate constantly and remain flexible. Adjust to what is happening and to your needs.

6) Look for weak spots in the crew and fill them. Pay attention to everyone's needs (especially the director who usually carries the heaviest load) and be prepared to shore up weak spots.

7) Be prepared to deal with major problems — whether it's that you're not getting the footage you want, you're going over time and budget, or you have serious personnel problems. Deal with them quickly when they arise — ignoring them won't make them go away.

8) Begin post-production liaison if you'll be editing during the shoot.

9) Get enough sleep and eat well. Keep your head clear — it's important that you function well.

Now, on to specifics.

CAST AND CREW

There are a number of things you'll need to do for the cast and crew during the shoot: 1) notify both cast and crew of the current schedule, 2) boss the crew and push to get the work done on time, 3) keep track of the needs of the crew and cast and make sure they are met, 4) keep track of the whereabouts of cast (and extras) during filming, 5) get the information you need from the crew, and 6) balance the needs of the cast, crew, and director within the budgetary limits of the film.

SCHEDULE

By now you should have decided what kind of written schedules you'll have — one for the entire film, or weekly or daily call sheets. Who will make these up (who will make the decisions they reflect and who will actually type and xerox the schedules)? How much additional notification will you do (such as calling to remind the cast the day before) and who will do it? How will you inform people of changes? Although I usually stick to my pre-announced call times, I like to give myself as much flexibility as possible so I make the final announcement about the next day's schedule at the end of the day. This lets me adjust for things like weather conditions and how the schedule is going.

Cast should also be kept informed. Remind actors the night before they work, and if you want them to bring any special clothes or props, remind them of that as well. Who will do this? Extras also need to be scheduled and reminded. Who will do this? Make sure cast and extras always have a phone number to contact you in case of questions, problems, or emergencies.

BOSSING THE CREW

Hopefully you've planned a schedule that's realistic. Now you have to stick to it. It seems like there's never enough time for what you want to do, but someone has to see to it that the filming is completed within the allotted time (or else find extra money if you go over schedule — which is usually harder). It's very important to decide who will keep them on schedule. To some extent this will depend on the size of the crew. Will you have an assistant director (AD) or will the producer or production manager or maybe even the director or DP do this?

The best tool you have to boss the crew is information. If the crew doesn't know what's up next, they can't be preparing for it. But if they know what's coming up, assuming you have more than a skeletal crew, they can be preparing for future shots. Crews work differently — some just want to know what's up next while others want to know the shots for the whole day (assuming the director has planned them out in advance). A xeroxed "shot list" might be useful for department heads. It's sometimes also useful to warn the crew if a certain day will be particularly difficult, or if it will be a light day where they can catch their breath a little (or work fast and go home early — I like to give them that option).

If the crew knows what has to be accomplished during the day, then they can pace themselves to make sure it gets done. Some crews think ahead and pace themselves better than others — and you might want to think about this at the hiring stage. If they do this well, great. If not, someone needs to do it. And, in any case, you need to watch over them to make sure they're doing it. Can the crew be setting up for the next shot in advance? Do they need to be reminded to do this? Although it's tempting to sit around and watch the filming, perhaps some of the crew can prepare for something later in the day, such as building scaffolding or set dressing or pre-rigging lights for another area.

Actors will also need to be kept informed. They, and crew people working with them such as wardrobe and make-up, will need to know how much time they have before they're needed. How long will the lighting take? When will they rehearse? When will the actual filming begin? Find out what the actors need to know. During long breaks they may want to take off their costumes and make-up. For difficult emotional scenes they may want a certain amount of time to prepare themselves. It's really important that the cast members have a quiet space in which they can relax.

To help things run smoothly, you'll need to keep track of how the crew division of labor is working. Is the work fairly evenly divided? Are there weak spots? Are some people standing around a lot? Do you need to re-assign people to get critical work done on time or simply to balance the workload better? If you have "swing" crew people whose tasks vary depending on daily needs, you have to make sure they're being used efficiently and know what they should be doing at all times. One day, for example, a production assistant may help with props, the next day with traffic control, and yet another with coordinating extras. The advantage of having people who can switch and do various jobs is that you can make do with fewer people, but you also have to make sure they know what they should be doing at any given time.

Keep track of any special equipment that will be used and make sure it's tested beforehand if necessary. We once planned a scene around a fog machine only to discover too late that no one could get it to work properly. This film's budget was too low to allow us to re-schedule so we had to make do without the fog. Advance testing could have avoided that.

MEET CAST AND CREW NEEDS

Cast and crew work hard and it's important to see that their needs are met, although I don't believe in the star system where you must cater to someone's every whim. You'll have to decide for yourself how much you'll meet individual needs (and desires), but some are very legitimate. Some people are aggressive about getting their needs met and others aren't, even though their needs may be just as real. The camera person who is working so hard that he or she doesn't have time to get a drink might really appreciate being brought one. The actor with a special diet might go hungry if not asked about his particular needs. Good meals, served on time, are important. A little kindness and consideration can make a shoot much more pleasant. On the other hand, pampering some people more than others who are working equally hard may cause resentment. Be aware of everyone's needs.

Watch out for the health and safety of the cast and crew. All the electrical equipment and rigging around a shoot are potential hazards. See that things are set up as safely as possible — and have someone in charge of maintaining safety.

Be aware of general health hazards such as sunburn or sunstroke if you're working in the hot sun (make sure you have sun lotion and sufficient drinks available) as well as specific problems such as allergies. We shot one scene for "Peter and the Wolf" in a lovely meadow only to discover later (when his face puffed up and he began sneezing) that the boy playing Peter had hay fever.

KEEP TRACK OF CAST

Make sure you know where cast and extras are when they're not on camera. If people leave the immediate vicinity, make sure someone knows where to find them. Tell them not to leave without notifying a specific person. Extras sometimes get bored and wander off, sometimes just when you need them.

GET INFORMATION YOU NEED

Get the information you need from the crew. For example, you need to know if you have to order more film or other supplies (and in time to obtain more before you run out). Know how much film you're using each day. Are you using more or less than expected? What is the problem? Are you doing too many takes, too many angles, or was the budget unrealistic to begin with? How much petty cash money are you and other people spending during the shoot? Are you on budget? If you're over budget, do you need to cut back? Can you cut back? Are all the expenses necessary?

Some of this information will show up on production reports. Although I think filling out the forms is a waste of time — you do need to have all the information.

Are any crew members having problems in their departments that you should know about? Are all the departments staying within their budgets? Are there any quality problems? Is the sound person getting the wild sound you need? Do you or the editor foresee any problems with the footage at the editing stage? Are you getting adequate coverage? Are you getting more coverage than you need (and can you cut back)? Are you on schedule? If you're not on schedule, what is causing the delays?

BALANCE

During the shoot you'll be most aware of the conflicting needs and wants of the various people, although that will have begun in the very early stages. The director wants time to plan action and camera moves, the actors need time to rehearse, the DP and gaffer need time to light, the camera operator and grip need to rehearse dolly moves, the assistant camera person may need to get focus marks, the set dressers need to dress the set but the lighting people want everyone out of the way so they can adjust the lights. The director wants the actors (and the set) for rehearsal but the lighting people need the actors to fine-tune their lighting and the make-up person also needs the actors. Crazy? Right! And someone has to juggle all this smoothly and efficiently — and prevent total chaos.

On top of this, people on the set (and during post-production) have different priorities. Individual crafts people may be more concerned about their specialty than the film as a whole. An actor may want to create a memorable character, a DP may want unique camera angles, a composer may want a distinctive score, an art director may want an imaginative look for the film, an editor may want a daring juxtaposition of shots. Each may hope to be singled out for his or her contribution by film reviewers. Or they too may be frustrated artists who have wanted for years to try some of their ideas. But, unfortunately, their needs may not fit for your particular film. And someone has to keep the overall needs of the film in mind.

It's usually the producer who has to balance all these needs and keep priorities straight in general — while it usually falls to the assistant director or production manager to do most of the actual juggling of details on the set. But again, who does it isn't as important as that it get done.

This juggling is key, both for an efficient shoot and for a happy crew. Because each person will be most concerned with their needs, and sometimes oblivious to the needs of others, it might help to make everyone aware of each other's needs, and the conflicts. They may then be more understanding than if you just juggle silently and announce your decisions.

LOCATIONS

During the shoot, someone will need to: 1) double-check all the location arrangements, 2) dress the set, 3) arrange traffic and/or crowd control if necessary, 4) maintain good relations with owners, tenants, and neighbors, 5) watch over the crew to prevent or minimize damage to locations, and 6) re-arrange the location so you leave it as you found it.

LOCATION ARRANGEMENTS

Most of the arrangements will be made before the shoot but someone has to double-check and make sure all subsidiary arrangements are made. Who will let you in (and what is their phone number)? Who will remind them the night before? Do you need to make any special arrangements for parking or to clear traffic? Do you need any permits, "No Parking" signs, or barricades? Have you checked central air conditioning, automatic fire sprinklers, lawn sprinkler schedules, lawn mowing schedules, street repairs, noisy neighborhood dogs, tree trimmers... anything that might interfere with your shoot?

Have you made all the necessary arrangements for your needs? Do you have space to set up (and store) equipment, rooms for dressing, resting, hair and make-up (with adequate light)? Will you be eating or preparing food at the location? Do you need any special equipment or services? Do you have a phone number to call if you have any problems? How about a back-up phone number? Where will everyone park?

SET DRESSING

The set dresser (or prop person or production assistant) will need to arrange the set, being very careful to keep track of exactly how everything was when you arrived so that it can all be put back, exactly as it was, when you leave. The traditional method is to use a Polaroid camera, but that can be expensive. Diagrams and labeling often work just as well. If a lot of people are moving things around (including non-prop people such as grips) you may lose track of what's been moved. Be very careful — you want to maintain good relations with the owner or manager.

TRAFFIC CONTROL

Will you need traffic, crowd, or noise control? For traffic control, do you need to make any formal arrangement to close a street and/or hire police or can you just stop cars informally as you require? Will you need special equipment for this (for example, walkie-talkies, traffic cones, or barricades)? How many people will you need for traffic control? Make sure you have enough people — and that the people you select can do the job. Traffic control often requires assertiveness and public relations skills in order to obtain cooperation and not antagonize people.

If you're trying to control on-lookers, be aware that they are probably simply curious. You're likely to get more cooperation if you allow them to see as much as possible. Show them where to stand to be out of your way. Explain the need for total quiet (no talking, foot shuffling, coughing, or clicking cameras) during filming. If you have time for more public relations, explain what is happening and what the various crew members are doing. You may make friends for the future as well as ensuring the cooperation you need.

Are there specific appliance noises you need to control, such as a refrigerator, air conditioner, or phones? Do they need to be turned back on whenever possible? If so, assign one person to that task. And double-check when you leave to make sure the appliance has been turned back on again (you might want to make a note to yourself in your "daily book").

PACIFY OWNERS

Be especially considerate of the owner or manager of the location if they're around. People who are not used to film crews are sometimes totally overwhelmed by the disruption and chaos, even if forewarned. If the owner or neighbors seem alarmed — reassure them. Have someone who will watch for this. Trouble-shooting is the art of noticing and taking care of problems *before* they happen.

While shooting one film in a fancy old Victorian house, I noticed the owners getting edgy as we turned their house upside down. They hovered as we filmed, watching the crew carefully. When the make-up person had finished her tasks, I asked if she could pamper the owners' teenage daughter. Soon after, the overjoyed daughter was getting her hair styled and the owners were thrilled and had turned their attention to their daughter.

DAMAGE CONTROL

Speaking of maintaining good relations, film crews can be notoriously insensitive and damage locations. Remember that you are a guest in someone else's home or place of business and act accordingly.   Even if you hope to work with careful and considerate crews, always keep an eye out for potential problems — and let the crew know your expectations ahead of time. Watch out for gaffers tape that may peel paint off walls, nails sunk into walls or woodwork, props that may be knocked over, and even simply trash and cigarette butts. If members of your crew smoke, provide smoking areas and ash trays. If the owners have requested that you not smoke or bring food or drinks into certain areas, enforce that with the crew and cast. If there are especially expensive or sensitive items, watch those carefully. You might want to keep them out of harm's way until you are completely ready for a take. Who will do all this — the set dresser, prop person, a production assistant, production manager, or producer? It doesn't matter who does it, as long as the job is done.

RE-ARRANGE

After you're finished, make sure that everything is put back exactly as it was when you arrived. Have someone responsible for checking this carefully — and then re-checking with the owner or manager the next day. Leave the place neat and clean and take your trash with you (unless you've made arrangements to leave it).

LOGISTICS DURING THE SHOOT

During the shoot you have to pay attention to all the little things mentioned in the earlier section on logistics.

LODGING

Make sure cast and crew are satisfied and have what they need.

FOOD

Make sure the food service works well — that the food is satisfactory and comes on time. It's tricky to plan so that lunch is available when the director decides (or can be persuaded) to break — but not so early that it's gotten cold. If you'll be serving both hot and cold lunches, there may be a logic about what days to have which. Plan cold lunches on days the schedule is harder to predict or where eating facilities aren't as comfortable. You might also want to plan cheaper and quicker lunches on days when you have a lot of extras.

TRANSPORTATION

Make sure that all people and equipment get to the set on time. Do you have to arrange for any special equipment that will arrive (or have to be returned) part way through the shoot? Film and sound stock will have to be sent to the lab and transfer studio, and viewing of dailies will have to be scheduled.

SUPPLIES

Make sure you have adequate supplies before you begin filming and set up a system so that you know when you're running low on any supplies, before you run out completely. Obtaining supplies on short notice can be costly and time-consuming.

PROPS AND WARDROBE

If props and wardrobe are well organized before the shoot, you should have little to worry about. For a large shoot you'll have to be more efficient — so that you always have the props and costumes you need with you and so that nothing is lost. Keep clear records of what is borrowed or rented from whom and for which scene each prop and costume is intended (little stickers or tags can indicate this but keep duplicate records in case the sticker comes off). Keep props and costumes in a safe place and guard against damage. Fragile or precious items should be treated with special care. Treat borrowed items as if they were your own — and make sure your crew does the same.

Wardrobe that belongs to cast members can present a special problem if something is to be worn for more than one day. Actors need to remember to bring all the same things again for the second day (and all days that match, which may not be consecutive days). You may want to have the wardrobe person take charge of their clothes, or simply remind the actors. If you don't have a wardrobe person on the set, you might want to make sure you at least have a sewing kit and safety pins.

MAKE-UP

Make sure the make-up person knows in what order and when you'll need each actor. And make sure that he or she has adequate space (and light) to work. Who will be responsible for make-up continuity on the set? When actors have to look the same on different days, plan that with them ahead of time. Pay special attention to hair, which may look different depending on how recently it was washed. Take Polaroid photos if necessary. If you don't have a make-up person, you should at least have a comb, face powder, and tissues on the set at all times. A production assistant can be in charge of this.

MONEY

Your book-keeping system, payment schedules, and petty cash system should all have been worked out before the shoot. During the shoot you just have to make sure it all works as planned. Make sure to have cash available when you need it.

Keep track of your budget as you go. How complicated this will be will depend on the size and complexity of your shoot. I always fill in the "actual" column on the budget as the shoot progresses. If the shoot is well-planned financially, then all you'll have to do is record changes from your detailed budget. In addition to entering exact figures, I also make notes about how much over or under budget I am on each item. I simply write "+$200" or "-$500" (circled so it stands out) in the margin. I can then go over the budget very quickly and see where I stand. If I have a lot of minuses, then I know I can afford to go over on a few things, or have a more elaborate cast party (or come in under budget!). If I seem to be going over budget, I can immediately look for places to cut. Since you'll know some (perhaps a lot) of your costs before the shoot, pay special attention to those that are uncertain. Keep close tabs on miscellaneous expenditures during the shoot (including petty cash) — they can add up fast. Requiring authorization for expenditures over a certain amount will help.

For short shoots (up to one or two weeks), I usually pay all bills at the end of the shoot and have the production manager handle petty cash. For "Hard Traveling" I did all the book-keeping (late at night) and had a production assistant who handled payroll details (I gave him basic figures and signed checks, he figured out deductions, wrote the checks, and handed them out). Neither of us spent much time at this. The production manager handled petty cash, including paying extras. She, in turn, gave money to both the prop department and the production assistant in charge of food. At the end of the shoot I collected all the receipts and went over them. This system worked pretty well and avoided the need for a payroll service (though it depended on a competent production manager and production assistant).

PUBLICITY

Don't forget stills!

SCRIPT AND EDITING NOTES

One of the key roles on the shoot is that of script supervisor. This job can include a variety of functions — primarily to aid the director, the actors, and the editor.

FOR THE DIRECTOR AND ACTORS

1) Accuracy. Dialogue must be spoken properly. The director should advise the script person as to what is acceptable and what procedure to follow for inaccuracies. For technical films, exact wording might be more critical; while for dramatic films there might be a lot of leeway. Missed lines and inaccuracies should be brought to the attention of the director (or the actor directly, depending on the director's preference). Ask ahead of time how the director wants this done.

2) Coverage. Make sure that all scenes and all lines are shot and recorded, including all angles the director had planned. You'd be amazed at how easy it is for a line to fall between the cracks, especially where a line from one scene is heard over another.

3) Screen direction. Screen direction means that if, for example, an actor is walking right to left across the screen (or looking to the left) in one shot, he should continue walking or looking in that direction in the next shot (unless we see him change). The script supervisor should double-check the director on this if necessary. Screen direction should not only match within a scene, but also with scenes before and after (which may be filmed weeks apart). Good script notes (and an annotated script) will help keep this straight.

4) Prompt actors. Actors need to be prompted if they forget their lines. Arrange beforehand with the director and actors how they prefer to do this.

5) Time shots. A script person may have a stop-watch to be able to time scenes. Sometimes timing is essential; for example, if a line is to go over other action, or for a commercial where every second counts. At other times, all that's important is to know if the film is generally going to come out the length the director assumed it would. It's important to know whether actors are talking much faster or slower than expected (and whether your 20-minute film will therefore turn out to be 15 or 30 minutes). Scenes with no dialog take up little or no space in the script but may take up a lot of time on film. It may be important to know how much time.

6) Continuity. Continuity means consistency — both within a scene and between scenes — of action, lines, props, wardrobe, hair, make-up, and mood.

A) Continuity within a scene. Make sure that if there's a glass of wine, it's filled to the same level for each take and each different angle. Same with other props such as cigarettes. Props need to be in the same place. Hair and wardrobe need to be the same. Words and actions need to match. If an actor enters a room, takes off his hat, says "Hello" and sits down in a wide shot, he has to do all those things in the same order and in the same places and the same way in any close-ups or shots from different angles. Otherwise he may say "Hello" in the wide shot and repeat it again in a close-up (after he sits) — and the editor will go crazy. Someone has to remember exactly what the actor did during each part of the scene. And the same for every actor in the scene. Seasoned film actors know to pay attention to this but actors who are new to film usually don't. Moods, as well as actions, need to match.

B) Continuity between scenes. Suppose that before the actor entered the above room, he approached the outside of the house, briefcase in hand. Suppose that scene was filmed three weeks earlier. Someone has to remember in which hand he had his briefcase. He must be wearing exactly the same clothes, with his hat at the same angle. And his mood must match. Because scenes that will follow each other in the finished film may be shot days or weeks apart, it's useful to take Polaroid photos to record details, or to review the key scenes on video if it's available. Someone should remember (or have reviewed) the previous scene so they have the information ready and no time is wasted on the set looking it up.

FOR THE EDITOR

1) Coverage. The editor needs to have basic information on what each shot is and what lines and action it includes. This can be indicated both in the editing notes and on a copy of the script. It's important to mark up a script during filming so that the editor knows what coverage he or she has on any given line or any section of the script. Note what lines are covered in the master shot, close-ups, reverses, etc..

2) Evaluation. The script person should note whether each take was complete or partial, good or bad (and why), and also note any irregularities. These can include lines said incorrectly, breaches of continuity (wine glasses not filled to the proper level), technical problems (fuzzy focus, extraneous noises, bumpy dolly move, boom or boom shadow in the shot), as well as any comments from the director on acting (quality of acting, delivery of lines, pace, mood, or expression). The script person should check with the director, camera person, and sound people after each take to see if they had any problems (this can be as simple as making eye contact with each one). Make sure that the director knows if there were any — and make sure there is at least one good take. Circle good takes.

Not all negative comments will mean that the take isn't useable, but it will alert the editor to potential problems. The director's comments might include things like, "beginning too slow" (which won't matter if you use another angle for the beginning), "acting forced," "laugh too loud" (it could be lowered in the mix, unless it overlaps other dialogue), "emphasis on wrong word" (perhaps you could substitute words with the correct emphasis from another take or recorded wild), "acting great," "Sam awkward" (which might not matter if another shot will be used for Sam's coverage). Possible problems should be noted as well as definite ones. For example, the camera operator might *think* the boom was seen in the frame. When you watch the dailies you can look closely at that take (alerted by the script notes) and check to see if the boom is indeed visible — or if any of the other problems really exist. You can then adjust the editing notes accordingly.

SCRIPT NOTES

Film: __Summer Adventure__   Script: __Maria Perez__   Date: __8/17__

scene	take	roll	roll	lens	comments
26	1	1	1		master framing bad (Bill sits on 'day')
	2x				cut
	③				false start, then again
	4				sound bad
	⑤				good
26A	1				c.u. David missed line
	2				said 'Ron' not 'Don'
	③				good. end slate
26B	1				c.u. Bill & Carl (Bill sits late)
	2				boom in?
	③				end bad, beginning good. nice laugh
	4	2			focus? expression great!
	⑤				beginning slow, end o.k. . check lines
	⑥				ok
26C	1				reverse on Sally too sad?
	2x				dog bark. cut
	③		2		2|| [2 starts]
	4				slower pan. acting?
	⑤				" " good
26D	1		MOS		c.u. Sally's hands
			→		+ wild lines & ambience

The script person should note if part of a take is good, even if another part isn't. If that take will be inter-cut with other angles, the good part might be usable. The more the script person understands how the film will be edited, the better he or she will know whether a particular take has to be used in its entirety or if parts can be used alone. For example, on a master shot that will be inter-cut with close-ups in the finished film, the bad section might be covered in close-up anyway. If that section of the master shot *is* needed, the director might prefer to re-shoot only that particular section and not the whole thing.

3) Variations. Sometimes the director will shoot alternatives in order to be able to make decisions at the editing stage. These should be noted for the editor.

The editing process may begin with the editor viewing the dailies with the director (and perhaps the producer). The director may select preferred takes at that time. Or the editor may begin to work with no more guidance than what is contained in the script notes. How this process will work for your film may affect the amount of detail needed in script notes. But even if the director selects the preferred takes, one of them may not work for some reason and the editor will need to select another. The script notes can be a guide in this selection. Script notes can be especially useful when the editor is working with a small editing screen and/or scratchy sound equipment and therefore might miss certain details unless alerted to them.

Other people (in addition to the script supervisor) may also be taking notes. The assistant camera person may take camera notes (usually as a guide for the lab on which takes to print) and the sound person may take sound notes (as a guide for what sound takes to transfer). These people should all communicate so their notes are consistent. If you're printing all takes, the camera and sound notes may be unnecessary (and a waste of time).

Because the script supervisor's job involves so much, I always try to simplify it as much as possible. Find out exactly how the director and editor plan to work on each film you do, and what information they'll need. Don't do anything unnecessary. If a scene won't have to match with any other scene, don't pay attention to beginning and end continuity. If time is unimportant, forget the stop-watch. If there will be a wardrobe person on the set at all times, you can give him or her the task of wardrobe continuity (although it never hurts to have a second person watching as well). Make sure, however, that the script person is getting all the necessary information.

The director, editor, and script supervisor should decide ahead of time how they will work together. For example, the director may trust the script supervisor enough to allow him or her to interrupt when something is wrong (and not waste film) or may prefer to be told only after the take is finished, or to be gently poked in the ribs mid-take. Again, there is no "right" way — figure out what works for your shoot and your crew.

I always prefer to stop a bad take as soon as possible to avoid wasting time or film. I try to hire crew people whose judgment I trust and rely on them. For example, if I hear a plane during a take, I'll look at the sound person and if he or she signals that it ruined the sound, I'll interrupt the take (by pre-arrangement with the director) — unless I know the take can be used without the sound. For this system to work, there has to be a high level of trust between director, producer, and other crew members.

DAILIES

The technical and editing processes of post-production will begin as soon as the first footage is shot. If you're shooting in film, the first step is to send the exposed film to the lab to be processed. The sound will be sent to a sound studio to be transferred to 16mm or 35mm magnetic stock. This is traditionally done daily (hence the name) and if you are near your lab there's no reason not to do it that frequently. You can then see the results quickly and make sure you're getting what you want. You can also discover if there are any problems, hopefully while it's still relatively easy to re-shoot. If you won't be able to view dailies promptly, let the lab and sound transfer studio know this and ask for their assistance. Ask them to watch your film especially carefully and to call you immediately if they spot problems. Work with a lab where you can get this kind of personalized service.

Talk with the lab ahead of time and let them know your plans for delivering the film and also what you'll want them to do. Do you want them to print everything (fairly standard with 16mm) or only selected takes (common with 35mm because it costs so much to print)? Do you want a "one-light" print (where they print the whole roll the same) or a "corrected" print (where the light is balanced for each individual scene)?

If you're shooting in video, you can view dailies whenever you want. You can even review a questionable take on the set immediately after shooting it. To do that after every take, however, will slow the process down. Make sure your director doesn't depend on this review during filming, although it might be useful to have some trusted person watching the video monitor.

HOW TO USE DAILIES

The reason to view dailies is obviously to see what you have filmed. Is the quality of the picture all right? Take into account that you'll probably be looking at a "one-light" print and you should know what the lab can and can't correct later. If in doubt, ask the lab about particular scenes. Are the framing, camera moves, acting, sound, etc. what you want? Do you have at least one good take for each shot — one in which both picture and sound are good? Is there anything that you need to re-shoot? Do you have sufficient coverage?

When viewing dailies, I use the script notes as a guide and I annotate them. Check the takes that the script notes indicate are the best. Are there any problems that weren't noticed during filming? If so, is there another good take? Perhaps you had a take on which the script supervisor noted a possible problem (for example, "boom in shot?"). Now is the time to look closely to see if there really was a problem. If not, you have another good take. Using the notes is valuable because you're generally watching for so many things when viewing dailies that it's easy to miss something unless you know what to look for. This may be the only time, until much later in the editing process, that you'll see the footage projected on a big screen. Take advantage of it. It will be much harder to see details like boom shadows, fuzzy focus, or even acting nuances on the smaller screen of an editing machine.

Once you've looked at the dailies, the editor is free to begin assembling the film. If this process will begin while you are still filming (common on feature films), you need to decide beforehand how the editor will work. Who will determine the good takes (the director and/or producer can do that during daily screenings or the editor can be given that discretion based on script notes)? How rough do you want the first cut to be? Some people prefer to cut scenes long while others prefer to have the first cut be as close to perfection as possible. Just make sure the editor knows what you want.

Once the editor begins piecing scenes together, he or she will be able to tell you if you are getting enough (and the right kind of) coverage and if there are any specific things that are missing. Take advantage of feedback at this stage — it can save you time and money later.

WHAT TO DO WHEN THERE ARE PROBLEMS

I began this section by saying that no matter how much planning you do, some problems are bound to arise. Hopefully, they'll be small ones and you'll be able to deal with them easily. But what if they aren't? What do you do when something goes wrong? If you think this out beforehand, you're a big step ahead. The following are the main types of problems you're likely to have: 1) technical problems, 2) script problems, 3) people problems, 4) time/money problems, and 5) "acts of God."

TECHNICAL PROBLEMS

Technical problems can include things such as camera or generator breakdowns or problems with film stock. There really isn't much to say about this type of problem. The best you can do is consult with as many knowledgeable technicians as possible, weigh your alternatives, check your insurance, and make the best decision you can. Often this simply means waiting for a repair or replacement.

If the problem can be solved by replacing an item, all you have to face is a delay in time. Keep the possibility of breakdown in mind when you make arrangements for your primary equipment (camera, sound, generators). Is the supplier close by or do you have someone on your crew experienced in repair? Do you have to sit idle while waiting for the replacement or are there things you can do while waiting? The more flexibility you have in your schedule, the easier to juggle and minimize lost time.

In "Beware the Jabberwock" our generator broke down leaving us in a dark redwood grove without lights. A call to the rental company assured us that they would send another generator out right away, but that would still mean most of a day without electricity. We quickly began to search for nearby alternate locations where enough light filtered through the trees so that we could shoot certain scenes using only reflectors. By the time the generator arrived, we'd shot all the scenes that could be filmed outside the main grove. We were still a little behind schedule, but not too much.

SCRIPT PROBLEMS

What if part way through your shoot you realize the story simply isn't working? Do you keep going, do you stop to re-write, do you try to re-write in the middle of the night for the next day's filming and hope the script will be finished in time, do you bring in someone else to help? Of course, at this point it doesn't help to say you should have fixed this *before* you began shooting. Think this one out carefully. Simply completing a film is much easier than completing a good, saleable film. The cost of stopping to fix problems may be high — but it may still be less than the cost of ending up with an unsalable film on your hands. You've put a lot of money into the project so far — make it as good as you can.

PEOPLE PROBLEMS

You may have people, either cast or crew, who just aren't working out in their jobs. Cast is harder to deal with because it may mean re-shooting. How much have you already shot? How central is the character? Can re-writing or cutting some scenes minimize the damage? Can the director spend extra time with the problem actor. For crew it's always a good idea to have back-ups in mind. Can you help the person do a better job? Can you shuffle jobs around? Is firing the person the only alternative? Firing people isn't easy — and may be costly depending on your contractual obligations (think about this before you begin hiring). Of course, it's always better to work with people you've worked with before but even that is no guarantee. Crew who may have worked out fine on a small shoot may simply be out of their league on a complex one. Or they may be wonderful but have personal or health problems that are hindering them on this particular shoot. There are no easy answers here, but you do have to face the possibility of firing people.

Maybe all the individual people are doing their jobs well — but they (or some of them) simply can't work together, whether for reasons of personality or because of power struggles. Can these be resolved by talking, by clarifying job definitions, or by re-shuffling jobs? How valuable are the people involved? Can firing one person resolve the problem or is it more widespread? How much energy is this problem taking away from the shoot?

TIME AND/OR MONEY PROBLEMS

Are you going over schedule (and therefore probably over budget)? You have four basic choices here: cut waste, work faster, cut out parts of the script, or raise more money and extend the shoot. This last option assumes the cast and crew don't have other commitments and can stay and work longer.

What is taking the time? Can you pinpoint a particular problem? Are dolly shots taking an inordinate amount of time? Is the assistant camera person blowing takes because of focus problems? Is the director indecisive? Is the gaffer slow? Are you simply shooting too much (too long a script, too much coverage of each scene, too many takes on each shot)? Are the actors blowing takes (because of incompetence, inattention, nervousness, inadequate direction, outside distractions, or insufficient rehearsal)? Once you pinpoint the problem, you might be able to find solutions. Perhaps there is no one easy solution.

Are you working as fast as possible or is there wasted time? Can you cut scenes? Can you simplify the script, consolidate shots, plan simpler shots (a pan, zoom, or cuts rather than a dolly shot, for example)? Would adding one or more people to the crew help (enough to make up for the added cost)? What are the money costs of the alternatives? The non-money costs? What would you sacrifice by pushing the crew faster, simplifying shots, or cutting

219

scenes? Sometimes you'd lose nothing — or just the writer's, or director's, or an actor's ego. But just because something doesn't cost money doesn't mean there's no cost — an unhappy cast and crew may not produce a good film.

Are you going over budget for reasons not connected to time? Why? Are you spending more than you anticipated for equipment or supplies? Have you added extra people or things that were not in your original budget? Were your original estimates inaccurate? Are unforeseen problems causing the extra expenditures? Did you simply leave things out of your original budget (people, equipment, technical services)? Is there waste (wasted supplies, equipment you could do without, unessential people)? It's too late now to say you should have been more careful with your original estimates (unless you're reading this book before making up your budget!). If there's waste, stop it! Who has the authority to order equipment and supplies? Do you (or someone) need to approve all expenditures (or those over a certain amount)? Do you need to re-evaluate your crew needs and perhaps let some people go?

Don't just continue to go over budget and assume you'll somehow deal with it later. Figure out now where you'll find the needed extra money. Have you built in enough contingency to cover this? Can you cut back the post-production budget (without sacrificing quality)? Do you know where to raise more money?

ACTS OF GOD

This category includes things such as tornadoes, earthquakes, the death or illness of an actor, or even unexpected rain. It also includes the lab accidentally ruining your film. By definition, these can't be prevented — but you can minimize losses by having flexibility in your schedule and a good insurance policy (talk to your insurance agent). Tornadoes and earthquakes are hard to predict but you can develop a good relationship with a local weather forecaster and call him or her often if rain will be a problem for your shoot. If you give your film to the lab in small batches as the shoot progresses you'll minimize losses if they do have an accident. Work hard to keep your actors and crew healthy during the shoot.

ROLE OF THE PRODUCER

The main tasks of the producer during post-production are: 1) to continue to balance the needs of all the people involved in the film and 2) to oversee the many processes involved in the post-production period and to ensure that these are carried out well — and efficiently and economically.

BALANCE NEEDS

In post-production, the needs of the various people working on the post-production phase of the film (editor, sound people, composer, — and director) may conflict, as during the shooting phase. The producer has to balance these needs and keep the overall needs of the film in mind. Be clear about who has the final say at various stages of post-production. Who controls the first cut? Who has the final cut? Who controls the music and effects? Who controls the mix? Who determines the color timing at the lab?

OVERSEE THE PROCESS

This job can be done by the producer, a post-production supervisor, the director, or the editor — it doesn't matter so much who the person is as long as there is such a person. Someone needs to control quality and expedite the various parts of the process to make sure all the pieces fit together within your time-frame — and your budget. This means, for example, making sure that the titles and music are begun in time to be available when the editor is ready for them.

Costs have to be watched very carefully at this stage, especially since post-production costs can easily get out of hand. Someone needs to know what's necessary and what isn't, given the budget you're working with. There's room for a lot of waste during post-production simply because there are so many technical processes and because filmmakers often don't understand them well enough to use them in the most efficient way. The trick is to know what you need and what you don't need — and how to get what you need in the most efficient way. For example, do you need a foley track or can you build an adequate effects track with library effects? Do you really need to loop a scene or will you be able to fix the sound adequately in the mix? Do you need fifteen effects tracks or will five suffice? The questions are endless. You may need all these things, but make *sure* you do, for your particular film. Remember that everything costs money.

Post-production is an area where it's easy to be led astray by "experts." It's also an area where technology is sometimes complex — and is constantly changing. But, as with many complicated subjects, the experts should be able to explain your options in relatively clear language so you can make decisions about what is best for your film.

Often the experts who have the necessary information and experience, such as editors and post-production personnel, have no reason to chose the most economical alternative. Their goal may simply be to do the "best" job possible — and best is a subjective term. Some may even hope to get more business and thus make even more money. Many technicians don't think about cutting costs. Those who work for others and don't pay the bills themselves can easily become accustomed to asking for whatever they think they need (or might need) and getting it. Find post-production people who will work with you to keep costs down. Tell them your budget limits and stick to them if at all possible.

STEPS IN THE PROCESS: FILM

An understanding of what physically happens to both picture and sound during the post-production process will help you control both quality and costs, so I'll go over the steps briefly for the benefit of those unfamiliar with this aspect of filmmaking.

FILM PROCESSING

After the film is shot, it's then sent to a laboratory and processed. First the film is developed and you get a negative. Then a positive print is made from that. This unedited footage is called "dailies." Dailies are usually a "one-light" print, which means that one color timing is arbitrarily selected for the whole roll, even though this means individual scenes may be too dark or too light or need color balancing. You can also request a "color corrected" print in which the color and light balance is adjusted for each shot. This is more expensive and seldom done unless there is a specific reason, such as to impress someone who will see the rough workprint or to make sure any color problems can be corrected in the lab and the scene won't have to be re-shot.

SOUND TRANSFER

The 1/4" magnetic tape that was recorded during filming is transferred (usually in a sound studio) to 16mm or 35mm magnetic tape with sprocket holes. These sprocket holes match those in the film stock and will enable you to go on to the next step which is to synchronize (sync up) the picture and sound. Picture without sound (MOS) and sound without accompanying picture (wild sound) are simply put on separate reels at this point.

SYNCHRONIZING DAILIES

When the film is shot, the "clapper," or "slate," or "sticks" which mark the beginning of each take was recorded on both the film and sound tape. Some cameras have a built-in electronic

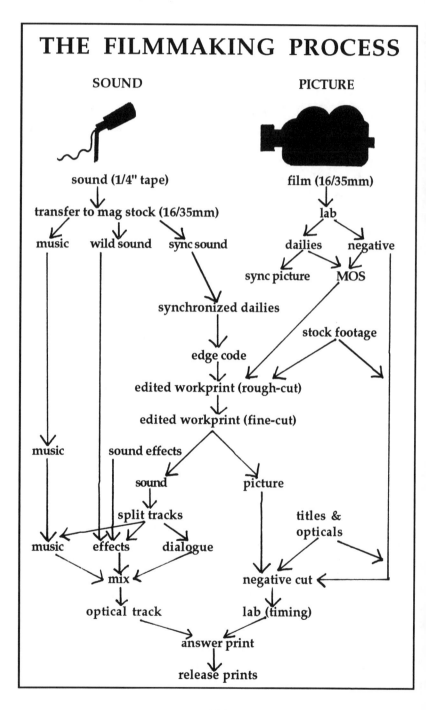

THE FILMMAKING PROCESS

SOUND

PICTURE

sound (1/4" tape)

film (16/35mm)

transfer to mag stock (16/35mm)

lab

music   wild sound   sync sound

dailies   negative

sync picture   MOS

synchronized dailies

stock footage

edge code

edited workprint (rough-cut)

edited workprint (fine-cut)

music

sound effects

sound   picture

split tracks

titles &
opticals

music   effects   dialogue

mix   negative cut

optical track   lab (timing)

answer print

release prints

flash/beep that serves the same purpose and saves a little film and time. To put them in sync, you line up the exact frames where you see and hear the clap. This can be done by your editor (or an assistant) or by a special service that specializes in this work. You now have dailies that are in sync — and these can be projected on a special "double system" projector so that you can see and hear what you've done.

I usually use this part of the process to put aside bad takes (those identified on the editing notes as having no usable parts). By eliminating them at this stage, I have less footage to edge-code, which saves money.

EDGE CODING

As a precautionary measure, to ensure that these two tracks (sound and picture) will always be matched throughout the editing process (where they may be moved around quite a bit), the two tracks are usually "edge-coded." This means that they are run through a machine that prints consecutive numbers along the edge of each roll of film about every foot. The same number is printed on corresponding frames of both picture and sound tracks. Then if at some future time the picture and sound tracks are separated (long after the sections with the clapper have been cut off and thrown away), you can re-match them without going through the tedious process of trying to read lips and put them back in sync that way (although that will work if necessary). Edge-coding does cost money and may not be necessary for certain small films (especially ones with very little voice sync) — but it will save time and aggravation (and help insure that your finished films will be in sync) if you can afford it. For larger films, make *sure* you can afford it.

To save money on films that have little sync sound, I do my own home-made edge coding by putting dot/dash codes at a few key points on each take on both tracks with an indelible marker.

EDITING

Now that you have all your takes in sync and edge-coded, your editor can begin the process of selecting the best takes and editing them together, using whatever combination of shots works best to create a coherent scene. This assemblage is called the "workprint," since it's what you work with in the editing process. The script may be followed closely at this stage or almost not at all, depending on the nature of the script, the available footage, and the desires of the director, producer, and/or editor. But somehow, out of all the footage, a '"rough-cut" emerges.

The rough-cut is precisely what it sounds like — a rough assemblage of the entire film. It may be more or less rough depending on the editor and on the preferences of the director and producer. The scenes will be in order but they may be cut long on purpose. There may be blank spaces to be filled in later with opticals or footage not yet available. The film may be very close to what it will ultimately be — or it may go through radical changes after this. Much of that depends on the skill of the director (in obtaining good, useable footage that will cut well together), the editor (in putting it together well), and the writer (in writing a script that will actually work). From here the editor, director, producer, and/or whoever else is part of the editing decision-making process, will polish the film — trimming, changing the order of things, or whatever is necessary until they eventually arrive at a "fine-cut."

The fine-cut is the film assembled as it will appear in the final product, although the final product will look and sound much more polished than the fine-cut as lab optical effects and more sound tracks are added. The work up to this stage has probably been done with one or two sound tracks (there is sometimes a reason to work with more than one track from the beginning, such as in a film where the music track is central to the film and much of the editing will be done to fit the music). There won't usually, however, be any titles, lab dissolves, added sound effects, or music. The picture and sound quality will usually still be rough at this stage, to be corrected later. But with the fine-cut the order of shots and sounds is theoretically locked in — so that the final polishing processes can begin. I say theoretically because you can always change things up until the last minute — but after this stage it becomes more complicated, more expensive, and your editor will hate you.

SOUND TRACKS

Once the picture is locked in, you begin the process of preparing the sound tracks for the final version. There are two parts to this: splitting the existing track(s) and building new ones.

SPLITTING TRACKS. The existing sound track, probably mainly dialogue, is split into its components — so that you can then re-mix them to obtain better quality at a later stage. This means, for example, that if you have two main characters, you will put each of their dialogues on a separate track, and any sound effects that don't overlap their voices will go on another track. The reason for this is that the voice quality (pitch and level) of the two voices is likely to be different and if they are separated now they can be adjusted and balanced when they are re-combined in the mix (see p. 236). You don't need to make a separate track for every character, but you do need to have enough separation between different voices so that the mixer can make adjustments in the mix. This will most likely mean alternating characters on separate tracks within dialogue sequences.

BUILDING TRACKS. The second task is to build more tracks — to make the sound effects fuller and more realistic, and to add music. In theory, you can have as many tracks as you want. The only limit is money. With a large number of tracks you'll have to pre-mix some of them together since the mixing studio will only be able to handle a limited number of tracks at one time (how many depends on the studio). But you often don't need lots of tracks. For a simple educational film you might have four or five tracks (2 dialogue, 1-2 sound effects, and 1 music). A feature film might have 10-20 tracks (some have many more but I'm not convinced that's not overkill in most instances). The reason for more tracks is to be able to overlay more sounds at once and to keep the different sounds separate until the mix in order to be able to have more latitude in the mix. For example, if you are building the sounds of a forest, you might have wind on one track, miscellaneous forest birds on another, an owl on another, a coyote howl on another, etc.. In the finished film these will all be mixed together to sound completely natural, with each sound at the appropriate level, but at this stage they may have to be pieced together one at a time on separate tracks. Or you might be lucky and find a sound effect of "forest sounds" that is exactly what you want and be able to use only that. Or you might find something that isn't perfect but will work adequately for your needs if you will only use it as very low background, behind dialogue and/or music.

The three main types of tracks you will have are 1) dialogue, 2) music, and 3) effects.

1) Dialogue. The dialogue tracks are generally recorded during the filming. You may also have a narration track, usually recorded separately. This is often treated as another dialogue track and kept separate, even if the same person also has on-camera dialogue, because the voice quality of the two recordings will usually be different. If the narration will intercut with dialogue by the same actor, you might want to be sure to record it under the same conditions (and the same location) as the dialogue to prevent matching problems at this stage.

If the sound quality of the dialogue recorded on location is not adequate, some dialogue may need to be re-recorded in a process known as "looping" or "automatic dialogue replacement" (ADR). For looping, the actors work in a sound studio where the original film (workprint) is projected before them. They listen to their original, flawed lines on earphones and then repeat them again in the studio, trying to match lip movements and the mood of the original recording. Depending on the skill of the actor, this can be more or less successful. If their lips aren't seen, the lines can simply be re-recorded without the film being projected (a cheaper process). This is a place where video might be used to save money, especially if you already have a video transfer. You might be able to re-record to video rather than film, which might give you a greater choice of recording studios.

The dialogue tracks need to be cleaned up at this time. That means that all extraneous sounds, such as loud breaths, coughs, sniffles, and miscellaneous bumps have to be removed. Someone may have hit something with their foot off camera and all you hear on the sound track is an unexplained noise. Or you may have a car horn or an airplane or other background noise that is not seen and is distracting. Cut them out if possible. Sometimes a line that is garbled or unclear will be clear on another take (or may have been recorded wild) and you might be able to substitute rather than loop the line.

2) Music. Music for a film will generally be recorded separately and added at this stage. Music can come from several sources: a) an existing recording to which you have obtained the rights, b) a music library, or c) music composed and/or recorded specifically for your film.

a) Existing recordings. If you are making a home movie, you can simply use a record from your collection, but if you plan to show the film anywhere you must obtain permission to do that. This may be simple and inexpensive for a little-known song or artist, but might be prohibitive for a well-known group. Don't ever incorporate music into your film before finding out if you can obtain permission to use it (and if you can *afford* to buy the rights to use it). Don't just assume you'll work it out. But also don't assume you'll always have to pay — use your negotiating skills.

b) Music libraries. Music libraries exist for the purpose of providing music for this kind of use. They have large collections of music written and recorded to go with a wide variety of films. Some music is an imitation of better-known music, some is their own recordings of classical music that is in the public domain, while much is original.

You can go to a music library, listen to music (sometimes there is a fee for listening time, sometimes not) and make your selections. They will then transfer the music to 1/4" tape or disc (or directly to 16mm or 35mm mag stock) and you agree to pay a set fee for its use. The fee depends on how much music you will use and in what markets (for example, you pay a higher fee for a theatrical feature film than to use the same music in an educational film). The fees are reasonable and this is often the cheapest way of adding music to a film. This process is also fairly fast. You can often select music for your film and have it transferred and cut into the film all on the same day. This method also allows you to have a lot of control over your music. You can select each piece and hear it exactly as it will sound. However, although the selection of available music is varied, you may not find what you want. Another drawback is that the music comes in pre-recorded lengths (although it is often written with a view to being easily cut at a variety of places). There are now music editing computer programs that allow you to customize music for your needs.

c) **Music recorded for your film.** The last alternative is to record music specifically for your film. This may simply mean recording existing music (which is in the public domain or to which you have obtained the rights) or it may mean composing original music. The later is generally fairly time-consuming and more costly, but don't rule it out because of cost until you check it out thoroughly because there are ways to obtain original music inexpensively. Your music can be composed by a big-name composer for a high fee, then arranged for a large orchestra (with separate parts copied out for each musician), then played by a large orchestra (for high rates), and recorded in a large studio. But that's not the only way to do original music. Talk with composers and musicians about alternatives. Many are anxious to work with film and are creative about cutting costs. Some can put together fairly complex sound tracks all by themselves, either by playing various instruments or by using electronic technology. Some have their own recording set-ups or access to inexpensive studios. We have used original music for educational films with very limited budgets several times.

For "Hard Traveling," we decided that relatively simple music would be most appropriate and our composer was willing to work with us to cut costs. Although we originally envisioned and budgeted for 8-10 instruments, we finally decided to try using only a guitar and a harmonica. We left ourselves the option of adding other instruments at any point during the process if the two instruments didn't seem sufficient, but we didn't need to add anything. We began talking with the composer about musical ideas early in the process and selected two of his songs to incorporate into the actual filming, sung by the actors. After the rough cut, the composer began fitting his ideas to the specific scenes in the film (using a rough video copy to work with and conferring with us often). By the time we had a fine cut, he was ready to fine-tune the music. We selected a harmonica player who began rehearsing with the composer (who also played the guitar). After a few days of rehearsal we decided we were ready to set up a recording date and did so at a small high-quality studio that had a VHS video set-up so we could watch the film as the musicians played. We recorded the guitar and harmonica, transferred it to 35mm mag stock and added it to the film. We liked the results and we were finished. Simple and inexpensive.

3) Sound effects. The third type of track you'll have is sound effects. Sound effects can be obtained in several ways: a) recording effects during the shoot, b) sound libraries, c) recording sound effects later, and d) foley.

   a) Recording effects during the shoot. The easiest way to obtain sound effects is generally to record them during the shoot if you can. You may want to make a point of recording effects clean, not overlapping any dialogue. Give the sound person a list of effects you know you'll need and make sure he or she gets them. Go out of your way during the shoot to record any extra sounds you might need, such as miscellaneous car sounds, doors closing, dog barking, footsteps, whatever. Be sure to record some ambient sounds or room tone for each location as well. A good sound person should do this as a matter of course, but make sure it happens.

It'll save you a lot of money (and save the editor a lot of grief) later.

b) Sound libraries. There are libraries for sound effects similar to those for music. They have a large selection of various sounds, all carefully catalogued. You can listen to sounds, select the ones you want, and have them transferred. If you'll use them often, you can buy records/CDs of some sound effects. In addition, some very standard background sounds will be available at the sound studio when you do your mix in the form of ready-made "loops." If, for example, you want to add some birds to an outdoor scene, you can ask the mixer to add a bird loop (there may be several different ones available) to the mix. This will save you adding background birds to your tracks, but check with the sound studio ahead of time to be sure they have the loops you need.

Sounds are not as standard and simple as you might think — and trying to find the right sound at a sound library can be a very frustrating experience. For "Physical Fitness" we needed two effects that I thought would be fairly simple to find. One scene needed splashes for two women swimming in an outdoor pool. Simple? Wrong. There were lots of listings under swimming pools — big noisy ones full of kids, small indoor ones, many with talking in the background. I finally found plain splashes for one person and used that twice, on two tracks, to create two people swimming.

The other scene was in a newspaper office. In order to obtain clean dialogue we didn't have anyone actually typing or talking, other than the principal actors, when we shot the scene. Everyone else was faking it. I had planned to record the sounds on location but we were running late and had to vacate the office. No problem, I thought, I can easily get office sounds at the sound library. Again, there were many office sounds listed in the sound library but none were right. Some had only women's voices (and we had several men visible), some were too big or too small. But the main problem was the typewriters. We had two manual typewriters in use and almost all the office sounds had electric typewriters. The closest was a loop that included a telephone ringing. It was the best I could find but we needed a long piece of it, which meant that the phone kept ringing and ringing. So our editor went through and cut out most of the phone rings, one by one. It worked

— but if you plan to use a sound library, make sure ahead of time that they have what you need.

c) **Recording effects later.** Another way to obtain effects is to go out with a tape recorder after the shoot and record the effects you need. This may mean going back to your locations or simply going around town. Give the sound person a very specific list of what you need. If possible, let them see the picture that the sound should match or go with them. This isn't usually an economical way to create effects, but you may need to do it to find exactly what you want.

d) **Foley.** The final way to create sound effects is by making what is called a "foley track." This involves going to a sound studio and recording effects while the film is projected in front of you in much the same way a film is looped. A sound studio that is equipped to do this will either have built-in pits or boxes that are brought into the studio containing different textures such as dirt, sand, and gravel so you can replicate footsteps on these different surfaces (as well as on others such as cement, linoleum, and wood). There will be other props at the studio and the "foley walker," the person who makes the sounds (many of which will be footsteps, thus the name), may bring additional materials to create sounds for your film.

When sound is recorded during filming, it's usually geared to capture the dialogue — the microphone is aimed at the speaker. If someone is walking at the same time, the steps may not be loud enough for the mike to pick them up. In the foley session, these footsteps can be replicated in such a way that they add a fullness and dimension to the track. In addition to footsteps, you can add almost any sound from the closing of a door to horses galloping. Experienced foley walkers know how to create many sounds, much like old radio sound effects people.

Foley is a slow, complicated, and expensive process. It's almost never done for an educational film, but it's common practice for features. You need a studio that is equipped for foley (with pits or foley boxes) and able to project your film (or, as in looping, this is a place where video could be used). But, most important, you need a good foley walker. And good in this case means someone who can not only duplicate a sound accurately, but who can do it quickly. A foley track for a feature can take days and days — at high hourly rates. If the foley walker can rehearse with the film beforehand (perhaps on video), you may save time during the foley session. You can also decide to keep your foley track simple and instruct the foley walker accordingly.

A cheaper variation on this would be to use the sound studio and its effects but without projecting the film. That won't help you get sounds in sync (your editor will have to do that), but it may allow you to use their props to create some effects that might be hard or more expensive to obtain otherwise.

THE MIX

Once all the tracks are separate, and every piece of music and every sound effect has been added in the proper place, it's time to mix all the tracks back together. This happens at the "mix" or "re-recording session." You take your workprint and all your tracks to a sound studio that is equipped to play a number of tracks simultaneously, in sync with the projected film. One or more mixers (depending on how many tracks you are working with) will mix the tracks together — balancing volumes, adjusting the pitch or the voices or sounds (treble/bass balance), and perhaps adding some special effects they have the ability to add (such as a telephone filter, which makes a voice sound as if it's being heard over a telephone). They can even fix some sound problems on your existing tracks, such as filtering out a low machine sound in the background. What the mixer can do is limited by the material (the tracks) you give him.

Cue sheets made up by the editor tell the mixer(s) which sounds are on which tracks at what points (marked according to footage). The mixer sits at the control board, watching the film and a footage counter — while at the same time looking over the cue sheets to see which sounds are coming up on which tracks and adjusting the sound levels and sound quality for each track. Too much for one human being to do? Seems like it, but they manage somehow. In another room there will usually be a technician (or several) who sets up the sound tracks and the picture on special machines. These machines are designed to stop at any time, back up, and go forward again, and always stay in sync (theoretically — and as long as your splices hold). The amount of time this process takes can vary greatly depending on the number and complexity of the tracks, and the skill of the mixer. Clean tracks and clear, legible cue sheets will really help.

Mixers can salvage a lot of bad sound at this stage — but it all takes time on their part (and therefore money on your part). Knowing what can be fixed at this stage is very valuable and may save you the necessity of looping and re-recording sounds (just as knowing the capability of the lab can help when you have poor picture quality). Spend time in a sound studio and learn what can and can't be done in a mix.

Sound studios and mixers are not all the same. Check the capabilities and technology of the studio and the skills of the mixer(s) and make your choices carefully.   Do they have the ability to do what you need? A studio that is fine for a simple film may be inadequate for a more complicated one. A fancy studio may be way more than you need for a simple film. Make sure your editor knows how the mixer wants cue sheets prepared. Legible cue sheets are essential.

If you have special needs, let the studio know ahead of time. Do you want to record in stereo? If you anticipate foreign sales, you might want to record a separate music and effects (M & E) track at this time. If you'll need an M & E track, make sure your original tracks are prepared appropriately, with absolutely no dialog at all on any music or effects tracks. After you're done, it's usually a good idea to make a 1/4" tape of the mixed track for protection.

Although the mixer is a highly skilled technician, many decisions here are artistic ones and the mixer will carry out the wishes of the director, editor, and/or producer (whoever is running the mix) in terms of what levels seem appropriate for various tracks and what quality you want. Know what you want in the mix — indecision costs time (and money). Mixers have a lot of valuable experience — if you want their advice, ask for it.

At the end of the mixing process you should have a sound track with all the voices, music, and sound effects nicely balanced in perspective (assuming, of course, that you went into the mix with all the necessary components). The mixing process is expensive, but essential. The best way to cut costs here is to come well-prepared (with clean tracks, legible cue-sheets, and a well-spliced workprint) and to choose your studio and mixer carefully.

OPTICAL TRACK

Once the composite sound track is made, it's converted it to a form that can be combined with the film. The standard method is to convert the magnetic track to an optical one. A cheaper (but lower quality) alternative is called an "electroprint." This may be adequate for an answer print, although usually not for a release quality print. When your answer print is timed, the lab will combine the two onto one piece of film. This is the end of the process for sound — now let's go back to the picture part.

COMPLETING THE PICTURE

Before the film can be finished, any graphics or missing elements such as opticals, animation, titles, or stock footage must be added. Sometimes these are not ready until the final editing stages, but add them in as soon as you can. New technology, including video technology, combined with better quality video to film transfers are opening up new possibilities in the way graphics are created.

Opticals. Opticals can be used for several purposes and are usually made by an optical house. Some opticals involve re-shooting footage that you've already shot (for example, blowing up a section to change the size or framing of the shot or to fix a mistake, such as a boom that can be seen on the edge of a frame). You can also freeze frames, either for special effects or to create a new shot. For "Hard Traveling," we decided in the editing process that we wanted an establishing shot of a farmhouse that we didn't have, in order to be able to shorten a scene. We were able to take one frame off another shot (a shot of the house after some people had walked out of the scene) and freeze it, thereby obtaining our establishing shot much more cheaply than if we had to go back and re-shoot. Be aware that the quality of the optical may differ somewhat from that of the original film.

Although fades and dissolves in 16mm are done in the lab at the answer print stage (with A & B negative roles), for 35mm they are done in an optical house beforehand. Some special effects are done completely in optical houses, usually frame by frame. All this is fairly expensive.

Animation. There are many variations on this process, from hand-drawn "cel" animation to manipulation of models or clay, to computerized animation. But the basic process is that each frame is photographed separately with each frame being slightly different from the one before so that the scene appears to move when the film is projected.

Titles. These may also be made by an optical house (or a place that specializes in titles). Costs can vary greatly depending on what kind of titles and end credits you want (what kind of type and whether they will be over a scene or simply against a plain background or a photo or graphic). Consult a title house to find out your options and costs. There are simpler alternatives, such as writing or printing titles on a card and shooting them when you shoot your film or shooting the titles as animation with an animation camera. There's no limit to your creativity here — just check out the costs carefully.

Stock footage. This is already existing footage that can be ordered from a variety of companies that sell stock footage. After telling them in general what you want, you look at possible footage and make your selection. They'll send you both a workprint and a negative. They usually charge a fee plus lab costs. You can sometimes save money by locating a fellow filmmaker who has the footage you need, instead of going to a specialized company.

NEGATIVE CUTTING

The workprint and all the original negative that until now has been carefully stored are taken to a negative cutter who will cut the negative to conform with the workprint, carefully matching up the numbers that are printed on both the negative and positive copies of the film (not the edge-coding numbers). This is done very carefully to make sure the negative doesn't get scratched. In 16mm, separate A and B (and sometimes C) rolls are made so the lab can make dissolves and fades or add titles.

ANSWER PRINT

The workprint and the conformed negative are then taken to the lab which will make an answer print, in which the colors will be properly balanced and the fades and dissolves will be integrated into the print.

The "timer" is the person at the lab who will control the color balance (and density of color saturation), generally in consultation with you (or the director or editor). Color timing is not just a mechanical process — it can involve artistic decisions. Do you want a neutral look or slightly warmer or colder?

Pay close attention to timing — it can influence audience response to your film. For "Hard Traveling," we chose a warmer look on purpose (beginning with art direction, but accentuated with the timing). We also made some scenes in the jail colder (bluer) than normal on purpose, perhaps too blue. The audience response to a first answer print screening was quite negative to the jail scenes, although no one mentioned the color. For the second answer print, we warmed up those scenes slightly (and trimmed some shots a little) and after that no one singled out those scenes.

Once the proper timing is obtained, the film will be processed and the optical sound track added along one side of the film. You'll then have your first answer print — your first test of the finished product. If the color didn't come out quite right, you may need to consult with the timer and make some corrections before trying a second answer print. Some labs charge higher rates but will make a second or third answer print free until the color is right. Other labs may be cheaper but charge for additional answer prints. Check with the lab. A hint — where your deal is for an "acceptable" answer print, you might be able to buy the "rejected" print for a much reduced rate (otherwise they'll keep it). This print, although not perfect, may be of use to you.

Answer prints are made from the original negative. To make many prints from the original would endanger the negative, so before quantity "release prints" are made, an inter-positive and a "dupe" negative are made, and then release prints are struck from that.

VIDEO EDITING

Video editing technology is changing rapidly enough that anything written here may be obsolete by the time you read it. But, in the hope that the basics will remain relatively constant, I'll give you an outline of the processes.

TYPES OF VIDEO EDITING SYSTEMS

There are two main types of video editing systems:

1. Linear editing. This is the traditional method that transfers selected cuts from the "source tape" onto the "edit master" tape in sequence. Because the cuts are on the tape, you cannot move them at will and if you want to lengthen or shorten a section, you must begin over (or cheat in a variety of ways I'll explain later). These systems can be used with or without computers.

2. Non-linear (digital) editing. This is fairly new technology, still very expensive, that is computer-based rather than tape based and therefore has much more flexibility. Once the material is digitized and entered into the computer, you can manipulate it in many ways. This technology is so new, and constantly changing, that if you'll be using it, ask a lot of questions and make sure you understand the processes and choices.

Off-line and on-line. The other primary terms used in relation to editing systems, "off-line" and "on-line" refer to the quality of the finished product. Off-line systems, which are usually less expensive, generally do not result in broadcast-quality material and thus are used as a first step. Some machines are not completely frame-accurate. The off-line edit is the equivalent of somewhere between a rough-cut and fine-cut when editing on film. Once the show is edited, the editing is repeated on an on-line system to obtain a high-quality finished product, including any special effects and titles. This is similar to conforming the film negative to the workprint in order to obtain an answer print.

241

For all the marvels of technology, editing on video is still editing. There is no magic to video editing — and it has disadvantages as well as advantages. Video editing won't automatically edit a film, nor will it transform a bad editor into a good one. They key to good editing is still to know what shots and takes to select, exactly where to make the cuts, how to combine the shots, and how to make the film or tape flow smoothly and produce the desired emotional effect. While I don't want to argue the merits of video vs film editing, I do want to give you a basic understanding of both the linear and non-linear video editing processes.

Talk to your lab, sound studio, editing facility. Talk to the experts. This is sometimes complicated technology, make sure you understand it well enough to use it to the best advantage — and not make mistakes.

LINEAR EDITING SYSTEMS

STEP 1: PREPARATION — TRANSFER TO VHS

Once you have finished the shoot, you'll transfer everything to 1/2" VHS (or whatever format you're using off-line — usually VHS). This is what you'll use for your off-line edit; you won't touch the original again until the on-line edit. At the time of the transfer, you'll add a time code "window dub," which means adding visible time code numbers to the VHS that match the numbers on the original tape. You want the VHS copy to have a visible "window dub" so that you can write these numbers down as you work. You'll work with these numbers throughout the off-line edit and they are what will be used at the on-line edit to find the exact corresponding segments on the original tape.

Film-to-tape transfers. If you're transferring from film, be aware that film and tape have different numbers of frames per second. That's what makes transferring from one to the other tricky. Film uses 24 frames per second, while tape uses 30 "frames." The process is too complicated to explain here but the essence of it is that frames are added when film is transferred to video, while when transferring from video to film, frames are lost. Talk to a video technician about this, especially if you will later transfer back to film. You want both systems to be compatible so that when you transfer back to film at the end, you remove the same frames that were added earlier. All transfer facilities are not equal — check quality, especially if you'll need to go back to film.

Sound. If sound was recorded separately, you'll need to add it (lay it in) to the tape in sync. Check with your lab about how to do this.

Tape logs. So that you know what footage you have — and so you can find it more easily — go through your tapes (on your home VHS to save money) and create a video tape log (see p. 292) that serves as an index. You can list each take, adding in information from the script notes, or you can just make a rough list of what scenes are on each tape. The more detailed your log is, the easier it will be to find things as you look for them during the editing process — and the more time you'll save then. Documentaries or complex films will most likely require more detailed logs than straightforward scripted films. If you're editing on expensive equipment, you'll want to waste as little time as possible finding your material during the actual edit, so log it carefully.

STEP 2: OFF-LINE EDIT

Edit the video, laying in one shot after the other, listing the time-code number carefully on an "edit decision list" (EDL) as you go (see p. 293). When you do the on-line edit, you'll rely on these time-code numbers so it's important to keep an accurate list as you go. This list will keep changing as you edit, but it's crucial. If your editing system is linked to a computer, the computer will keep track of these numbers and create the edit decision list.

Off-line systems can only do cuts and not dissolves and special effects. Make notes to add these on-line.

Because linear editing actually lays the edits onto the tape, you are limited in how you can edit. You must edit in a linear sequence, you can't simply go back and insert five more frames someplace or add another shot. This gives you an incentive to edit carefully as you go along rather than do a somewhat sloppy first edit that you'll tighten later. There are, however, some ways to cheat. Although you can't just snip out four frames someplace and tighten everything up, you can have some inaccuracies on your tape — as long as you keep an accurate edit decision list. In that case, what you see off-line won't be exactly what you'll get on-line, but if your EDL is accurate, when you do the on-line edit (or a second pass on the off-line), you'll get what you want. If you just take out four frames, you'll have a black space instead and you would have to re-lay in everything after it to get rid of that space. As I edit, I often ignore those details and live with some black spaces or even some missing frames. I might even re-build a section on another tape, to be added later. I just make sure that my EDL is correct and the next time I re-lay things in I get it right.

You will probably be working with a picture and two sound tracks at this point. And your sound and picture at any given point may not be from the same tape. Just make sure that your EDL clearly shows the source for all sound and visuals. If you're not using a computer system and you have a lot of overlapping sound or picture (from different shots), it may be difficult to get the EDL clear since the sound numbers will not be visible on the screen — but make sure you get it right. A computer will get correct sound numbers automatically.

Some editors only note approximate frames at this point and plan to fine-tune at the on-line edit. That can get very expensive and I recommend getting as accurate as you can (within the limits of your off-line machine; some aren't frame-accurate). Sometimes you may not be able to hear a sound clearly enough off-line and you'll have to fine-tune on-line, but (unless you're very rich) that should be a last resort, not a general practice. The closer to an exact cut you get on the off-line edit, the less money you'll waste in an on-line facility.

As you build your video, you can add in any stock footage or extra sound (wild sound, effects, or music) you have at this time. If you don't have everything you need at first, add it in at any point before you're finished. You have to have all your elements ready before the on-line. And make sure everything fits and your EDL numbers are accurate.

Computer editing. If your editing system is linked to a computer, the computer automatically keeps track of your EDL numbers. Then, as you make changes, the computer can re-edit the film for you without you having to lay everything down again. When you go to do your on-line edit, just plug in the disk. Magic. Wonderful. Unfortunately, it costs money and everyone doesn't have it.

Even if you don't have a computer linked to your editing system, you can use a computer program to enter your EDL on a disk after you've completed your off-line edit. You then take the disk to the on-line, which can save you time and money there.

STEP 3: ON-LINE EDIT

The on-line edit is generally very expensive and you want to go into it as prepared as possible. Make sure all your tapes are in the proper format, clearly labeled, and organized. You can do an on-line from a computer generated EDL stored on a disk or from a hand-written EDL. Either way, you want your EDL to be clear and accurate. If you don't have a computer list, make sure your hand-written list is legible. The on-line edit will be very high-pressure and the last thing you want is to waste expensive time looking for tapes or trying to decipher your notes. Get plenty of sleep the night before the on-line — you'll want to be awake enought to catch any problems and make quick decisions about how to fix them.

The on-line edit is the place to add special effects, graphics, titles, and any of the other wondrous things the on-line machine can do. When you select an on-line facility, know your technical requirements and find a studio that can do what you need (and ask what that will cost!). Discussing your needs (and at what point they fit in your show) will allow the facility to plan ahead to have the equipment you need available when you need it. It will also let them reserve special equipment for you *only* when you need it so you don't have to pay for it the whole time. Make sure ahead of time that the on-line facility is compatible with your off-line computer system.

If your video doesn't call for many fancy optical effects, you might be able to use a less expensive facility. If you're unfamiliar with what on-line facilities can do, ask for a demonstration. It may give you ideas. After seeing a demonstration, I was inspired to add a few special effects to "Turnabout," which was a fairly straightforward documentary.

Special effects. Be aware that complex effects can take a lot of time. How much are they worth to you? You might have some things you'd like to try if you can do them relatively fast, and skip or simplify if it seems that they'll take too long or you're behind schedule. You can discuss some key options before the edit, especially if it'll affect your numbers. Ask the video technician. Video titles are done at this stage with a "character generator."

At the end of the on-line edit, you'll have your master tape, in whatever format you choose, such as 1", D-1, D-2, or Betacam. If you're using a computer, it can also generate a "negative cutting list" that your negative cutter will need if you're going to go back to film .

STEP 4: SOUND TRACKS

After your on-line edit, you'll finalize your sound tracks, usually at a sound studio. If your audio tracks are simple enough to be done with the on-line edit, you need to have the sound exact at that time. Off-line, you usually only have room for two tracks. After the on-line, you can add any other music or effects you want.

This is also the time to smooth out your sound tracks and electronically "sweeten" the sound. Know what your sound studio can do and what you have to prepare beforehand.

STEP 5: FINAL STEPS

Your final step will be to make a duplicate master (for protection in case anything happens to the original) and then any other copies you may need at this point. If you want the final product to be in film, you'll need to conform the film negative or do a tape-to-film transfer (see p. 249).

NON-LINEAR (DIGITAL) EDITING SYSTEMS

STEP 1: PREPARATION — DIGITIZE YOUR MATERIAL

The first step is to transfer your tape or film onto computer disks. This process, called "digitizing," takes up a lot of disk storage space and is expensive, so you might want to only digitize selected takes. You can also digitize material from other sources such as CDs, photographs, and computer graphics. If you're transferring from film to tape, see page 243.

STEP 2: OFF-LINE EDIT

Once all your material is in the computer, you can begin your edit. Editing with this process does not have to go in a linear sequence.

You can begin anywhere, and remove or add frames anywhere with ease. In this sense, non-linear editing resembles film editing.

Non-linear editing allows you to change your mind easily and to keep many versions of a given section so you can make final decisions at a later time. You can also get overwhelmed if you keep too many alternatives.

Some systems can produce complex visual effects. But be careful — to duplicate those on-line might be difficult expensive. Check this out beforehand.

There is no need to keep a hand-written edit decision list because the computer will do that automatically. When you're done, it will produce a computerized EDL that you can use for your on-line edit. You can also make an off-line copy of your edit on tape. Since the quality of this tape depends on the recorder you use, it can sometimes be quite good.

You may be working with many sound tracks at this point, depending on the capability of your system. Some off-line systems can produce excellent sound tracks.

STEP 3: ON-LINE EDIT

This should proceed fairly smoothly, working from the computer-generated edit decision lists. As with a linear on-line, you'll add any desired graphics, titles, or effects at this stage. Again, don't forget to make sure the on-line facility is compatible with your off-line system and to talk out what you will need carefully ahead of time with the technicians.

STEP 4: SOUND TRACKS

The process here is similar to that for linear editing, if you haven't already done it off-line. You want to flesh out the sound by adding music and effects, sweeten it (if necessary), then mix it down.

STEP 5: FINAL STEPS

This will also be similar to those for a linear edit. Think out ahead what you'll need.

TAPE-TO-FILM

If you want your final product to be on film, you have two choices, depending on how it was shot to begin with.

Conform the negative. If you originally shot on film, you can conform the film to the edited video. The computer can provide a "negative cut list" but make sure you plan for this from the very first stages. Talk to your lab. Although technically you could go straight from tape to conforming the negative, it's wise to confirm a workprint first to catch any possible mistakes and then conform the negative to the workprint.

Tape-to-film transfer. If you originally shot on video, you can use a process called "tape-to-film transfer" to end up with 16mm or 35mm film. This is tricky because of the difference in the number of frames on film and video but the results can be quite good. Several labs specialize in this, using various methods. Check out Image Transform (Los Angeles), Palmer Lab (Belmont, CA), and Du Art (New York). The labs should be able to show you a sample of their work.

We originally shot our documentary "Turnabout" on Betacam SP because we had a limited budget and a project we though would have a limited audience and be sold only to television, schools, and home video (and therefore not require film). After it was finished, we realized the show had a wider market than we originally envisioned and we were urged to transfer it to film to enable it to be shown at more festivals, as well as theatrically. We did, and although the 16mm transfer is not as polished as if we'd shot on film (or even planned from the beginning to transfer it), it has been quite adequate and enabled us to show the film in places we would not have been able to if it was only on video.

DISTRIBUTION

Filmmaking is more than simply making a film — it includes getting the film into distribution. As hard as it is to raise money and actually make the film, it may be even harder to get it distributed — at least in a way that will let you make back anywhere near your costs. The harsh reality is that many films just don't get distributed. So, although this is the last chapter, it's really one that you should think about from the very beginning (unless, of course, you just want to make a film for the sake of it and don't care who sees it or if you ever make any money from it).

Whether you will distribute the film yourself, find a distributor on your own, or turn the film over to a "producer's representative" who will hopefully find you a distributor, you'll need to be aware of the possible markets for films in general, and for your film in particular.

The two main "rational" criteria for distributing a film are the quality of the film and how well it fits into distribution categories (which means the type of market and the audience to which it's geared). Some types of films are easier to sell than others. A mediocre film that appeals to a teen-age crowd, or a horror film, will probably be more marketable than an excellent film that has no obvious specific audience, either because of content, style, or length.

MARKETS

The following are the primary distribution markets. Remember that each of these exists both in the U.S. and abroad.

1) Theatrical. These films, generally 1 1/2 to 2 hours in length, will be shown in either large "first-run" theaters, neighborhood theaters, or "art houses." Most theaters can only accommodate 35mm, although some are equipped to show 16mm films.

249

2) Television. There are a number of sub-categories in this area — "pay cable" (such as Home Box Office and Showtime for which cable customers pay special rates), "free cable" (such as Nickelodeon, that may come free with your cable subscription), network television (CBS, NBC, ABC), public television (PBS and its affiliates), and "syndication" (licensing shows to individual local stations on a station-by-station basis).

3) Home video. These are the VHS tapes that you can buy or rent to show on your home video recorder. They are now also used in schools and libraries (which may conflict with educational sales).

4) Non-theatrical. This category includes sales or rentals to schools (colleges, high schools, elementary schools), libraries, corporations, and the government. This is the primary market for educational films. This also includes a number of other very specific markets, such as "in-flight" movies (those you see on airplanes) and doctors' offices and hospitals (both for patient education and also entertainment for the waiting room).

5) Festivals. This is not really a "market" but festivals can be useful in the distribution process, either to help obtain a distributor or to get the film known and exhibited after you have a distributor. For some types of hard-to-market films, festivals might be a primary means of exhibition. Some festivals give prizes and/or pay the filmmakers' expenses to the festival while others are fairly costly to enter (entrance fees and shipping costs, not to mention the time your print is tied up). Some festivals have film markets connected with them where films are sold to buyers of various kinds.

6) Other markets. New technology is creating new markets. Check out if your film could be adapted for CD ROM.

There are also various potential markets for spin-offs from your film. Usually films are made from books, but the reverse is also possible. Documentary films, especially those with a lot of interesting source material, can often be successfully made into books. Our education film, "The Immune System: Your Magic Doctor" was so successful that I adapted it as a book. And then there's the dolls, toys, T-shirts, etc..

Once you've decided which markets your film fits into, you can find out more about those particular markets, how they work, and who the distributors are. Each market is usually serviced by a different set of distributors (although some handle more than one market). And the different markets use very different "standard contracts" (as much as there is such a thing) and work in different ways. There are also different levels of distributors within each market — big and little, established and brand new, reputable and not so reputable. The companies change, personnel within them changes, and their interests and reputations change — making it very hard for someone on the outside to understand it all. One of your best sources of information about distributors will be other producers, especially producers of recent films similar to yours.

Filmmaker organizations such as the Independent Feature Project (IFP) in New York and Los Angeles, the Film Arts Foundation (FAF) in San Francisco, or the Association of Independent Video and Filmmakers (AIVF) in New York can also be very useful for obtaining information and making connections for distribution and festivals. The New York IFP runs a very large and successful sales market for independent feature films every fall where many new films are exhibited and many deals made.

Be creative in deciding which markets your film might fit. Distributors can sometimes pair up one or more films to create a longer program or series. Or you might have several films of your own that logically fit together. We produced three half-hour children's films narrated by Ray Bolger. We later filmed a few connecting segments and linked them together and were successful in obtaining a home video sale and additional television sales for the combined show ("Peter and the Wolf and Other Tales").

Can you alter your film? Can you change the length to make it appropriate for another market, for example cut a feature film down to a one hour TV show? Can you cut parts out of your film to change the nature of it — for example, to change an educational film into entertainment? Or can you add educational material to an otherwise hard to categorize film to make it fit that market? Of course, the best time to think about this is *before* making the film, but sometimes you can also do it after the film is finished. Weigh the costs of changes against potential sales.

If the distributors can't see quite how to market your film or what audience it might appeal to, help them out. Tell them who you think it will appeal to, and why. Better yet, show it to them at festivals and test screenings with an audience.

EVALUATION

To help you sell your film, go back to the old formula for evaluating your project (see p. 35), this time looking at it from the distribution point of view. Forcing yourself to formally assess your film might let you see angles you have otherwise overlooked or taken for granted. You can make this assessment by yourself — and you can also ask for feedback from others. Show the film to people and take surveys. Even though you've worked on this film a long time, there is probably still a lot you can learn about it once you begin showing it to other people.

An assessment of your film should look at strengths, weaknesses, resources, needs, and market potential — much as you did earlier.

Strengths. What are the strengths of the film? How can you use publicity to maximize these and let people know about them? To whom will the film appeal? Are there any special groups that might be especially excited about the film (and might, in turn, help you publicize it)? How can you reach these groups?

Weaknesses. What are the weaknesses of the film? Can any of these be fixed by additional editing or a re-mix? Is it practical (and financially possible) to fix any of them now? Can you compensate for any of the faults (for example, publicity might be used to clarify plot points that are unclear)?

Resources. What are your resources at this time? How much money do you have left at this stage? Do you have enough (or can you raise enough) to do a lot of publicity, set up screenings, go to festivals, perhaps even pay some or all of the distribution costs (which makes it easier to find a distributor — or lets you distribute the film yourself if you want to do that)? Do you have friends who can and want to help you? What influence or skills do they have? Do you know any distributors, film reviewers, journalists? Can they help you? How much time and energy do you (and others connected with the film) have to promote the film at this stage — and how good are you at that sort of thing?

Needs. What are your needs, financial and emotional? How much money do you need to recoup and how fast? Is visibility, prestige, money, or free time to go on to the next project most important?

Market potential? Now that the film is completed, for what markets does it seem appropriate? What is the likelihood of those sales — and what is the potential income (given current market conditions and prices)?

Once you've completed this evaluation, you can look at your options again and figure out the best ways of proceeding. Remember that you can test things on a small scale to see if they work. Keep your assessments handy, especially the list of strengths. You might want to refresh your memory before talking to distributors — or even write it up in some form.

SELLING YOUR FILM

Once you've finished your evaluation, you can set your priorities and figure out your strategy. You can use mailings, individual meetings with distributors, screenings of various kinds, film festivals, the press. You can approach distributors one at a time in a pre-determined order (perhaps you met with them early on and have determined which you would prefer to have handle your film), or you can approach them all at once and see who responds most quickly and favorable (or who responds at all). You can approach distributors right away or you can work to build word of mouth about your film first. There's no right way — each film is different and each salesperson is different.

Being a salesperson is very different than being a filmmaker. If you're going to be the person "selling" your film, make sure you have it in you to do this. Otherwise think seriously about finding a producer's representative or someone else to do the selling for you. A producer's rep may (or may not) already have contacts with many of the distributors you're trying to reach. This may give them easier access to the distributors than you might have, especially if they are liked and respected. A producer's rep (or some other third party) might have an easier time lauding the film precisely because they have some distance from it, and their praise might be taken more seriously than yours. On the other hand you probably know your film better and care more about it than anyone else — which may make you a better salesperson than someone you hire. Distributors are always eager to find good films, so they should be willing to see anyone with a film to sell (although that isn't always the case — they do get flooded, and all films are not worth their time).

But getting them to see the film is only the first step. Even if they love it, they'll want to know if and how they can sell it. And what they really want to know is, "Can I make money with this film?" That's what you need to prove to them.

With "Hard Traveling" we did an audience survey after a couple festival screenings. We asked people to rate the film and some of it's parts (acting, directing, cinematography). We then asked them it they'd recommend the film to their friends — and how they would describe it. We left space for 1-2 sentences. We also asked what they liked best (and least) about the film. The result was some very complimentary statistics and some great quotes. We also asked people a little about themselves (age, sex, occupation) so we could show the distributor what kind of people liked the film. We sent a brief summary of the survey results, along with a page of the best quotes, to potential distributors. They were impressed and several called who hadn't shown interest earlier. We also got a couple offers from distributors who saw the film at festivals (with appreciative audiences).

Always present your film at its best. Distributors, festivals, and press people are notorious for claiming that they can judge a film from a video cassette (or even a rough-cut). Don't believe them. You may sometimes be stuck and have no choice about how you show the film (35mm is especially difficult) — but be forewarned that if you send a video casette, they may view it in their office as they're answering calls and doing other business. Is that how you want your film judged? You'll probably get a better reaction if you show a good finished print, in the best format (film rather than video), in pleasant and relaxed surroundings, perhaps with an audience. Do you want to risk not showing your film at its best? You may not get a second chance.

Take care of yourself during this process. You may be lucky and sell your film quickly and easily. But you may not. Selling is hard work and it can be frustrating and create lots of tensions (especially if you're under financial pressure to sell the film quickly). Try to alleviate as much pressure as possible. Allocate plenty of time and money to sell the completed film when you first begin your planning. If you're exhausted and depressed, you won't be a good salesperson — so take care of yourself for the sake of your film as well as for your own sake!

PUBLICITY

This is not a new topic but it's very important at this stage of the game, especially for a feature film. Decisions you make at this time are critical — they can affect the perception of the film by distributors, the press, and audiences. Both the words you write and the graphics you use will convey a sense of the film. Until people see your film, this is often all they'll know about it. Your PR campaign may determine whether people see your film at all and how they perceive the film if and when they do see it. How do you want to influence them?

Your publicity material is very important — give yourself plenty of time to prepare it carefully. Remember that people may draw conclusions about the quality of your film based on the quality of written or oral presentations. Put as much care into this material as you put into your film. You can do the publicity yourself or hire a publicist to create a publicity campaign and place stories. Publicity will cost money — plan for it when you make up your budget. Make sure you not only have money in the budget, but that it stays in the bank until this stage. To finish a film and not have money to sell and promote it is foolish and self-defeating.

Beware of too much hype. You want to get people interested in your film — but don't build expectations up so high that they'll be disappointed when they actually see it.

Creating an image. Most films have several aspects. Your film may be a love story, with some mystery to it, set in an interesting locale or historical period. What do you stress? Do you play it up as a love story, a mystery, a glimpse at an exotic location or historical period? Do you stress the gentle parts or the action-oriented ones? Or do you stress the quality of the acting, the famous name star you may have, or an issue raised by the film? Or the talent of a new actor or director? Each approach may attract a different type of audience. Remember that you're trying to sell your film to a distributor at this stage. You want to let the distributor know its strengths, its appeal, and how *they* may be able to pitch it. You don't want to mislead them — you want to attract the type of distributor who might really be interested in distributing your film.

Lists. Mobilize your resources. You've made lists of them, now use them. Ask friends for their assistance and let them know what help you need. Go over the lists you've compiled of distributors, press, festivals, and miscellaneous contacts. Find out not only who the distributors are but also any information about the influential people in those companies. Who makes the decisions? These are the people you want to reach. The lower level people can only say "no" or pass you up the line. The top people can say "yes." See if you can get through directly to the top people, rather than just calling cold or sending out mailings.

Sometimes simply sending out a mailing is your only option and sometimes it works. For "Peter and the Wolf," we sent out a simple flyer and cover letter to various distributors and directly to some television buyers when we were almost finished with the film. By the time we had an answer print, we had a sizeable list of people who were eager to see the film. We showed it to all of them, letting them know we were getting a lot of interest and urging them to make their offers quickly. Many did, and within a few weeks we had an educational distribution deal (with a large advance), a good sale to HBO, and a television distributor who would handle other domestic and foreign sales. We then went on a long overdue vacation. This is almost an ideal scenario — but it doesn't always work that easily.

Publicity materials. The following are some specific materials you might want to prepare: a basic press release, a synopsis of the story, a list of cast and crew credits, short biographies of primary cast and production personnel, and a poster (this can be full-sized as is used to publicize feature films or simply a small version of it to show how the film might be publicized). Postcards with a photo or graphic of your film can come in very handy.

Select the main still photos you want to use to represent the film (and prepare some with captions identifying actors and the production company on the back). Are there any reviews or articles that have been written about the film that you want to reproduce and distribute? You might also want to have preselected video clips of your film available and perhaps an interview or two (with the director, producer, actors, or whoever would be good for publicity). The publicity materials you compile now might be used later by your distributor, so this is a chance to influence and aid their publicity campaign.

Which of the materials you have put together will you include in a press kit? Which will you send out with a press release? Before you send out a press release, remember that the simple existence of your film isn't news, you have to focus on some specific timely event — such as the launching of a film project, the beginning of production, the end of principal photography, completion of the film, invitations to (and successes at) film festivals, and screenings of the film. You can be creative in thinking of reasons to put out press releases but do have a reason. Different press releases might have different emphases. Some might focus on the actors, the director, the story, an interesting sidelight, or audience responses to the film.

Screenings for friends, specially invited guests, or test screenings for an unknown public can also be important for publicity. They cost money (to rent the theater and for publicity if necessary) and take time and energy to set up, so plan ahead. Think of what kind of screenings you want. Do you want to fill a theater so that the distributors can see the film with a live audience? Do you want to prove that folks in Oshkosh will come to see your film? Do you want to get feedback from any particular kinds of people? Do you just want to have people there or do you want to take a survey (long or simple) afterwards? Do you want to speak at the screening or hide in the background? Be aware of what you want from the screening and set it up accordingly.

THE DEAL

Although there is no such thing as a "standard deal," there are general types of agreements that are often made for different markets. These differences between them reflect the way each market operates — primarily in terms of the costs involved in distributing to that market. Within these generalities, there is room for much variation — usually based on how eager the buyer is to obtain the film and how desperate you are to sell it.

Theatrical. Theatrical distributors have very high expenses for both prints of the film and for advertising, with no guarantee that they'll ever make it back. This can make them very cautious about what films they take on for distribution, and deals in this market are perhaps the most unpredictable. This also usually makes the distributors want to acquire other (more lucrative) markets as well. Distribution expenses can vary greatly depending on the type of film, the type of release it will get (wide or just a few key cities; all at once or slow), and the distributor. Major studios might spend $10,000,000 for 1,000 prints of a film and a national advertising campaign while a small distributor may make do with a few prints that will be circulated from city to city, along with a very modest advertising campaign that will rely more on reviews and word of mouth than on expensive television ads or huge newspaper ads.

Educational. Educational film companies also have to lay out a lot of money for prints (less for video copies) and advertising. These distributors usually keep the largest share of the revenues, giving the filmmaker an average royalty of 10-25%. If the filmmaker receives cash, it will be either in the form of an advance against future royalties or a complete buyout (in which case the filmmaker receives no further money).

Television. For television sales, the distributor's expenses are relatively low compared to the theatrical and educational markets — and the filmmaker gets a much higher percentage of the revenues, often 60-75%. This is also an area where it's easier for the filmmaker to go directly to the buyers without going through a distributor (this is much less practical for theatrical or educational markets because of the large number of potential buyers — theaters or schools— and the large expenses involved).

Home video. Although distribution expenses are relatively low, so are sales prices. Typical deals may give filmmakers 20-30%.

NEGOTIATING THE DEAL

When making a deal with a distributor, there are a lot of important questions to ask in addition to, "How much do I get?" What rights does the distributor want and for how long? Are they offering an advance or just a percentage of income? If a percentage, is it a percentage of "gross" or "net" income? The difference between "gross" and "net" is expenses. What expenses will be deducted? Will there be limits on what are reasonable expenses or is the company free to do what it wants with what is essentially your money (you might even end up paying for their vacations in Cannes or for expenses on other films)?

What is the distributor offering for each market, if they want rights to more than one? For example an educational company might want television rights as well, but since the typical distribution fees for television sales are very different than for educational sales, make sure your contract reflects this. You might also want to know how experienced the company is in making television sales and how good their contacts are before giving them the rights for this market. Will income from the different markets be kept separate or will profits in one area be used to offset losses in another? For example, a distributor might want to use profits from television sales to offset possible theatrical losses, especially since the theatrical market involves relatively high costs and high risks. This is known as "cross-collateralization" and you want to avoid it whenever possible.

What are your needs in the deal? Do you need money immediately — or would you prefer to hold out for a higher percentage down the line (which is often the trade-off)? Do you want a guaranteed payment or are you willing to take a risk on how well the film will do financially? Part of that decision may rest on how much you trust the distributor (and their book-keeper), as well as your needs. Read the fine print. Pay special attention to words such as "gross" and "net", and gross and net of *what*. You don't automatically need a lawyer to understand a simple contract, but make sure you understand every clause and possible loophole. If you don't, that's what lawyers are for. You can also ask advice of other producers who may have had similar experiences.

An offer is only as good as the company that makes it. What do you know about the company — its capabilities, financial stability, and honesty? A company that distributes exploitation films to drive-ins may have the best intentions in the world when they say they want to distribute your esoteric art film, but they may not have the appropriate contacts and knowledge to distribute it well. An offer that looks very enticing and generous on paper, promising you a large percentage of profits, may be meaningless if the company practices "creative book-keeping" or goes bankrupt. Again, the best protection here is to talk to other filmmakers about their experiences.

AFTER THE DEAL

Closing the deal should not be the end of your involvement with your film. You can work with the distributor to produce the best possible publicity materials (poster, trailer, press kit). Provide them with any material and ideas you have. Follow what they are doing and argue with them if you don't like their ideas. Some distributors will be more receptive to you than others (think of this when you make the deal).

After we sold "Hard Traveling" to New World Pictures, I worked closely with them to urge them to produce the type of publicity we thought would aid the film. Although they had experience and resources we didn't have, most of their experience was with a different type of film — and we knew our film and its potential audience. The first poster idea they had was similar in design to the final one (see p. 5) but the photos they had selected gave the impression that the film was a murder thriller (which is isn't, although it does include a murder). Upon receiving a copy of the proposed poster, I called them and then drove to LA for a meeting the next day. They listened and agreed to change the photos. The same thing happened with the proposed trailer and again I drove to LA and sat with the editor as we re-cut the trailer.

You can also go on the road with the film to help promote it. A feature film distributor may pay your expenses to do this, but you can — and should — do it anyway. Attend festivals where your film will be shown. Go to openings/screenings in various cities. Get there in time to do press interviews. This can be grueling work after the novelty wears off, but try to pace yourself and build some fun and vacation time into it. With "Hard Traveling," we turned festival invitations into vacations in Moscow, Spain, and Italy (which led to film sales to both the USSR and Spain).

And when you've finally sold your film, you can go back to the beginning of this book, adding in all that you've learned in the meantime, and begin all over again on your next film.

BUDGET

Production:_____
Prepared by: _____Date:_____
Length of film: _____ minutes
Days shooting: _____Days rehearsal:_____

BUDGET SUMMARY

	budget	(deferred)*	actual	(deferred)*
Script & rights				
Producer's unit				
Director's unit				
Talent				
ABOVE THE LINE TOTAL				
Extra talent				
Talent expenses				
Casting & rehearsal				
Production staff				
Art department				
Set department				
Prop department				
Special effects				
Wardrobe department				
Hair & make-up				
Still photography				
Camera department				
Sound department				
Lighting department				
Grip department				
Transportation				
Crew expenses				
Location expenses				
Location office				
Film & lab				
PRODUCTION TOTAL				
Film editing				
Video editing				
Titles				
Music				
Post-production sound				
Film & lab post-production				
POST-PROD. TOTAL				
Insurance				
Office expenses				
Legal & accounting				
Fund-raising expenses				
Distribution				
Contingency				
OVERHEAD TOTAL				
GRAND TOTAL				

* List deferred amounts in parentheses.

	detail	budget (deferred)	actual (deferred)
SCRIPT & RIGHTS			
Writer			
Rights purchased			
Research			
Secretary			
Technical consultant			
Storyboard			
Xerox			
Travel			
Fringes			
Other			
TOTAL			
PRODUCER'S UNIT			
Producer			
Executive producer			
Associate producer			
Secretary			
Travel, pre-production			
Travel, production			
Travel, post-production			
Fringes			
Other			
TOTAL			
DIRECTOR'S UNIT			
Director			
Casting director			
Choreographer			
Acting coach			
Dialogue coach			
Secretary			
Travel, pre-production			
Travel, production			
Travel, post-production			
Fringes			
Other			
TOTAL			

	detail	budget (deferred)	actual (deferred)
TALENT			
Stars			
Supporting cast			
Day players			
Stunts			
Musicians (on screen)			
Welfare worker/teacher			
Looping			
Overtime			
SAG pension			
Fringes			
Other			
TOTAL			

EXTRA TALENT			
Extras/ stand-ins			
Special extras			
Welfare worker			
Drivers (with cars)			
Travel allowance			
Overtime			
Fringes			
Other			
TOTAL			

TALENT EXPENSES			
Hotels			
Meals (per diems)			
Travel, air			
Travel, gas allowance			
Phones			
Other			
TOTAL			

CASTING /REHEARSAL			
Casting space			
" publicity			
" travel			
" video tapes			
Rehearsal space			
" travel			
Other			
TOTAL			

	detail	budget (deferred)	actual (deferred)
PRODUCTION STAFF			
Production manager			
Production assistant			
" " #2			
" " #3			
Location manager			
Prod. office coordinator			
Production secretary			
Publicist			
1st assistant director			
2nd " "			
Script supervisor			
Auditor/ Accountant			
Book-keeper			
Research			
Technical advisor			
Runner			
Overtime			
Fringes			
Other			
TOTAL			

	detail	budget (deferred)	actual (deferred)
ART DEPARTMENT			
Art director			
Assistant art director			
Set designer			
Overtime			
Fringes			
Other			
TOTAL			

	detail	budget (deferred)	actual (deferred)
SET DEPARTMENT			
Set decorator			
Assistant set decorator			
Construction labor			
" materials			
Set striking			
Set rentals			
Purchases			
Painter			
Greensman			
Loss & damage			
Overtime			
Fringes			
Other			
TOTAL			

	detail	budget (deferred)	actual (deferred)
PROP DEPARTMENT			
Prop person			
Assistant prop person			
Animal trainer			
Animal wrangler			
Prop manufacturing labor			
" " materials			
Purchases			
Rentals			
Animals			
Cars (with drivers)			
Cars (without drivers)			
Major props			
Loss & Damage			
Overtime			
Fringes			
Other			
TOTAL			

	detail	budget (deferred)	actual (deferred)
SPECIAL EFFECTS			
Operating crew			
Manufacturing labor			
" materials			
Rentals			
Purchases			
Permits			
Police/Firemen			
Overtime			
Fringes			
Other			
TOTAL			

	detail	budget (deferred)	actual (deferred)
WARDROBE DEPT.			
Costume designer			
Wardrobe person			
Wardrobe assistant			
2nd assistant			
Manufacturing labor			
" materials			
Purchases			
Rentals			
Alterations & repairs			
Cleaning & dying			
Loss & damage			
Overtime			
Fringes			
Other			
TOTAL			

	detail	budget (deferred)	actual (deferred)
HAIR & MAKE-UP			
Hairdresser			
Assistant hairdresser			
Hair consultant			
Make-up person			
Assistant make-up person			
Make-up consultant			
Purchases			
Rentals			
Overtime			
Fringes			
Other			
TOTAL			

STILL PHOTOGRAPHY			
Still photographer			
Film			
Develop & print			
Overtime/Fringes			
Other			
TOTAL			

CAMERA DEPARTMENT			
Director of photography			
Camera operator			
1st assistant camera			
Loader			
2nd camera operator			
2nd camera assistant			
Camera rentals			
Video assist			
Camera truck			
Other rentals			
Overtime			
Fringes			
Other			
TOTAL			

SOUND DEPARTMENT			
Sound mixer			
Boom operator			
Equipment rental			
Extra sound rental			
Walkie-talkies			
Purchases			
Overtime			
Fringes			
Other			
TOTAL			

272

	detail	budget (deferred)	actual (deferred)
LIGHTING DEPT.			
Gaffer			
Best boy			
Utility #1			
Utility #2			
Lighting package rental			
Extra lighting rental			
Expendables (lamps, gels)			
Generator rental			
" operator			
" gas and oil			
Electrical line drop			
Overtime			
Fringes			
Other			
TOTAL			

	detail	budget (deferred)	actual (deferred)
GRIP DEPARTMENT			
Key grip			
2nd grip			
3rd grip			
Dolly grip			
Grip truck rental			
Dolly rental			
Crane rental			
Other equipment rental			
Purchases			
Overtime			
Fringes			
Other			
TOTAL			

	detail	budget (deferred)	actual (deferred)
TRANSPORTATION			
Car rentals			
Truck rentals			
Dressing room rentals			
Drivers			
Gas & oil			
Fringes			
Other			
TOTAL			

	detail	budget (deferred)	actual (deferred)
CREW EXPENSES			
Crew travel, air			
" " , gas allowance			
Crew hotels			
Crew meals (per diems)			
Other			
TOTAL			

273

	detail	budget	(deferred)	actual	(deferred)
LOCATION EXPENSES					
Location rentals					
Studio stage rentals					
Location scouting					
Permit fees					
Janitors					
Security					
Police					
Firemen					
Other location people					
Meals, breakfast					
" lunch					
" dinner					
" snacks					
Wrap party					
Damage and Loss					
Overtime					
Fringes					
Other					
TOTAL					

LOCATION OFFICE					
Location office rental					
" " equipment					
Location phone					
First Aid					
Shipping					
Other					
TOTAL					

FILM & LAB					
Film stock					
Develop negative					
Forced processing					
Daily printing					
Corrected prints					
Test film stock & process					
Video tape					
Video transfers					
Audio tape stock (1/4")					
Transfer sound, labor					
" " mag stock					
Shipping					
Other					
TOTAL					

	detail	budget (deferred)	actual (deferred)
FILM EDITING			
Editor			
Assistant editor			
Sync editor or service			
Edge coding			
Sound editor			
Dialogue editor			
Music editor			
Editing room rental			
" " equipment			
" " purchases			
Leader/slug			
Projection			
Location screening costs			
Trailer editing			
Shipping			
Overtime			
Fringes			
Other			
TOTAL			

VIDEO EDITING:			
Off-Line			
Editor			
Assistant editor			
Editing room rental			
Equipment rental			
Video transfer			
Time code/window dub			
Tape stock			
Digitize video			
Computorize EDL			
Other			
On-line			
Edit suite rental			
Operator			
Tape stock			
Titles			
Special effects			
Other			
TOTAL			

TITLES			
Title design			
Main titles & credits			
Other titles			
Foreign sub-titles			
Other			
TOTAL			

	detail	budget	(deferred)	actual	(deferred)
MUSIC					
Composer, conductor					
Lyracist					
Arranger					
Copyist					
Musicians					
Singers					
Music library					
Music rights					
Rehearsal space rental					
Instrument rental					
Recording studio rental					
Tape stock					
Mag stock & transfer					
Overtime					
Fringes					
Other					
TOTAL					

	detail	budget	(deferred)	actual	(deferred)
POST-PROD. SOUND					
Sound effects library					
Extra sound recording					
Narration					
Foley crew & facilities					
Foley walker					
Looping crew & facilities					
Mixing crew & facilities					
Pre-mix					
Sound Sweetening					
Mag stock, effects					
" " foley					
" " looping					
" " final mix					
" " M & E track					
Protection tape					
Optical track					
Leader/slug					
Stereo costs					
Other					
TOTAL					

	detail	budget (deferred)	actual (deferred)
FILM & LAB POST-PROD			
Stock footage purchases			
Reprints			
Opticals			
Animation			
Optical track			
Negative cutting			
Answer print			
2nd answer print			
Reels & cans			
Shipping			
Inter-positive/inter-neg			.
Dupe negative			
35mm blow-up			
Video transfer			
Video cassettes			
Video-to-film transfer			
Other			
TOTAL			

	detail	budget (deferred)	actual (deferred)
INSURANCE			
Cast insurance			
Negative insurance			
Third party property			
Misc. equipment			
Faulty film, camera, equip			
Auto			
Errors & Ommisions			
Workers' Compensation			
Completion bond			
Other			
TOTAL			

	detail	budget (deferred)	actual (deferred)
OFFICE EXPENSES			
Office rental			
" equipment			
" supplies			
Overhead fee			
Phone			
Xerox, pre-production			
" production			
" post-production			
Research materials			
Postage			
Interest on loans			
Other			
TOTAL			

	detail	budget (deferred)	actual (deferred)
LEGAL & ACCOUNTING			
Prospectus, legal fees			
" printing			
Other legal fees			
Accounting			
Payroll service			
Tax accountant			
Other			
TOTAL			

FUND-RAISING EXPENSES			
Printing/xerox			
Postage			
Travel			
Entertainment			
Commissions, finders' fees			
Other			
TOTAL			

DISTRIBUTION			
Release prints			
Video cassettes			
Trailer			
Preview expenses			
Screenings			
Festival entrance fees			
Publicist			
Publicity materials			
Publicity photos			
Travel			
Shipping			
Foreign versions			
Producer's rep			
Other			
TOTAL			

CONTINGENCY			
TOTAL			

278

SHORT BUDGET

Production:_____
Prepared by: _____Date:_____
Length of film: _____minutes
Days shooting: _____ Days rehearsal: _____

BUDGET SUMMARY

	budget	(deferred)*	actual	(deferred)*
Script & rights				
Producer/Director				
Talent				
ABOVE THE LINE TOTAL				
Production department				
Crew				
Equipment				
Sets/Props/Wardrobe				
Location expenses				
Film & lab				
PRODUCTION TOTAL				
Video editing				
Film editing				
Post-production sound				
Lab				
POST-PRODUCTION TOTAL				
Office expenses				
Contingency				
OVERHEAD TOTAL				
Contingency				
GRAND TOTAL				

* List deferred amounts in parentheses.

279

	detail	budget (deferred)	actual (deferred)
SCRIPT & RIGHTS			
Rights			
Research			
Script			
Typing & Xerox			
Travel			
Other			
TOTAL			

PRODUCER/DIRECTOR			
Producer			
Director			
Secretary/assistant			
Travel			
Other			
TOTAL			

TALENT			
Principals			
Bit Players			
Extras			
Narrator			
Welfare worker/teacher			
Hotel			
Meals			
Travel			
Casting expenses			
Overtime			
SAG pension			
Fringes			
Other			
TOTAL			

PRODUCTION DEPT.			
Production manager			
Production assistant			
" " #2			
" " #3			
Assistant director			
Location manager			
Secretary			
Travel			
Fringes			
Other			
TOTAL			

	detail	budget (deferred)	actual (deferred)
CREW			
Director of photography			
Camera operator			
Camera assistant			
Second camera			
Second camera assistant			
Sound mixer			
Sound boom			
Gaffer			
Best boy			
Key grip			
Grip #2			
Grip #3			
Utility person			
Script supervisor			
Art director			
Prop person			
Wardrobe person			
Hair/make-up person			
Driver			
Runner			
Overtime			
Fringes			
Other			
TOTAL			

	detail	budget (deferred)	actual (deferred)
EQUIPMENT			
Camera			
Extra camera equipment			
Sound equipment			
Lighting package			
Extra lighting			
Grip equipment			
Dolly/crane rental			
Generator rental			
Special equipment			
Expendables			
Truck rental			
Gas, oil			
Other			
TOTAL			

281

Short budget 4.

	detail	budget (deferred)	actual (deferred)
SETS/PROPS/WARDROBE			
Set construction			
Prop rental			
" purchases			
Wardrobe			
Hair, make-up expenses			
Cars			
Animals			
Special effects			
Other			
TOTAL			

LOCATION EXPENSES			
Location rentals			
Permits			
Police/Fire			
Hotels			
Meals, breakfast & snacks			
" lunch			
" dinner			
Other crew expenses			
Location phone			
Car/truck rentals			
Gas			
Other			
TOTAL			

FILM & LAB			
Film stock			
Process			
Print			
Audio tape stock (1/4")			
Transfer sound			
Mag stock			
Stills, stock & process			
Video transfer			
Window dub			
Shipping			
Other			
TOTAL			

VIDEO EDITING			
Editor			
Off-line equipment			
On-line edit suite			
Titles, special effects			
Other			
TOTAL			

	detail	budget (deferred)	actual (deferred)
FILM EDITING			
Editor			
Assistant editor			
Sound editor			
Edge coding			
Editing equipment			
" supplies			
Stock footage			
Opticals			
Titles			
Negative cutting			
Fringes			
Other			
TOTAL			

POST-PROD. SOUND			
Sound effects			
Music			
Library music			
Looping			
Mag transfers			
Recording studio			
Mix			
Mag stock			
Other			
TOTAL			

LAB			
Answer print(s)			
Optical track/electroprint			
Release prints			
Video transfer/cassettes			
Other			
TOTAL			

OFFICE			
Office rental			
" equipment			
" supplies			
Overhead fee			
Phone			
Xerox			
Postage/shipping			
Book-keeping			
Insurance			
TOTAL			

CONTINGENCY			

283

BUDGET

	detail	budget (deferred)	actual (deferred)

TALENT BUDGET DETAIL

role	cast name	weeks	days	rate	total pay	hotel days	per diem days	other

PROP BUDGET DETAIL

scene	prop	special notes	material cost	rental	purchase

MONEY BOOK

																		date			
																		check #			
																		paid to:			
																		TOTAL			
																		rent			
																		phone			
																		printing			
																		postage			
																		office supplies			
																		talent			
																		crew payments			
																		equipment rentals			
																		production services			
																		film supplies			
																		location expenses			
																		props/wardrobe			
																		travel			
																		entertainment			
																		publicity			
																		legal			
																		insurance			
																		taxes			
																		miscellaneous			
																		owner draw			

WEEKLY CALL SHEET

date	time	location	scenes	cast	misc.

CALL SHEET

Film: Day:
Director: Crew call:
Producer: Pick-up crew call:
Production manager: Office phone:
Assistant Director: Location phone:

Set Description	Scenes	Pages	Cast	Location

Cast	Character	Pick-up	Hair/MU	Wardrobe	On Set	Transportation

Extras	Props/Vehicles

Special equipment or instructions

CREW CALL: on location	(or pick-up — PU)	
Director	Set dresser	
ADs	Props	
PAs	Grip	
Camera	Electric	
Sound	Wardrobe	
Stills	Make-up	
Food service: AM ready at:	Lunch ready at	

PRODUCTION REPORT

Film:	Date:	Day #:
Producer:	Director:	
Assistant Director:	Production Manager:	

Scenes shot today:
Location(s):
Set(s):
Crew Call: Shooting call: Lunch: Finish time:
Special crew call:
Special equipment:
Comments:

CAST

Cast	Character	*	Make-up Wardrobe	Work On set	Dismiss	Meals Begin	End	Travel To set	Leave

EXTRA TALENT

#	Rate	On set	Dismiss	Notes	#	Rate	On set	Dismiss	Notes

SUMMARY

	Days	Scenes	Pages	Minutes	Set-ups	Added Scenes	Film rolls
Total in script							
Shot Prev.							
Shot today							
Total to date							
Still to shoot							

Days scheduled: Days actual: Ahead: Behind:

* W=work, S=start, F=finished, R=rehearsal, H=hold, TR=travel

290

SCRIPT NOTES

Film: _____Script: _____Date: _____

scene	take	roll	roll	lens	comments

TAPE LOG

Film: _____ Date: _____ Tape: _____ Page: ____

tape				scene/take			subject	notes
	:	:	:					
	:	:	:					
	:	:	:					
	:	:	:					
	:	:	:					
	:	:	:					
	:	:	:					
	:	:	:					
	:	:	:					
	:	:	:					
	:	:	:					
	:	:	:					
	:	:	:					
	:	:	:					
	:	:	:					
	:	:	:					
	:	:	:					
	:	:	:					
	:	:	:					
	:	:	:					
	:	:	:					
	:	:	:					
	:	:	:					
	:	:	:					
	:	:	:					
	:	:	:					

EDIT DECISION LIST

Film: _____ Editor: _____ Page: _____

	VIDEO			AUDIO	
	: : :			: : :	
	: : :			: : :	
	: : :			: : :	
	: : :			: : :	
	: : :			: : :	
	: : :			: : :	
	: : :			: : :	
	: : :			: : :	
	: : :			: : :	
	: : :			: : :	
	: : :			: : :	
	: : :			: : :	
	: : :			: : :	
	: : :			: : :	
	: : :			: : :	
	: : :			: : :	
	: : :			: : :	
	: : :			: : :	
	: : :			: : :	
	: : :			: : :	
	: : :			: : :	
	: : :			: : :	
	: : :			: : :	
	: : :			: : :	
	: : :			: : :	

INDEX

ORDER FORM

Additional copies of **BEFORE YOU SHOOT** are available from Shire Press, 26873 Hester Creek Rd., Los Gatos, CA 95030 (use order form below). Cost: $12 each (plus $1.50 postage and handling).

Also available from Shire Press: packet of **PRODUCTION FORMS**, including budget forms (feature budget, short budget, blank budget page), breakdown sheet, breakdown chart, call sheets, petty cash forms, money book page, storyboard form, script notes, tape log, and more. All forms are 8 1/2" x 11" — ready to duplicate. Cost: $8 (plus $1.50 postage and handling).

_____BEFORE YOU SHOOT   ($12 each)

_____PRODUCTION FORMS   ($8 each)

_____Please send information on "Hard Traveling" and "Peter and the Wolf" videos.

Send to:

_____

_____

_____ zip _____

Please enclose payment for book(s) plus $1.50 postage and handling per book. California residents add sales tax.